Plenty of Nothing

*

Plenty of Nothing

*THE DOWNSIZING
OF THE AMERICAN DREAM
AND THE CASE FOR
STRUCTURAL KEYNESIANISM*

*

THOMAS I. PALLEY

PRINCETON UNIVERSITY PRESS

PRINCETON, NEW JERSEY

Copyright © 1998 by Princeton University Press
Published by Princeton University Press, 41 William Street,
Princeton, New Jersey 08540
In the United Kingdom: Princeton University Press,
Chichester, West Sussex
All Rights Reserved

Library of Congress Cataloging-in-Publication Data
Palley, Thomas I., 1956–
Plenty of nothing : the downsizing of the American dream
and the case for structural Keynesianism /
Thomas I. Palley.
p.   cm.
Includes bibliographical references and index.
1. United States—Economic policy—1981–1993. 2. United States—
Economic policy—1993–   3. United States—Economic conditions—1981–
4. Keynesian economics. I. Title.
HC106.8.P345 1998
ISBN 0-691-04847-9 (cl : alk. paper)
338.973—dc21 97-34907 CIP

This book has been composed in Galliard

Princeton University Press books are
printed on acid-free paper and meet the guidelines
for permanence and durability of the Committee
on Production Guidelines for Book Longevity
of the Council on Library Resources

http://pup.princeton.edu

Printed in the United States of America

1   3   5   7   9   10   8   6   4   2

FOR THE NEXT GENERATION

ESPECIALLY DAVIA AND SOPHIE

✳

❋ *Contents* ❋

❊ *Tables* ❊

✳ *Preface* ✳

MILTON AND Rose Friedman's *Capitalism and Freedom* (1962) is one of the great books of modern political economy. As a classic, it rightly appears on undergraduate reading lists, and it has influenced the minds of two generations. I, too, remember reading it as an undergraduate, and remember being swayed by its compelling rhetoric. Yet, even while enjoying the text and argument, I had a feeling that something was amiss. It was not the logic of the Friedmans' argument that was troubling, but rather their vision of the process they were describing.

Later, in graduate school I learned the essence of the Friedmans' economic argument, now albeit in the sophisticated language of mathematical economics. I also learned the critiques of their argument. However, these were of an internalist nature, in the sense that they challenged the technical economic assumptions rather than the vision.

The writing of this book has been an attempt to articulate a different vision of how a dynamic capitalist economy works. It is not intended as a criticism of capitalism per se, and I would be disappointed if that were to be the reception. I am a convinced believer in the productive power of capitalism and the social good it can generate. As such, I do not see the economic problem as a choice between capitalism and something else. Rather, it is a matter of what type of capitalism we are going to have. It is this dimension that is missing from current debate, and its absence threatens to mislead us about possibilities for our future.

Capitalism comes in a range of forms, where these forms depend on social choices regarding laws, governance structures, and economic policies. To understand how these factors affect the working of a capitalist economy, it is necessary to have a grasp of the anatomy of the economic process. This anatomy is what I have sought to illuminate.

I am not philosopher enough to have stuck with an entirely abstract account. Instead, I have lodged my account within an analysis of the performance of the U.S. economy. This has involved describing the U.S. economy's economic performance over the last twenty years, as well as examining economic policy. I hope that this placement of the abstract account within a real world setting gives concreteness and relevance to the former.

When it comes to policy and performance, I am a critic. I believe there has been a sea change (for the worse) in economic performance, and much blame for this change rests with misguided policy. The basis of this criticism is rooted in an understanding of the economic process. This is an essential feature: in the absence of such understanding, policy analysis either reduces to ad hoc commentary or wishful thinking. Finally, criticism alone would be churlish: I have therefore sought to develop an explicit set of alternative policy prescriptions that I believe can restore a widespread and deepening prosperity.

I would like to thank a number of people. My thanks to Marty Wolfson and Jamie Galbraith for providing careful and encouraging readings of the initial manuscript. My thanks to David Smith with whom I had some very helpful conversations about economic policy that tied up a number of loose ends. My profound thanks to Peter Dougherty who was a wonderful editor from start to finish. And last, thanks to Teresa Carson who did a magnificent job of copy editing.

Plenty of Nothing

✳

✳ CHAPTER 1 ✳

Debunking Economic Naturalism

THIS BOOK is about the American economy and the gradual dismantling of mass prosperity that has been taking place over the last twenty-five years. The focus of the book is on "long-term trends" that continue to operate on the economy independently of the temporary ups and downs of the business cycle. Though the economy periodically experiences cyclical booms, underlying the booms of the last twenty-five years has been a persistent downward trend.

This interaction of trend and cycle makes understanding the economy a difficult task. When the economy is up, it is easy to forget about the recent down. Moreover, this proclivity to short-term memory is compounded by the fact that people are optimistic, and all too ready to believe that each economic recovery marks a new beginning. That optimistic psychological disposition then inclines them to believe that their earlier concerns were misplaced, and that there is no longer any need for altering their economic course. In this fashion, Americans have ridden the economic roller coaster that has seen the majority slip behind while the few have prospered.

This proclivity to believe that each new business cycle marks a fresh start is dramatically reflected in our current experience. In April 1997, the U.S. unemployment rate fell to a twenty-three-year low of 4.9%. Following the release of this report, newspapers were filled with stories about how the U.S. economy had successfully reinvented itself.[1] Yet, just fourteen months earlier, Americans had been wrestling with the trauma of rising economic insecurity and the disappearance of the middle class: The *New York Times* even ran a week-long special (March 1996) titled "The Downsizing of America." Moreover, even as the unemployment rate was hitting 4.9%, average hourly wages actually fell fractionally. As documented in chapter 4, the purchasing power of average hourly wages has actually fallen during the most recent business cycle and remains far below the peak level of wages reached in 1973.[2] If this is economic reinvention, something is lacking.

Capitalist economies have always had booms, and they will continue to do so. The current economic boom is therefore not at odds with the claim of an on-going erosion of the American Dream. Indeed, the character of this boom provides some confirmation. In past booms, there would have been significant wage gains at this stage of the business cycle. In the current boom, there has been welcome relief on the employment front, but wage stagnation persists; hence the claim "plenty of nothing."

The fundamental thesis of this book is that restoring widely shared and growing prosperity will require major changes in the direction of economic policy. Effecting such change will require that people reassess their thinking about the economy, for economic policy is ultimately the reflection (albeit indirect) of popular thinking as expressed through the collective choice process that is politics. In the absence of these changes, the economy may continue to grow, but economic polarization between rich and poor will also continue to expand.

Sixty years ago, the great British economist John Maynard Keynes struggled to change popular understandings of the causes of the Great Depression. The orthodoxy of the day promoted an economic fatalism that opposed attempts to stimulate spending despite the overwhelming presence of unemployment: the orthodox claim was that any government attempt to increase spending would merely displace an equal amount of private spending. For Keynes, the difficulty in persuading people lay "not in the new ideas, but in escaping from the old ones, which ramify, for those brought up as most of us have been, into every corner of our minds."[3] A similar argument can be made today regarding an array of issues ranging from the claim that a dose of economic austerity is the prerequisite for restoring economic prosperity, to the claim of a binding inflation constraint that compels us to live with permanently high interest rates and unemployment.

Despite temporary relief, most Americans are apprehensive about the economy, and they have reason to be. For the last twenty years, the wages of the average worker have been falling, economic insecurity has been growing, and the prospects for future prosperity have been receding. This is not a matter of progress at a slower pace: rather, we are going backward. The existing configuration of economic arrangements and policies has produced this outcome, and the belief that the market will suddenly reverse its existing course in an act of goodwill is tantamount to the fatalist thinking that characterized the depression era.

The restoration of the shared and growing prosperity that marked the immediate post-World War II era requires the restoration of an appropriate balance of power within our economic system. The technological and organizational changes of the last thirty years have upset the previously extant balance of power among government, big business, and labor. As a result, there is a need to recalibrate our system so that it again delivers for all.

STRUCTURAL KEYNESIANISM

The notion that we need to recalibrate our economic system gives rise to an economic philosophy that I call "structural Keynesianism." Like traditional Keynesianism, it shares the fundamental proposition that capitalism is the most powerfully productive social system that has ever been created. Capitalist economies are capable of generating a greater bounty of goods and a higher standard of living than any economic system heretofore, or any economic system we can currently imagine.

Like traditional Keynesianism, structural Keynesianism also shares the core proposition that capitalist economies have a fundamental tendency to generate a deficiency of demand for the goods and services that they are capable of producing. Moreover, this deficiency of demand can occasionally be severe enough to generate economic depressions and mass unemployment. A large class of problems in capitalist economies can therefore be understood by reference to the principle of aggregate demand—that is, by understanding the economic forces determining the total demand for goods and services in an economy. Keynes and his followers understood this principle, and in the period after World War II they applied it in guiding economic policy. The result was an unequaled period of full employment during which the scourge of mass unemployment was replaced by mass prosperity.

This period of success led Keynesian economists to believe that demand management, conducted by government through its control over interest rates (monetary policy) and government spending and taxes (fiscal policy), was sufficient to eliminate permanently the problems of the business cycle and unemployment. Behind this belief lay an implicitly static view of the world, in which the structure of the economy was fixed so that monetary and fiscal policy would always be feasible, effective, and sufficient means of managing demand and ensuring prosperity.

The last twenty years have been marked by the return of higher rates of unemployment and the withering of popular prosperity. This has undermined the sanguine prognosis of traditional Keynesianism. Thus, it has

5

become increasingly difficult to apply expansionary monetary and fiscal policy, and, even when applied, the results have not been as in the earlier period. It is true that expansionary monetary and fiscal policy are still able to reduce unemployment, but the reduction has proven temporary. Moreover, Keynesian demand management policy has been impotent with regard to the problems of widening income inequality and stagnating wages. It has also become increasingly difficult to pursue expansionary policies owing to mounting government debts and the threat of a sell-off in bond markets, which raises interest rates.

Structural Keynesianism builds on the analytic inheritance of traditional Keynesianism. Thus, it recognizes both the unequaled productivity of capitalist economies and the tendency of capitalist economies to generate problems of insufficient demand. However, it supplements the Keynesian argument in two important ways. First, just as there is a proclivity to generate insufficient demand, uncontrolled capitalist economies also have an unyielding tendency to generate exploitation of ordinary people that results in a distribution of income in which a few have vast riches and the many have some or none. This skewing of income distribution in turn feeds back adversely on the level of demand. As a result, income distribution takes on a profound import, because running a system of mass production at full employment requires a robust mass market, which requires a healthy distribution of income to support demand. From a policy standpoint, income distribution is of concern not just for ethical reasons of equity, but also for reasons of economic prosperity.

Second, structural Keynesianism recognizes that capitalism is a dynamic system in which business seeks to promote an economic environment that maximizes profits. This means that business will seek to influence policy by such activities as political lobbying. Even more importantly, business will also innovate with regard to production technologies and methods of business organization, and these innovations will change the economy's structure. Though the abstract driving forces of capitalist economies remain unchanged, the specific visible economic arrangements and production techniques are constantly changing. This economic dynamic is summarized as follows: "the more things change, the more they remain the same," while at the same time "one can never step in the same river twice."[4]

This recognition of the dynamic process governing economic activity has momentous implications for the conduct of economic policy. Traditional Keynesians believed that demand management was sufficient to ensure full employment and popular prosperity, and their early success convinced them of this belief. However, the reality is that the period immediately after World War II was characterized by a configuration of structural factors that was highly conducive to successful demand management. This structure included strong trade unions, controls on international movements of financial capital, limited ability of business to relocate jobs, and strong domestic demand conditions.

Over time, these favorable conditions have gradually been eroded, and replaced by unfavorable conditions that render demand management policies less effective and less feasible. This change did not happen by accident or bad luck: rather, it reflects the systematic workings of the free market. Thus, through a combination of technological innovation, organizational innovation, and political action, business has succeeded in asserting dominance over both government and labor. As a result capitalism's proclivity to unequal income distribution and demand deficiency is reasserting itself with a refound vengeance.

Such an analysis gives rise to three fundamental propositions of structural Keynesianism.

Proposition I. Keynesian demand management can only solve the systemic problem of deficient demand if an appropriate economic structure is in place.

Proposition II. Keynesian policies of demand management must be supplemented by regulatory policies that ensure an appropriate economic structure. This requires regulation of business (both industrial and financial), regulation of international financial markets, and regulation of labor markets. These regulatory structures must be designed so as to preserve the incentives for productive enterprise that are the source of capitalism's bounty.

Proposition III. These regulatory policies need to be periodically updated because capitalism is a dynamic process that will persistently seek to evade them. If regulation is successful, it means that it is binding in the sense of restraining business from doing something it would have freely chosen to do in the absence of regulation. This sets up an incentive to innovate (technologically or organizationally) so as to circumvent the regulations.[5] Over time, this process of innovation will be successful, which means that regulations have to be periodically updated. In effect, successful regulation always sows the seeds of its own destruction.

CHAPTER 1

Politics before Economics

Structural Keynesianism elevates the significance of structure and policy, and in doing so it forces politics to the forefront of the stage. Structure is inevitably a political matter: the establishment of a structure conducive to widespread prosperity can only be accomplished by individuals acting in concert; achieving prosperity within that structure then becomes the province of individuals acting on their own account.

This is the great paradox of free-market capitalism. Though driven by the pursuit of individual self-interest, all free-market economies require some collectively agreed upon structure. The popular myth is that free markets are free of structure, but this is a fabrication. Even the most radically laissez-faire economy rests on laws and institutions governing and enforcing the rights of property and the obligations of contract: at a minimum, there is always a "policeman," a "judge," and a "jailer." It is also true that such a minimalist structure will never generate the widespread prosperity that is the hallmark of the American dream.

The failure to recognize that widespread prosperity rests on appropriately designed market rules and regulations is the cancer that is killing the American dream. Thus, as the old regulatory structure that promoted the success of Keynesianism has withered, we have failed to update it. Instead, by a combination of default, misunderstanding, and apathy, Americans have gotten locked into a new set of market structures that set worker against worker to the disadvantage of all but big business. This new structural environment generates a cruel paradox: the pursuit of self-interest, which is both individually rational and the source of the bounty of free markets, ends up hurting ordinary workers. Worse still, none can escape: not to pursue one's self-interest while others do, is to consign oneself to an even worse economic predicament. This is the logic of the infamous "prisoner's dilemma," and it is easily illustrated.

The Stock Ownership Dilemma. Many Americans own small amounts of stock. Each individual wants higher profits at the company in which he owns stock, as this will increase the stock price. If these profits come from reduced company wages, that's all right because the individual does not work there. However, when all adopt this mentality, everyone is worse off. The increased stock value pales by comparison with the decreased value of wages, which represent the dominant source of income for working Americans. The sole beneficiary is the small group of the wealthiest

8

Americans who own most of the stock. Despite this, each of us has a private interest to canvas companies in which we hold stock to seek higher profits through wage reductions—as long as it's not at our own place of employment.

The Rat Race Dilemma.   Most people want to make it to the top, and win the prize of a high salary that goes with being at the top. To get there, they try and distinguish themselves by working harder, which involves putting themselves under increased strain and stress, reducing their community involvement, and shortchanging their families of time and attention. However, when their colleagues see them working harder, they too have an incentive to respond by increasing their effort because they also want to get to the top. Consequently, a rat race develops in which each tries to outwork the other. From the start, only one can be top dog: yet, all have an incentive to participate in a rat race that makes all but one worse off.

The Wal-Mart Dilemma.   During the 1980s, the Wal-Mart chain of discount stores spread across rural America. In its wake, it decimated downtown business districts as local retailers and merchants could not compete with Wal-Mart's buying power, which enabled it to offer lower prices. Local residents, including the local merchants who were being driven out of business, had an incentive to shop at Wal-Mart to get these lower prices. Yet at the end of the day, communities were worse off, with downtowns destroyed and higher paid dignified local business employment replaced by low-paying service work at Wal-Mart.

The Automobile Dilemma.   Most people want cars that are safe and have good gas mileage. To get a little more safety, people may buy a slightly bigger car, and sacrifice a bit of mileage. However, when one person buys a bigger car, it makes persons driving smaller cars less safe as they are more likely to be hurt in collisions. Drivers of small cars then have an incentive to buy slightly larger cars, so that none are safer. In this fashion, people may end up driving large low-mileage cars that leave everyone worse off.

These are a few examples of how prisoner-dilemma-type problems permeate markets. Each person rationally pursues his self-interest, which is exactly what free markets are supposed to thrive on. Yet, at the end of the day, this can make everyone worse off. However, not to pursue self-interest while others do, makes individuals even worse off: consequently, there is no opting out.

Not only do these problems apply to individuals, but they also apply to governments as can be seen from the following examples.

The Tax Auction Dilemma. Recently, many state governments have been giving generous business tax exemptions either to attract new business or to get existing business to stay. However, when the state next door (consider New York and New Jersey) sees that its neighbor is giving such exemptions, it too has an incentive to give exemptions. As a result, an auction of tax exemptions develops. By such means, New York may ultimately be able to persuade business to stay, but the resulting lower tax revenues must be made up by additional property taxes on households.

The High Interest Rate Dilemma. Financial capital is highly mobile in today's globalized financial markets. International money now flows between London, New York, and Tokyo in search of the highest interest rate, and these flows can trigger an exchange-rate crisis if they happen in large sudden fashion. To guard against this possibility, countries try to keep their interest rates fractionally above the global average. However, if one country follows this strategy, then others are obliged either to follow or face an exchange-rate crisis. Yet, when every country adopts this strategy, the result is to push up the global average interest rate, resulting in higher interest rates everywhere.

The implications are clear. The prisoner's dilemma is a problem that pervasively afflicts both individuals and governments, and it derives from the structural arrangements governing markets. During the course of this book, we shall see it reappearing over and over again. Resolving the problems it poses, requires establishing market governance structures that prevent destructive pursuit of self-interest that ends up harming all. Establishing such governance structures is a matter of collective choice rather than individual action, and it is in this sense that politics comes before economics.

STRUCTURAL KEYNESIANISM VERSUS ECONOMIC NATURALISM

Structural Keynesianism recognizes the need for institutional design that promotes economic well-being. This recognition of the significance of "design" contrasts with the dominant economic philosophy of the day, which I term *economic naturalism*. The latter rests on an appeal to nature and views the economy as a product of nature: hence, the appeal to the notion of a natural rate of unemployment, a natural rate of interest, and a natural rate of growth. This appeal brings with it rhetorical advantage because, by implication, everything else is unnatural. More than that, it brings with it an economic mentality that can be termed *economic fatalism*. If the economy is fixed by nature, then there is little we can do about it. Instead, we just have to lump it and live with it. Of course, this appeal to nature is not politically neutral: it ends up favoring the status quo.

The triumph of economic naturalism over the American mind is the ultimate source of our current fatalistic attitudes, which maintain that the economy is beyond our influence. Hence, globalization and the dominance of business are viewed as inevitable outcomes, and we should be grateful that there are jobs and that wages do not fall.

Structural Keynesianism stands in stark contrast to economic naturalism. Whereas the latter sees the economy as predetermined and given, the former sees it as the outcome of choices. Whereas the latter promotes policy fatalism, the former promotes policy activism that seeks to create prosperity by design. There are constraints on prosperity: these are people's attitudes to enterprise, the wealth of a country as measured by its natural resources and factories, and the level of knowledge and technological advance. However, that said, the extent to which these endowments produce prosperity, and the manner in which that prosperity is shared, depend on the design of our economic institutions and laws and the economic policies we adopt.

ECONOMICS AND THE END OF THE COLD WAR

Economic naturalism dominates the American mind. Its dominance was reinforced by the Cold War, which continues to exert an influence despite its finish. A widely held belief is that the end of the Cold War signaled the triumph of free-market capitalism, and that henceforth only one type of economic system would be viable.[6] Moreover, that economic system is the one we already have, so that the economic question is settled de facto and there really is no choice.

For those at the top of the income distribution, this is a comforting story. However, this claim rests on a false dichotomy that contrasts a utopian laissez-faire capitalism with extreme Soviet-style authoritarian-

11

ism. The reality is that capitalism has always come in a range of forms, and today we are edging toward a return to the extreme form that characterized conditions before the New Deal. The triumph of this "no choice" mentality has therefore become another obstruction obscuring the real problem of establishing "the capitalism" that works best.

Scanning the world's economies is revealing of the range of capitalisms, and the same is true for the history of the American economy. Thus, the capitalism of the period 1950–1970 represents a different capitalism from that of today. Whereas the former worked for Main Street America by sharing the fruits of economic growth, current arrangements pit citizen against citizen in a vicious struggle that redounds to the benefit of the few who own and manage America. Viewed in this light, the message from the end of the Cold War is not the end of choice, but rather that America must choose whether it wants yesterday's Main Street capitalism or today's Mean Street capitalism.

During the Cold War, both sides engaged in vigorous ideological propagandizing on behalf of their respective economic systems; the Soviets peddled utopian communism, whereas America peddled utopian capitalism. The collapse of the Soviet Union left the propaganda of utopian communism completely discredited, but America's triumph left the propaganda of utopian capitalism intact. As a result, America remains burdened by its Cold War ideological baggage.

The ideological character of the Cold War meant that discussion of the fundamental nature of the economy was out of bounds, and instead America claimed to have permanently solved the economic problem. This claim was reinforced by historical circumstance after World War II, whereby military spending, the rebuilding of Europe and Japan, the reforms associated with the New Deal and the G.I. Bill, and the accumulation of five years of pent-up World War II consumer demand, all combined to push the U.S. economy onto a trajectory that provided twenty years of growth and spreading prosperity. The result of this confluence of events was that Americans came to believe their own ideological rhetoric, claiming to have permanently solved the economic problem. In the process, the very language needed for talking about the economy was forgotten. The end of the Cold War therefore poses a challenge that requires Americans relearn how to talk about the economy. Rather than signalling the triumph of a fictitious utopian capitalism, the choice is between Main Street capitalism and Mean Street capitalism.

12

LESSONS FOR EUROPE

Though this book is principally about the American economy in that it uses American economic data to make its arguments, both the central thesis and many of the specific arguments also apply to the economies of Western Europe. The transition to Mean Street capitalism is more advanced in America, but there are powerful forces seeking to accelerate the transition in Europe. The arguments are therefore directly relevant to European debates over free trade, the role of unions, and the role of government in ensuring full employment and a fair distribution of income. Taken in isolation, each of these policy debates can appear as specific and contained in nature. Considered collectively, their resolution will determine whether European Main Street capitalism is replaced by its Mean Street cousin.

Fortunately, there are a number of reasons to be optimistic about the outcome. These include the existence of the European Community, the foundations for which were established in the 1950s. The Community's institutions embody the optimistic outlook that characterized that period of European renewal, and this outlook is built into its legal charter and organizational culture. A second reason for optimism is the structure of European politics. In Europe, there exist well-defined mainstream labor parties, and trade unions view themselves through a historical lens that commits them to broad concerns with national economic and social policy. This widens the scope of public debate and contrasts with America, which lacks a labor party. However, Europe has its own political problems. Whereas cultural politics is America's great distraction, in Europe there is the persistent danger of reactionary nationalist politics, which can be used to hijack the economic debate.

13

* CHAPTER 2 *

Making Sense of the Economy and Economics

As ECONOMIC advance has waned for larger and larger numbers of people, an understanding of the roots of prosperity has become ever more vital. In this climate of economic stagnation and insecurity, politicians and economists have pushed competing and conflicting policies. Naturally, all claim to be acting in the best interests of ordinary Americans. However, ordinary Americans seem ever less certain of how the economy actually works, what is the cause of the vanishing American dream, and whose policies will really improve their economic condition.

This confusion is manifested in two ways. First, there is an increasing skepticism with the rosy prognostications of professional economists, whose analysis is so deeply at odds with most workers' real-world experience. Second, the lack of an alternative intellectual framework promotes a tendency to fall back on an uncritical faith in the ingrained myths about market economies and the "invisible hand." All that is good is then ascribed to the invisible hand, whereas all that is bad is ascribed to government or other scapegoats such as trade unions, affirmative action, or womens' participation in the labor force.

In making sense of the economic world, ordinary Americans are caught in a bind: they neither know who to believe, nor how to thoughtfully evaluate the conflicting policy prescriptions they are offered. The goal of this book is to fill this void, and provide a simple coherent framework for understanding how the economy works, how we have gotten to where we are, and how we can make viable policy changes that will restore a rising standard of living for all.

There are many popular books on the economy. Some sell on the basis of their sensationalism, be it optimistic or pessimistic, whereas others tap into particular issues in a timely fashion. In these books, authors provide their own interpretations of the issue at hand and usually end with a lament that everything would be so much better if policymakers would only follow their recommendations. No doubt there is some of this in the current book. However, where as other books provide a set of arguments related to a particular issue, they provide no overarching framework for thinking about the economy that can be used to address other questions as and when they arise. Providing such a framework is an intrinsic goal of this book.

For professional economists this framework is called a *model* of the economy, but in lay parlance it simply means a view of how the economy works. I hope that readers will find the suggested framework useful in many other instances, be it watching the Jim Lehrer News Hour or reading an economic feature in *Time* magazine. Getting things right requires that ordinary people be able to assess the logic of the competing economic policies they are offered.

THE ECONOMY: CREATIVE DESTRUCTION AND CONFLICT

Behind the slow dismantling of prosperity and the return of economic insecurity, stands the economics of business domination that is built on unfettered tooth-and-claw capitalism. Accounting for the revival of business domination involves two interacting components: (1) the underlying economy in which the forces of market competition and conflict are played out, and (2) economic policy and its impact on the economy.

At the core of the argument developed in the ensuing pages lies a vision of the economy. My friend and former colleague Bob Heilbroner has a wonderful saying about economics, which is that "The best kept secret in economics is that economics is about the study of capitalism." This book is about the economy, and it is therefore unabashedly about capitalism. Such economies are characterized by a process that Joseph Schumpeter called "creative destruction."[1] According to this process, entrepreneurs and firms are motivated by the desire for profits, and they engage in a constant search for new products and methods of production. This search is the mainspring of technological progress and economic growth, but just as it brings new products to market and increases the efficiency of production, it also renders existing products and methods of production obsolete: hence, the combination of "creation" and "destruction."

A capitalist economy is also a place of conflict, with different groups competing over income distribution. In effect, this conflict determines how the fruits of creative destruction are divided. Modern economics is full of talk about capital and labor as "physical inputs" in the production process. However, though it is happy to use these categories to describe inputs, it denies their social dimension. In doing so, it suppresses the essential presence of conflict within the economic process.

15

This presence of conflict is not incidental to the operation of free-market economies; rather, it is of central import because conflict determines the distribution of income between wages and profits. The distribution of income in turn affects the purchasing power of households, and this determines the robustness of mass-consumption markets on which modern industry is predicated.

Moreover, not only does the distribution of income affect current economic conditions, it also affects the speed and character of creative destruction. Income distribution affects business conditions and employment, and both of these act as spurs to innovation. Robust business conditions mean that firms can confidently launch new products, while full employment provides an incentive to reduce labor costs through technical innovation.

This process of conflict, with all its ramifications for economic prosperity, is deeply affected by the pattern of business organization because the pattern of organization can affect the balance of power between capital and labor. The pattern of organization is itself subject to persistent change because business is dynamic and constantly evolving. Sometimes this change is extremely rapid, and sometimes it is glacially slow.

The leitmotîv of this evolutionary process is the search for profit. Thus, firms have evolved from single-owner family businesses, to partnerships, to privately owned limited-liability companies, to publicly owned limited-liability companies quoted on public stock exchanges. Production has been governed by different regimes ranging from artisan-based craft production to mass production. *Taylorist methods* of production focus on detailed time and motion studies of worker activities: *Fordist methods* of production focus on maximizing output from mass-production assembly lines. Horizontally diversified conglomerates own businesses in unrelated industries: vertically integrated conglomerates own businesses that cover every stage of production from initial fabrication of parts, to assembly, to distribution. The multinational corporation conducts business in many countries.

Within these corporate forms, the excercise of control may be centralized or decentralized: control over some activities such as manufacturing assembly may be decentralized, whereas control over finance and research and development may be centralized. Today, organizational innovation continues at a rapid pace through the development of subcontracting, use of temporary workers, the creation of strategic alliances between firms, and production licensing arrangements.

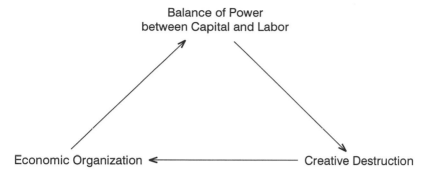

Fig. 2.1. The interaction among economic organization, the balance of power between capital and labor, and the process of creative destruction.

The evolution of business organization is both cause and consequence of the process of creative destruction. This interactive process is illustrated in figure 2.1. The process of creative destruction changes the pattern of business organization, which then changes the balance of power between capital and labor. Changes in the balance of power in turn loop back and affect the underlying process of creative destruction by giving firms fresh incentives either to innovate and consolidate their advantages, or to remedy their disadvantages.

The search for profits is the impulse behind creative destruction. This search can either take the form of interfirm competition in which firms seek to drive out their rivals, or it can take the form of a struggle between capital and labor with firms seeking a relative advantage over their workers. Interfirm competition enlarges the national economic pie, and has the potential to make everyone better off. Capital-labor struggle is more ambiguous: frequently, it is not the size of the pie that is at stake, but rather the division of the pie and how it is sliced in terms of profits and wages. Indeed, firms may even adopt organizational techniques with large supervisory bureaucracies that produce a smaller economic pie, if this increases the size of the slice going to profits.[2]

Viewed from a Schumpeterian perspective, the economy is never in stasis. Instead, it constitutes a dynamic world in which firms struggle with firms for competitive advantage, and business struggles with labor to reduce the wage share. An underlying argument of this book is that the industrialized economies have been undergoing a process of rapid structural change that has put labor at a disadvantage in its unspoken contest

17

with business. This process has been especially prominent in the U.S. economy, and it has destroyed the Golden Age that characterized the period from 1945 to 1970. This golden age of prosperity was marked by stable employment, low unemployment and a distribution of income favorable to labor: it has been replaced by unstable employment, higher unemployment, and a distribution of income favorable to capital.[3]

Behind this shift in power lies such developments as the maturation of the multinational corporation, the decline of trade unions, the development of global subcontracting that allows firms to rapidly shift production across countries, and free trade that has exposed U.S. workers to the threat of replacement by the hundreds of millions of pauperized workers around the world. The exploration of the causes and consequences of these developments is a core element of this book.

THE SIGNIFICANCE OF ECONOMIC POLICY

Consideration of the causes of structural change serves to introduce economic policy, which has also played a prominent role in the emergence of Mean Street capitalism. Economic policy is extremely important for the operation of the economy. Monetary and fiscal policy directly impact economic activity: the former concerns the control over interest rates by the Federal Reserve, while the latter involves control over government spending and tax rates to influence economic outcomes. Both monetary and fiscal policy affect how much after-tax income people have, the level of government employment, interest rates, and the cost of borrowing. These factors in turn impact the level of demand for goods and services, thereby directly affecting employment and unemployment.

In addition to directly affecting the level of economic activity, policy influences the economy's structure. Thus, the economic climate affects labor's bargaining power: tight labor markets strengthen labor's position, whereas high unemployment weakens it. Labor legislation and industrial regulation also affect labor's power by determining the ease with which firms can lay off their workers. Welfare legislation and unemployment benefits affect labor's power by reducing the cost of unemployment to workers, thereby giving workers greater confidence and bargaining power in their dealings with firms. Lastly, labor's power is also affected by firms' ability to replace strikers, by the rules governing union formation and union busting, and by tariffs affecting the relative profitability of locating production overseas.

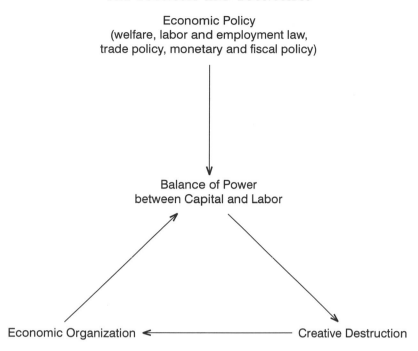

Fig. 2.2. The effect of economic policy on the balance of power between capital and labor, and thereby on the process of creative destruction.

These impacts of economic policy are captured in figure 2.2 which shows how policy influences the balance of power between capital and labor. Welfare and labor market regulations have a direct influence by providing workers with protection against the threat of unemployment: monetary and fiscal policy have an indirect influence that works by lowering unemployment and making more jobs available to workers.

As is shown in the ensuing chapters, the political dominance of business and the intellectual dominance of laissez-faire has meant that economic policy over the last twenty years has consistently worked against labor and in favor of business. Economic policy has therefore been a significant ingredient in the establishment of business domination, and economic policy bears significant blame for the demise of the American dream.

This feature represents a dramatic reversal from the period 1945 to 1970, during which policy was predicated on a stance that was tilted in favor of labor and explicitly directed toward acheiving full employment. During this period, the value of welfare and unemployment benefits increased, thereby strengthening labor's bargaining power. Simultaneously, monetary policy kept interest rates low, while fiscal policy pumped spending on defense and the nation's infrastructure into the economy. Expansionary monetary and fiscal policy therefore contributed to keeping unemployment low, and this also helped labor.

ECONOMIC KNOWLEDGE AND THE FORMATION OF ECONOMIC POLICY

The above observations reveal the major significance of economic policy. This prompts the question of why the direction of economic policy has changed. It is at this point that the economics profession enters. Paradoxically, today economists stand somewhat discredited and accused of irrelevancy: yet, they have played a real albeit concealed role in the drama of the downsizing of the American dream. In an often quoted passage at the end of his magisterial *General Theory,* Keynes wrote: "[T]he ideas of economists and political philosophers, both when they are right and when they are wrong, are more powerful than is commonly understood. Indeed the world is ruled by little else. Practical men, who believe themselves to be quite exempt from any intellectual influences, are usually the slave of some defunct economist. Madmen in authority, who hear voices in the air, are distilling their frenzy from some academic scribbler of a few years back."[4] Today, as ever, both policymakers and the public are guided by the scribblers, whose influence is so gradual and imperceptible that it goes unnoticed and unexamined.

The importance of the economics profession lies in the fact that it produces what society takes for economic knowledge, and it thereby determines our vision of how the economy works. This vision is central to the establishment of economic policy, because it defines what policies are deemed viable and appropriate. In this fashion, economic knowledge indirectly sets the bounds of policy, and policy then impacts the economy. Moreover, the effect of the economics profession is often immediate and direct, because in many instances the actual policymakers are themselves economists or are directly advised by economists.

Today, the economics profession has adopted an intellectual view that is implicitly anti-labor and pro-business. The reasons for this shift involve a complex sociology that includes the fact that big business is now the dominant social force. Business also pays many of the bills in academia by endowing professorships and directly funding economic research and the establishment of business schools. This inevitably promotes a pro-business agenda because business is not keen to fund research that is critical of it. Lastly, there has been a generalized conservative drift in society at large, and as members of society, economists have themselves been affected by this drift.

As a result of this pro-business leaning, economists have consistently advocated policies that have disadvantaged working America. The evidence is visible across a wide range of issues. Thus, there has been widesprcad adoption of theories claiming that monetary and fiscal policy cannot lower unemployment and that government and the Federal Reserve should not try to stabilize the economy in the face of business cycle fluctuations. Government is itself characterized as a burden on the economy, rather than as contributing to economic well-being through the provision of infrastructure, education, and public health, and through the provision of a social safety net that removes the threat of impoverishment.

Economic theory is also anti-labor, with economists consistently claiming that high and rigid wages are the cause of unemployment. In effect, labor is blamed for the scourge of unemployment, a scourge which would be eliminated if workers would just take pay cuts. Unions are consistently presented as driving up unemployment by raising wages: similarly with minimum wages. Both are presented as distortions of the natural market, and the economist's policy recommendation is that government should seek to eliminate them.

Side by side, economists have been pro-business in their support of free trade, without regard to its adverse effects on employment, wages, and the distribution of income. Moreover, this support is in complete disregard of conventional trade theory, which unambiguously shows that by uniting American labor markets with the surplus labor markets of the Third World, free trade will inevitably drive down wages.[5]

The philosophical core of modern economics is laissez-faire. This philosophy embodies the belief that market outcomes are the product of autonomous forces. Moreover, these forces ensure that all (workers, corporate executives, and owners of industry) get paid what they are worth. Behind this story is the assumption (euphemistically referred to as perfect competition) that no one has any power in the market, so that labor and capital supposedly stand on an equal footing when it comes to the battle over the distribution of income. Adam Smith, the creator of the invisible-hand metaphor, knew better. Thus, over two hundred years ago, he wrote:

21

[T]he common wages of labor depend everywhere upon the contract usually made between two parties, whose interests are by no means the same. The workmen desire to get as much, the master to give as little as possible . . . It is not, however, difficult to forsee which of the two parties must, upon all ordinary occasions, have the advantage in the dispute . . . In all such disputes the masters can hold out much longer. Many workmen could not subsist a week, few could subsist a month, and scarce any a year without employment. In the long run the workman may be as necessary to his master as his master is to him, but the necessity is not so immediate.[6]

THE NEED FOR A NEW ECONOMIC VOICE AND A NEW ECONOMIC CONVERSATION

The significance of the economics profession extends beyond its technocratic impact on economic policy because economists also inform the popular understandings of the economy held by ordinary people. Every year, hundreds of thousands of students absorb this vision of the economy. In this fashion, undergraduate training in economics has become a conditioning of the American mind that promotes acceptance of the economic status quo.

This conditioning helps explain the public's acceptance of laissez-faire policies regarding labor laws and the treatment of trade unions, the role of government, and free trade. Within the conventional undergraduate training, big business is represented as the efficient outcome of a natural order based on the market's invisible hand, whereas interventions to redress the uneven balance of power are represented as unnatural. According to laissez-faire, markets naturally ensure that people get what they deserve, unemployment is the result of high wages, and collective action by labor is bad because it interferes with the individual exchange on which the market process depends. However, though both collective action by labor and labor market regulation are represented as unnatural distortions, the same is not true when it comes to the interests of business. Thus, corporate capitalism, predicated on pooled holdings of capital and the legal protections conferred by the law of limited liability, is not represented in these terms.

Despite the partisanship embuing the current state of economic knowledge and education, there are grounds for optimism regarding the possibility of opening thinking about the economy, the causes of our past successes, and the changes needed to ensure future prosperity. Within popular culture, there have always been two voices for speaking about the economy. The first is the voice of laissez-faire individualism. This voice links with other culturated images of American history in which frontier individualism produced American greatness. The second is a darker voice that speaks of the economy as a site of conflict and exploitation. According to this voice, low wages and unemployment can arise owing to an uneven balance of power that gives rise to unequal income distribution. Somewhat surprisingly, these two voices are used by both rich and poor, by the broker on Wall Street and by the machinist in Peoria, Illinois.

The voice of laissez-faire individualism remains dominant. Yet, many people are increasingly skeptical regarding its claims of a natural economic order. The "silent depression" of the last twenty years has produced too many job losses, too much economic insecurity, and too many years of stagnant wages and declining prospects.[7] This has produced a combination of skepticism and anger: both are double-edged. Skepticism can signal a willingness to listen to an alternative voice: it can also produce apathy. Anger can provide the energy for change: it can also result in scapegoating and a backlash that experiments with an even more extreme version of laissez-faire. Indeed, this may well characterize recent political conditions that have been marked by moves to repeal the structures implemented during the New Deal era, institutionalize deflationary policy, cannibalize the regulatory role of government, and expose labor to the full threat of expatriate production based in the Third World. The danger is that, even if only temporary, such a backlash can lock in institutional arrangements that will prove hard to reverse.

* CHAPTER 3 *

Plenty of Nothing: An Overview

CHAPTERS 1 and 2 have laid out a broad canvas describing the anatomy of the economic process. It is now time to begin blocking in the details of how the hollowing of the American dream has come about. The underlying thesis is that there has been a slow dismantling of mass prosperity in the American economy. The driving force behind this process is a precipitous reconfiguration in the balance of power among business, government, and labor, and this has produced an economics of business domination. The result has been increased economic insecurity and inequality of income distribution, with a small minority garnering the lion's share of economic growth, while the rest see no gain and even considerable slippage.

The American economy remains the largest economy in the world. Continental in scope, stretching from the Atlantic to the Pacific, it inevitably dwarfs the economies of other smaller countries. It is also an extraordinarily productive economy, and in 1994 the Council on Competitiveness said that the U.S. economy had regained its ranking as the most competitive economy in the world.

Though the American economy consistently produces a massive and expanding output, this does not mean that ordinary Americans are prospering. Far from it, many Americans are struggling economically. The few at the top have seen consistently large increases in income over the last twenty years. Contrastingly, the mass of the American middle class has experienced stagnant incomes, while the size of the middle class has been shrinking.

A starting point for making this claim is the evolution of median family income, which is shown in table 3.1. The median family represents the family that is exactly in the middle: 50% of families receive more income, and 50% receive less. The table reveals two things. First, there is a downward trend in the rate of growth, which was 2.8% per annum in the period 1947–67, and has fallen steadily since then. Second, in the most recent period, 1989–95, median family income fell 0.6% per annum: this is evidence of outright economic regress.

TABLE 3.1

Median Family Income and Growth of Median Family Income, 1947–95 (1995 dollars)

Year	1947	1967	1973	1979	1989	1995
Income	19,088	33,305	38,910	40,339	42,049	40,611
Period	1947–67	1967–73	1973–79	1979–89	1989–95	
Annual growth	2.8%	2.6%	0.6%	0.4%	−0.6%	

Source: Mishel et al., 1997, p. 44.

TABLE 3.2

Shares of Family Income Going to Various Groups,
1947–95 (percent)

	1947	1973	1989	1995	*Percent Change* 1973–95
Lowest fifth	5.0	5.5	4.6	4.4	−20.0
Second fifth	11.9	11.9	10.6	10.1	−15.1
Third fifth	17.0	17.5	16.5	15.8	−9.7
Fourth fifth	23.1	24.0	23.7	23.2	−3.3
Top fifth	43.0	41.1	44.6	46.5	+13.1
Top 5%	17.5	15.5	17.9	20.0	+29.0

Source: Mishel et al. (1997, p. 53).

Table 3.1 reveals the deterioration in economic performance for the median family. However, concentrating on a single family fails to reveal the full scope of the problem. This becomes more evident from inspection of the distribution income shown in table 3.2. This table shows a massive increase in income inequality and is revealing of the about-face in economic performance. During the Golden Age that ran from 1945 to 1973, every income group except the top fifth saw their income share increase. Moreover, within the top fifth, the share going to the very top 5% also declined. Since then, the situation has completely reversed. Every income group except the top fifth has been losing income share, and the composition of the top fifth has itself become more unequal, with the top 5% increasing their share. All the gains of the Golden Age have been reversed, and America is more unequal than it was in 1947.

An interesting feature is that this process of declining well-being and increased income inequality is now starting to eat its way up the food chain. Tables 3.1 and 3.2 provide some indication of this. Median family income grew until 1989, albeit at a declining rate, but has since declined:

TABLE 3.3
Family Income Growth, 1979–94

	Average Family Income* (1994 dollars)			Percent Change	
	1979	1989	1994	1979–89	1989–94
Lowest fifth	10,088	9,741	8,875	−3.4	−8.9
Second fifth	24,527	24,224	22,151	−1.2	−8.6
Third fifth	38,254	39,031	36,641	2.0	−6.1
Fourth fifth	53,775	57,914	55,792	7.7	−3.7
Top 80–90%	72,210	81,055	79,386	12.2	−2.1
Top 90–95%	91,816	105,674	107,504	15.1	1.7
Top 5%	166,465	241,862	259,093	45.3	7.1

Source: Mishel et al. (1997, p. 60).
* Includes single-person families.

though the rich have gotten richer, income inequality has increased among the top 20%, with the top 5% gaining more than the next 15%. Table 3.3 confirms this claim. It shows that only the bottom 40% lost income during the period 1979–89, and everybody else gained. In the period thereafter, however, everybody except the top 5% has lost. Having cut out the bottom, the process of expanding profits and top incomes at the expense of the rest has started moving up the food chain. This new reality is reflected in middle management's fears of downsizing. The lesson is that middle and upper-middle class households are vulnerable to the same process that has afflicted lower-income workers: we are all in the same economic boat, though we may get tossed out at different times.

The deterioration in income distribution is mirrored in the buying power of wages (which economists refer to as *real wages*). Thus, average real weekly wages (measured in constant 1995 dollars) of production and nonsupervisory workers (who make up 80% of wage and salary employment) was $469.44 in 1973: by 1995, weekly wages had declined to $395.37, a decline of 15.8%. Average hourly wages of production and nonsupervisory workers peaked in 1973 at $12.72 (constant 1995 dollars): by 1989, they had fallen to $11.87. The decline has continued through most of the 1990s, reaching $11.46 in 1995. Hence, the 1994 cover story in *Time* Magazine of "Boom for Whom?"

This ongoing decline is captured in table 3.4, which shows median (i.e., the middle person's) hourly wages for both men and women. These figures show a decline of 6.1% for men over the period 1989–94, while women's wages stagnated. The table also shows a narrowing wage differ-

TABLE 3.4

Trends in the Median Hourly Wage for Men and
Women, 1989–94 (in 1994 dollars)

	Median Hourly Wage			Percent Change
	1989	1992	1994	1989–94
Men	11.98	11.47	11.24	−6.2
Women	8.76	8.84	8.74	0.0
Ratio	0.73	0.77	0.78	6.8

Source: Baker and Mishel (1995).

TABLE 3.5

Distribution of Household and Individuals' Income Relative
to the Median (percent)

	1967	1979	1989	1995
Household Income in 1995 dollars				
Under $15,000	24.0	21.0	20.2	21.0
$15,000–50,000	56.2	49.7	46.8	47.0
Over $50,000	19.8	29.3	33.0	31.9
Individuals (income relative to median)				
Less than 50%	17.9	20.0	22.1	22.6
50–200%	71.2	68.0	63.3	61.2
Over 200%	10.9	11.9	14.7	16.2

Source: U.S. Bureau of the Census (1996) and unpublished tables
by John McNeil, cited in Mishel et al. (1997, p. 77).

ence between men and women, but this narrowing occurred only because
men's wages fell. Such conditions have provided fertile ground for the
white male backlash that has provided the fuel for the nation's culture
wars. Regrettably, this backlash has only served to obscure the real cause
of middle-class decline, which is a shift in the balance of power in favor of
capital over labor. The argument that will be made in the balance of this
book is that this shift has been brought about by the process of creative
destruction, and it has been furthered by economic policies that have favored business interests.

These adverse trends in income distribution and wages have been accompanied by growing economic insecurity reflected in the shrinking of
the middle class. This shrinkage is captured in table 3.5, which shows that
America has been splitting into two societies of rich and poor. Thus, the

TABLE 3.6
Distribution of Families by Income Class (constant
1990 U.S. dollars)

	Percent of Families	
Income Class	1973	1990
Upper, Above $75,000	8.6	12.3
Middle, $25,000–$74,999	59.7	54.5
Lower, $0–$24,999	31.8	33.3

Source: Peterson (1994, p. 57).

share of households making between $15,000 and $50,000 has declined from 56.2% in 1967 to 47.0% in 1995, while the number of persons earning 50% to 200% of the median income has shrunk from 71.2% of all persons to 61.2%.

A similar tale is revealed in table 3.6, which shows how the percentage of families earning between $25,000 and $74,999 shrunk between 1973 and 1990 from 59.7% to 54.5% of all families. The middle class therefore contracted by 10%. At the same time, the lower class increased. True, there was also a large increase in the percentage of upper-income families, but it must be remembered that remaining middle-class families are increasingly clustered in the lower middle class (i.e., closer to $25,000 incomes rather than $74,999 incomes) owing to the decline in median wages. The shrinking of the middle class, combined with a declining share of income for all but the top 20% of households, means that not only are most Americans not participating in the growth of the American economy, but many are actually receiving a shrinking slice of the national pie.

Such a pattern marks a break in the history of the American dream, and contrasts with the Golden Age of prosperity that marked the twenty-five years between 1945 and 1970. During this period, the American economy expanded at the tremendous rate of 3.5% per year, and there was an enormous democratization of prosperity as huge numbers entered the middle class. Indeed, an entire new working middle class was created, as blue collar workers came to enjoy the benefits of home ownership, and high wages gave them the ability to pay for household appliances, new cars, and regular vacations.

Why has this process of expanding and spreading prosperity come to an end? This is the question that this book addresses, and this chapter provides an overview of what has caused the demise of the Golden Age.

Though the story makes for dismal reading, there is a silver lining: it is possible to restore the Golden Age. However, doing so will require Americans to recognize that mass prosperity can only be restored by design. Relying on the hope that markets automatically work in the interests of all flies in the face of the evidence of the last twenty-five years.

CAPITAL MOBILITY AND THE RISE OF BUSINESS POWER

A key element behind the emergence of the disordered economy is a shift in the balance of power within the economy. As noted in the previous chapter, capitalist economies are marked by a process of creative destruction, which continually gives birth to economic innovations that are the ultimate foundation of our prosperity. However, who gets to enjoy the fruits of these innovations depends on the bargaining process between workers and business that determines the distribution of income.

Sometimes this bargaining process is explicitly visible, as in the case of bargaining between big unions (such as the auto and steel workers) and large corporations (such as General Motors and U.S. Steel). However, most of the time it is an invisible process, as small groups and individual workers implicitly bargain with firms over pay. In these situations, workers use the threat of quitting or reducing work effort and job commitment if pay conditions are inadequate. The relative bargaining strength of workers and business is therefore crucial to the outcome of this subterranean conflictual process.

The relative bargaining strength of business and workers depends on a host of factors. One critical factor is the state of the economy, because unemployment serves to weaken worker power. Thus, running the economy with persistently higher rates of unemployment hurts workers. In this regard, obsessive anti-inflation policy predicated on high interest rates has consistently and systematically injured workers' bargaining power. Other dimensions of economic policy have also reduced workers' power, and these include reductions in the scope and scale of the social safety net and the promotion of wage competition through free trade.

Economic policy is one important ingredient in the emergence of the disordered economy; increased capital mobility is another. Business corporations are driven by the search for profits, and these can be earned either through innovation and head-to-head competition with other firms or by attacking labor and cutting wages. The ability to redistribute from wages to profits depends on the ease with which firms can threaten to fire and replace existing workers with unemployed workers, or the ease with which they can relocate production to other sites where cheaper labor is available. The greater this ease, the more powerful is business relative to labor because the threat to replace becomes credible, and workers are therefore compelled to make wage and benefit concessions.

Over the last twenty-five years there has been a remaking of the structure of the American economy, which has increased the mobility of production and lowered the costs of replacing workers. This restructuring has been the result of forces internal to the market process, as well as the result of politically sanctioned economic policies of deregulation and free trade. With regard to the former, the process of creative destruction has been directed to the creation of new technologies that facilitate replacement. It has also enabled flexible production that can be moved from region to region, both within and between countries. These are the hallmarks of the new lean and mean corporate environment.

This increased flexibility is built on the new microelectronic technologies that have vastly improved communication and information-processing capabilities. These technological advances have made it feasible to manage production in multiple distant locations, so that multinational corporations are now the rule rather than the exception. The new technologies have also contributed to the automation of production, which has lessened reliance on labor. Together, the changes have increased the relative power of firms, which is built on the credible threat of either replacing existing workers with unemployed workers or shifting production to other locations.

In addition, there have emerged new firms such as Manpower, Inc., which specialize in the supply of temporary workers. Thus, firms have easy access to temporary replacement labor that can be used to undermine the power of existing employed insider labor. In the 1980s, temporary agencies accounted for 4.4% of U.S. job growth, whereas in the 1990s they have accounted for 13.8%.[1] In 1973, the temporary and personnel services industry accounted for 0.3% of total employment: by 1995, it had risen to 2.1%. Though not a huge number, the effect of this new industry comes from its threat effect: firms do not actually have to use such services; they just need them available as an option. In this case, the threat of replacement is credible, and the power of firms relative to that of workers is increased.

This increased threat has been rendered more potent by the higher rates of unemployment that have prevailed since 1974. In such an environment, scarcity of jobs means that laid-off workers must face longer periods of unemployment in the event they are let go, and this makes workers more willing to grant concessions. Moreover, these changed circumstances have been exacerbated by an increase in corporate America's willingness to replace workers. This new willingness to replace was given official sanction in the early 1980s when the Federal government openly and visibly crushed the strike by air-traffic controllers (the PATCO strike), and used the massive resources of the government to quickly and clinically find replacement controllers.

UNIONS, LABOR LAW, POLITICAL CULTURE, AND THE DECLINE OF SOLIDARITY

Another important element in the shift in the balance of power between labor and capital has been the decline of solidarity among American workers. Ultimately, the causes of this decline are sociological and political, but it has had important consequences for the distribution of income. This is yet another example of how sociology and politics affect economic outcomes. In essence, the decline in solidarity has facilitated a corporate strategy of divide and rule, and has increased the credibility of replacement threats as a means of getting wage concessions. With the demise of solidarity, workers know that replacement is a real possibility, because the taboos against scabbing no longer serve as a constraint on potential replacement workers.

The most visible sign of the breakdown of solidarity is the decline in trade union membership. Unionization rates peaked at 35% of the total employed workforce in 1955 and have fallen to a mere 14.5% of the total workforce in 1996. Moreover, 42% of unionized workers were employed in the government sector in 1996. Thus the private sector is almost completely free of unions, having a unionization rate of only 10.1% in 1996.

The decline in unionization among private sector workers is vividly captured in figure 3.1, which shows how private sector unionization rates steadily increased from 1933 to 1953. In the next seventeen years (through 1970), unionization rates gradually fell from 35.7% to 29.1%. Since 1970, however, the decline has been precipitous and persistent, so that by 1994 the private sector unionization rate was a mere 10.9%—well below what it was in 1933.

This decline in the size of unions has had major consequences for wages and employment security because unions have a positive impact on wages in both unionized and nonunionized industries. The reason for the posi-

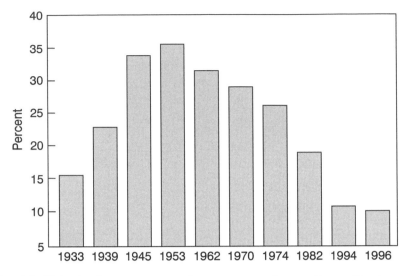

Fig. 3.1. Unionization rate among private-sector employees. *Source*: Dembo and Morehouse 1995; 1996 data provided by Bureau of Labor Statistics, "Union Members in 1996," January 1997.

tive effect on nonunion wages is that nonunionized firms are willing to pay higher wages to reduce the incentive for their workers to join unions. Consequently, when unions were a significant force in the private sector, nonunion private sector wages received a major boost.

As unions have declined in size, workers in the nonunion sector have suffered since firms have taken back the higher wage ("wage premium") they previously paid to prevent unionization. Within the unionized sector, unions have been forced into a persistently defensive stance, so that union workers have not shared in productivity gains as they did in the years of the Golden Age. However, union workers still receive higher wages and benefits than workers in the nonunionized sector. Table 3.7 shows the extent of the union wage and benefit premium earned by union workers.

Unfortunately, this premium has all too often been interpreted as cause for envy and resentment: the reality is that strong unions pull up all wages. Tables 3.2 and 3.3 showed how the greatest loss of income share has been in the bottom two quintiles of the income distribution. At the same time, the decline in unionization rates has also been greatest among workers in the bottom two quintiles of the income distribution.[2] The connection is clear: where unionization rates have declined the most sharply, wage stagnation and worsening income distribution has been most pronounced.

TABLE 3.7
Union Wage and Benefit Premium in 1995 (U.S. dollars)

	Wages	Insurance	Pension	Compensation
All Workers				
Union	16.69	2.24	1.15	22.40
Nonunion	13.35	0.98	0.42	16.26
Premium (%)	25.0%	128.6%	173.8%	37.8%
Blue collar				
Union	16.81	2.34	1.31	23.07
Nonunion	11.21	0.94	0.31	14.14
Premium (%)	50.0%	148.9%	322.6%	63.2%

Source: Mishel et al. (1997, p. 199).

The reasons for the decline of unions are multiple. Certainly some blame lies with the unions, which allowed themselves to become perceived as a special interest, while some unions have also had problems with corruption. The most extreme example of this was the Teamsters Union with its links to the Mafia, which ultimately led to a temporary government takeover of the union under Federal racketeering laws. Such cases tended to tarnish the entire union movement, and the politics of the union movement are such that it is difficult for individual unions to speak critically about events in other unions.

However, the real causes of the decline in unions have been labor laws and our national economic and political culture. With regard to law, the 1930s was a period of advance for unions with rights to form unions, bargain collectively, and strike being enshrined in the Wagner Act of 1935. This right was soon undermined by the Supreme Court's decision in National Labor Relations Board v. Mackay Radio & Telegraph Co. (1938), which gave employers the right to permanently replace striking workers. In doing so, it gravely undermined the substance of the right to strike. Even more important was the Taft-Hartley Act of 1947, which profoundly and lastingly undermined union strength. First, it prohibited secondary boycotts (i.e., sympathetic strikes); second, it extended the concept of unfair labor practices to include actions by unions; third, it made the closed shop illegal, preventing unions from requiring firms to make union membership a condition of employment.

Employers have been able to exploit the deep conflict of interest among workers unleashed by the outlawing of closed shops. This conflict of interest is built on the prisoner's dilemma, illustrated in figure 3.2. There are

INDIVIDUAL A

	Join Union	Not Join Union
Join Union	1. Closed shop/ Solidarity	2.
Not Join Union	3.	4. No closed shop/ No solidarity

INDIVIDUAL B

Fig. 3.2. Union membership as an instance of the prisoner's dilemma.

two individuals, A and B. Each can choose to join a union or not join a union. Joining a union is costly because one must pay dues to support the union organization and strike fund. If both join, then they get maximum wages (box 1); if neither joins, then they get minimal wages (box 4). Closed-shop laws would ensure that both join. In the absence of such laws, firms can exploit private interest to undermine unions. Thus, they can offer nonunion workers a slightly lower wage while saving them union dues: individual workers then have an incentive to defect from the union. In this fashion, box 4 comes to dominate. However, as workers defect from unions, union power erodes and so does the union wage. As the union wage erodes, employers can lower the wage they pay their non-union workers, and the economy ends up in box 4 with low wages. In the absence of closed shops, the problem of the prisoner's dilemma relentlessly asserts itself.

The illegality of sympathetic strikes has also profoundly undermined union power relative to firms. Moreover, this prohibition is becoming increasingly important in our globalized economy, in which firms are multinational in character and have production facilities around the world. The adverse consequences for union workers are illustrated by the 1997 strike against the Goodyear Tire & Rubber Company. In response to a strike at its U.S. production facilities, Goodyear simply declared that it would increase production at its Brazilian and Mexican operations and import this substitute production. The only way to stop this tactic would be a secondary boycott by dock workers, who would refuse to unload Goodyear's tire imports. However, this is illegal. In the new globalized environment, dock workers must now de facto actively help companies in defeating other unions.

Antiunion labor law is one cause of the decline in union power; our national economic and political culture has been another. The closed shop is one way out of the prisoner's dilemma; solidarity among workers is another. If workers have a sense of solidarity, understand the necessity of trade unions, and see how firms actively seek to divide and rule, then they can voluntarily join unions and frustrate business in its attempt to increase profits at the expense of wages and benefits. However, achieving such an outcome requires an understanding of the economic realities.

Such understanding is filtered through popular economic and political culture. Within the United States, this culture has worked against unions. In the early 1950s, the environment of high employment promoted wage growth and employment security, in stark contrast with the depression years before World War II. During this period, corporate America was willing to pay higher wages owing to the strength of unions, and because it sought to prevent a revival of an active political left such as had begun to emerge in the 1930s. These objective social and political conditions provided the basis for what many still refer to as the "social contract" between business and workers. The important point is that this social contract did not come into being because of a sudden bout of goodwill on the part of corporate America. Rather, it was a result of strong unions combined with the political threat that had been generated by the Great Depression and which remained in place through the existence of the Soviet Union. The underlying anatagonism between business and labor remained fully intact, but labor temporarily had the upper hand.

Unfortunately, the success of the social contract led Americans to believe that the essential conflict of interest between business and labor was an issue of the past. Rather than recognizing that the strength of labor was the reason for the social contract, Americans chose to believe that corporate America had changed the color of its spots. The economic prosperity of the 1950s in turn led working Americans to believe that the economic scourges of unemployment and depression had been permanently eliminated by a combination of the institutional reforms of the New Deal and the new economic stabilization policies associated with the Keynesian revolution in economic governance. In this environment, it was easy to believe that there was no longer a need for unions to even the balance of power between labor and capital.

Unions also bought into this point of view. Hence, they became increasingly inward looking, with each union focusing on the particular group of industrial workers it represented, with little regard for the interests of other workers. These industrial unions were then able to ride the coattails of American industry, which was enormously profitable owing to strong demand conditions and the absence of foreign competition resulting from the destruction of European and Japanese industry in World War II.

Despite their positive impact on wages throughout the economy, the growing differential between union and nonunion wages led to wage envy. This envy, combined with the perception of unions as a special interest, led to increasing alienation between unionized and nonunionized workers. Corporate America also actively sought to drive a wedge between union and nonunion workers. This has been particularly evident in corporate America's promotion of a job competition between the Rust Belt and the Sun Belt. This has involved shifting Rust Belt union jobs to the nonunionized Sun Belt, while simultaneously fostering the claim that high-paid union workers are inefficient and raise prices at the expense of everybody else's well-being: the reality is that unions raised wages for all and held down profits.

The belief that the social contract rendered unions no longer necessary, the special interest tag acquired by the union movement, and the anti-union offensive of corporate America have all taken their toll. The result has been a lack of interest in unions and an unwillingness to support the codes of solidarity and opposition to scabbing that are the foundation of union strength.

Instilling such an attitude requires reversing the popular economic construction of unions, which derives from conventional economics. The latter represents unions as a form of "market failure," interfering with the natural process of free and voluntary exchange based on individual preferences. Behind this view lies the philosophy of economic naturalism discussed in chapter 1. Institutions such as unions, and interventions such as the minimum wage, are represented as distortions to the natural market: the policy recommendation is that government should seek to eliminate them.

The reality is that unions are a correction of market failure, namely the massive imbalance of power that exists between individual workers and corporate capital. The importance of labor market bargaining power for the distribution of income, means that unions are a fundamental prop for widespread prosperity. Weakening unions does not create a "natural" market: it just creates a market in which business has the power to dominate labor.

The notion of perfect natural markets is built on the assumption that market participants have no power. In reality, the process of labor exchange is characterized not only by the presence of power, but also by gross inequality of power. An individual worker is at a great disadvantage in dealing with large corporations that have access to massive pools of capital and can organize in a fashion that renders every individual dispensible. Recall the earlier quote from Adam Smith, who, even in the age of artisan production, wrote: "In the long run the workman may be as necessary to his master as his master is to him, but the necessity is not so immediate." Unions help rectify the imbalance of power in labor markets, and they therefore correct market failure rather than causing it.

Another important element explaining the decline of unions has been American political culture. The period of communist paranoia initiated by Senator Joseph McCarthy in the 1950s, turned the climate against labor in general. During the 1930s, when millions of Americans had been unemployed, unions grew enormously and were in the forefront of struggles to prevent firms from using the threat of unemployment to drive down wages. As representatives of labor, trade unions inevitably shared some of the rhetoric and symbols of the Soviet Union, which had unilaterally cast itself as the nation of industrial workers. It did not matter that there was no similarity between democratic unionism and authoritarian communism: it was enough that the Soviets used some of the same symbols. As a result, the anticommunist fervor that infected most Americans, also tainted attitudes toward unions. In effect, the legitimate opposition to the totalitarianism of the Soviet Union was exploited to undermine the standing of trade unions in the American mind.

Ironically, this "Red scare" mentality likely contributed to the drift toward narrow industrial unionism. In the paranoid political environment of the 1950s, the anticommunist campaign which was notionally against the Soviet Union, was used to attack all forms of progressive and social democratic political action. Traditional unionism, which strove for economic justice and better pay and working conditions, inevitably fell within the purview of this anticommunist campaign. Consequently, the political climate of America in the 1950s demanded that union leaders retreat from a social democratic program inclusive of all workers and instead become narrow industrial unions. In conforming to the mentality of the Red scare rather than confronting it, unions sowed the seeds of their own future weakness. This was because narrow industrial unionism inevitably got cast as a parochial special interest without connection to the interests of nonunionized workers.

In sum, the widespread prevalence and strength of unions was an important component in the spread of mass prosperity in the twenty-five years after World War II. Yet, the role of unions in this process was little understood, and the culture became increasingly hostile toward them. Thus, once prosperity was achieved, unions increasingly came to be seen as an anachronism that could readily be done away with. The ensuing decline in unions, combined with the growth in business power arising from increased capital mobility, have both contributed to the ending of Golden Age Main Street capitalism and promoted a return to an earlier Mean Street capitalism. Such an interpretation of the causes and effects of declining union membership reveals the significance of public understandings and attitudes for the establishment of economic prosperity.

THE INSTITUTIONALIZATION OF DEFLATIONARY BIAS

As mentioned earlier, an important element in the determination of the balance of power between workers and firms is the rate of unemployment. The higher the rate of unemployment, the greater the relative strength of firms: workers are intimidated by the consequences of job loss in an economy with high unemployment. Moreover, when unemployment is high, it is harder to enforce taboos against scabbing because unemployed workers have families to support and must find work.

During the period of the Golden Age, the rate of unemployment in the American economy was persistently below 5%, but since then it has steadily risen. In the period 1951–74, the average unemployment rate was 4.65%: in the period 1975–93, it was 6.97%. At the moment, the United States is enjoying an economic boom, and the average unemployment rate for the period 1994–6 was 5.7%. The temporary presence of this boom can obsure the longer trend, which is that the average unemployment rate since 1974 has been almost 50% higher than it was in the earlier Golden Age period.

The combination of high unemployment and weakened unions have in turn allowed business to use the threat of replacement to intimidate labor. Two recent highly publicized instances where firms defeated strikes by using replacement workers were the 1994 strikes at Caterpillar and Firestone Rubber Company.[3]

Why has unemployment been so much higher? An important part of the explanation is change in the direction of economic policy. During the period of the Golden Age, economic policy had an expansionary tilt, and full employment was deemed a national priority. Since then, there has been a retreat from full employment, which has become increasingly characterized as a special-interest policy designed to help those who cannot help themselves in a competitive market economy. In place of full employment, the Federal Reserve has substituted an obsessive concern with inflation that has given monetary policy a persistent deflationary bias. Thus, the Federal Reserve now treats a 1% increase in inflation as if it were worse than an increase of 1% in unemployment.

The Fed's elevation of inflation as public enemy number one has been facilitated by popular misconceptions about inflation. The public roundly dislikes inflation. In part, this is due to the incessant claims of politicians, economists, and the media that inflation is bad. In part, it is attributable to the fact that the great stagnation of the 1970s coincided with higher inflation, and this coincidence led people to believe that higher inflation caused the stagnation. Most importantly, it is because people have conflated the "wage squeeze" with inflation. Inflation refers to rising prices; the wage squeeze refers to prices rising faster than wages. However, people tend to call any situation in which prices are rising faster than wages as one of high inflation, even though prices are rising slowly.

This changed policy stance is illustrated in the Fed's response to improved employment conditions. Whenever there have been indications of a tightening of labor markets, which is to the workers' advantage, the Fed has responded by raising interest rates. This was vividly illustrated in 1994. Over the course of the year, the Federal Reserve raised its target interest rate six times, with the first increase coming in February, and the last coming in November. This was followed by a further half-point raise in January 1995, and as a result short-term interest rates almost doubled from 3% to 5.9%, while the six-month T-bill rate rose from 3.25% to 6.5%. These increases in interest rates came just as the economy finally began to show promise of a real recovery that would help ordinary American families through rapid job creation and tightening labor market conditions. Such developments presaged a swing in the balance of labor market power favoring workers and offered the prospect of higher wages: it was exactly this outcome that the Federal Reserve was opposed to.

The official justification for the increase in interest rates was that the economy was showing signs of increasing inflation. Thus, once again, inflation was placed ahead of jobs on the Fed's priority list. However, as Papadimitriou and Wray (1994) have shown, there was absolutely no plausible evidence that inflation was accelerating. Instead, the Federal Reserve was simply flying blind, merely choosing indicator variables reflecting nothing more than a hunch that inflation was about to rise in order to justify interest-rate hikes.

Recently (1996–7), the Fed's motivations have become even more transparent owing to its new policy focus on the employment cost index (ECI). This index measures the costs of wages, salaries, and benefits, and it is a favorite inflation indicator of Fed Chairman Alan Greenspan. The index has been rising at an annual rate of just under 3%, but there is still no evidence of an actual acceleration in price inflation. Despite this, many at the Fed have been claiming that the ECI suggests that such an acceleration is imminent, and interest rates should be raised in anticipation. Their argument is that prudence demands that the Fed act now, because an ounce of prevention is worth a pound of cure.

The Fed's focus on the ECI reveals its true colors. In effect, the Fed has taken on for itself the role of regulating the distribution of income and seeks to do so in a manner favorable to business. If working Americans are to share in the growth of productivity, then wages must grow. The need for wages to grow is illustrated in equation (3.1).

$$\text{Growth of purchasing power wages} = \text{growth of} \\ \text{dollar wages} - \text{inflation} \qquad (3.1)$$

The growth of the purchasing power of wages is equal to the growth of dollar wages minus the rate of inflation. Dollar wages must therefore rise at the rate of inflation just to hold people's standard of living intact. If people are to actually enjoy a rising standard of living, then wages must rise even faster.

If workers are to share equally in productivity growth, then wages must grow at the rate of inflation plus the rate of productivity growth. With the Fed seeking to hold wage growth equal to the rate of inflation, it has effectively locked working Americans into a situation of stagnant wages.

The Fed's focus on the ECI is even more harmful because much of the increase in the ECI is attributable to higher medical insurance costs, which are themselves driven by the increased profits of the insurance companies, the managed-care providers, and the drug companies. Thus, what looks like a wage gain turns out, on closer inspection, to be a profit gain.

National income consists of wages, interest, and profits. Since 1988, the corporate profit rate has almost doubled, and the increase in profit income has far exceeded the rate of inflation. Much of this increase has come at the expense of wage growth. In 1996, the before-tax profit rate was 11.39%, while the after-tax profit rate was 7.57%. The previous peak in the before-tax profit rate was 11.29% in 1966. Since 1988, both the before- and after-tax profit rates have increased almost 50%. When profits have been growing rapidly, the Fed has felt no obligation to act and slow down such growth. Only when wage income begins to hold its own does the Fed step on the economic brakes.

Why has the Federal Reserve shifted to this antiworker policy? The argument, developed in detail in chapter 7, is that the Federal Reserve is committed to monetary policy with a deflationary bias because such a policy advances the interests of Wall Street and financial capital. In effect, the Federal Reserve has been captured by special interests representing the banking and financial community, and these special interests are now projected as national interests. The incessant beating of the inflation drum provides a cloak that obscures how our most powerful economic policy-making institution has been captured by America's financial community to the detriment of working family prosperity.

How did this capture come about? Explaining this capture involves a complicated train of investigation that shows how conservative economic theory, developed by laissez-faire economists under the rhetoric of free markets, came to dominate the economics profession and the counsels of economic policy making. This theory now provides the justification for the deflationary and antilabor policies followed by the Federal Reserve. Initially restricted to right-wing think tanks, the free-market ideology of conservative economics spread into the academy during the 1970s. This spread was facilitated by the economic turmoil caused by the successive oil shocks of the 1970s. These shocks generated unavoidable inflation and economic dislocation, and conservative economists opportunistically exploited them to blame the policies of the Golden Age as the cause of inflation. The dislocations of the 1970s therefore provided a critical window of opportunity for the revival of conservative economics, and today it dominates the economics profession, with the profession in turn validating conservative economic policy.

DEFLATIONARY FISCAL POLICY AND THE ATTACK ON GOVERNMENT

Fiscal policy is another area where conservative economic theory is now being used to institutionalize deflationary policy. The policy arguments being advanced to justify deflationary fiscal policy are examined in detail in chapter 8.

41

CHAPTER 3

Fiscal policy is concerned with government spending and tax policies. Understanding how fiscal policy affects the economy is somewhat technical. The basic principle is that government spending increases economic activity by pumping spending into the economy. Tax cuts can also increase economic activity if they put money into the pockets of the middle class, but they have less effect if they are directed toward the wealthy, who tend to save the tax cut rather than spend it. However, both tax cuts and government spending need to be financed by government borrowing. This causes the national debt to grow, and government then has to pay interest on the debt. Thus, tax revenues increasingly become used to pay debt interest. Moreover, since the government debt is largely owned by the wealthy, interest on the debt becomes a way in which middle-class tax payments are paid over to the wealthy. This is one of the dangers of excessive debt accumulation.

During the 1980s, fiscal policy had a strongly expansionary tilt as the U.S. government ran huge budget deficits. This expansionary tilt was based on defense spending and tax cuts, and it helped mitigate the deflationary stance adopted by the Federal Reserve. However, the 1980s policy mix of high interest rates (tight monetary policy) and big deficits (loose fiscal policy) was unwise and unsustainable. It was unwise because high interest rates reduced corporate investment spending and capital accumulation, which are the lifeblood of economic growth. High interest rates also contributed to the redistribution of income, as ordinary households had to make higher interest payments on their mortgages and consumer debts. The policy mix was unsustainable because the deficits caused a massive increase in the national debt that ultimately threatened to bankrupt the government.

Given this, there has been a move to eliminate the budget deficit, but now the pendulum has swung to the opposite extreme, with proponents of laissez-faire seeking to downsize government and institutionalize deflationary fiscal policy. The proposed new policy threatens to generate an equally unwise policy mix in which both fiscal and monetary policy are pointed in a deflationary direction, and the new mix risks sending the economy into a prolonged tailspin. What is needed is balanced fiscal policy that addresses some of the inequities in income distribution, combined with looser monetary policy that will lower interest rates and promote growth.

With regard to the fiscal policy of the Reagan–Bush presidencies, it should be noted that, though they had a temporary favorable effect on the economy, the policy was never intended as a policy for helping working

TABLE 3.8

Publicly Held Federal Debt and Interest Payments (billions U.S. dollars)

	Publicly Held Federal Debt	Interest Payments	Interest as Percent of Government Spending	Interest as Percent of Government Revenue
1980	$709.8	$52.5	8.9	10.2
1992	$2,998.8	$199.4	14.4	18.3

Source: Economic Report of the President (1997, p. 367) and author's calculations.

people. The fact that policy did stimulate the economy was an accidental by-product of the financial raid on the Treasury. This raid awarded huge personal tax cuts to the wealthiest echelons of society, while leaving middle-class tax burdens unchanged. In addition, corporations were given enormous tax breaks (in the form of accelerated depreciation allowances) and the right to sell tax losses among themselves. The result was a huge tax subsidy to corporate profits, and, because the wealthy own corporate America (the top 5.2% of households own 51.1% of all directly and indirectly held stock, including mutual funds, IRA or Keogh plans, and defined contribution pension plans), this subsidy effectively went to the rich and contributed to the worsening of income distribution.

From an eagle-eye vantage, the wealthy were given a massive tax cut that enabled them to buy the government debt needed to fund the deficit created by the tax cut. This debt was sold at extremely high interest rates (owing to the tight monetary policy pursued by the Federal Reserve), and the U.S. government is now burdened with paying it back. The effects of these policies are captured in table 3.8, which provides data on the government debt and interest payments. Between 1980 and 1992, Federal debt increased 300%, and interest payments as a percentage of government spending and revenues rose approximately 80%. In 1996, the federal deficit was $107.3 billion: the increase in interest payments over the twelve years of the Reagan–Bush presidencies was $146.9 billion; in the absence of their deficits, there would be a budget surplus today.

Though not normally talked about in such terms, the Reagan–Bush budgetary and interest-rate policies effectively set in place a process for recycling middle-class tax payments into the pockets of the wealthy because ownership of bonds is massively concentrated among the wealthy. Wolff (1996) showed that the top 1% of wealthiest households own 62.4% of all bonds: the next 9% own 28.9% of bonds. Thus the top 10% own 90.3% of bonds; whereas the bottom 90% own 8.7%. Massive deficits, financed at historically high interest rates, have therefore been a means of effecting a major adverse redistribution of income and wealth. In this fashion, policy has exacerbated trends that were already in place in the private sector.

The policy of massive deficits has had lasting negative consequences on both the economy and American politics. Ordinary Americans were offered the rhetoric of tax cuts, but never received any, so that their tax burdens remained unchanged. At the same time, to prevent the deficit from exploding, there have been cuts in social programs, cuts in infrastructure investment, and cuts in education spending. These forms of spending are the channels through which the middle class gets value for its tax dollar. The net effect of these combined developments has been to erode middle-class support for government.

Interest payments on the debt have now boxed in government and restrict it from playing its historical role as an economically expansionary and progressive force. Concern with the deficit and the huge national debt, combined with the induced disenchantment with government, now fuel the push for a balanced budget amendment. By this means, economic conservatives hope to disable government permanently and knock it out of the economic picture.

If passed, the balanced-budget amendment would institutionalize deflationary fiscal policy. The traditional textbook interpretation is that the policy would be destabilizing because it would promote tax cuts during booms, which would further fuel the boom by increasing consumer spending. Taxes must be cut in booms because tax revenues go up in booms, and to balance the budget government would have to cut taxes. Similarly, in recessions when tax revenues go down, government must raise taxes, thereby reducing consumer spending and worsening the recession.

An even greater impact would likely come through the effect on the size and quality of government. Because the Federal Government is running a deficit, obtaining budget balance will require fiscal tightening. With tax increases being political suicide, such tightening will likely be achieved by permanent expenditure cuts, which will take government spending out of the economy. It will also further diminish the quality of government services, and contribute to the continued vicious circle whereby government is underfunded so that government does not solve the problems it claims to. This in turn makes it look like government should be abandoned.

Moreover, the reduction in the size of government will likely have reverberating adverse effects for workers throughout the economy. Not only will government workers lose, but private-sector workers will also be adversely affected because the expansion of the government sector has historically been a structural factor promoting higher wages and employment security in the private-sector. Government employment has provided an alternative to private-sector employment, thereby setting a baseline for wage and benefit conditions. In a sense, government employment has had a positive effect on private-sector employment in the same way that unions have a positive effect on wages in the nonunionized sector. Moreover, government employment is largely immune to economic fluctuations, and this has helped stabilize the economy by providing a significant bloc of employment that is not subject to cyclical fluctuation. Thus, shrinking government will not only undermine conditions of employment in the private-sector by removing the option provided by government jobs, but it will also increase the insecurity and uncertainty of private-sector employment by reducing government's stabilizing influence on the economy.

THE INTERNATIONALIZATION OF DEFLATION

Another area where there has been increasing institutionalization of deflationary bias is the international economy. These developments concern both the arenas of international trade and international financial markets. The issue of international trade is examined in detail in chapter 9, while the question of international finance is taken up in chapter 10.

In the realm of international trade, there has been an increasing push for globalized free trade, as evidenced by the passage of the North American Free Trade Agreement (NAFTA) and the General Agreement on Tariffs and Trade (GATT). Most economists have asserted that free trade is good for American workers, and they have persistently pushed for the elimination of tariffs. However, these economists draw no distinction between types of trade, so that trade with West Germany is treated as if it were identical to trade with Indonesia or India.

Without doubt trade can be beneficial by promoting product choice and lower prices through international competition. However, trade ceases to be good when it rests exclusively on wage differentials. In this case, it becomes an implicit instrument for battering down wages and pushing up profits. This possibility forces a reconsideration of free trade that involves distinguishing trade between different types of countries and different economic systems. Conventional economics argues that because domestic trade (i.e., trade within the United States) is good, international trade must also be good. But such logic misses a critical point, namely, that all domestic trade takes place within a common economic system. However, international trade often takes place across different systems, and this introduces the notion of *systems competition.*

The key feature of trade based on systems competition, is that free trade can become a force for implementing the lowest standard, thereby setting in place a race to the bottom. Consider the case of United States–Indonesia trade. The Indonesian system is based on pauperized wages, no environmental protections, no worker safety laws, and no employer obligations to provide for social security and other employee benefits. Consequently, costs of production are lower in Indonesia, and free trade therefore sets up competition between the Indonesian and U.S. systems. Thus, trade becomes a means for promoting wage concessions. Moreover, to the extent that the American system of social and environmental protections becomes viewed as a cause of cost disadvantage and job loss, it unleashes political pressures for repeal. In this fashion, ill-considered free-trade arrangements promote a race to the bottom, with trade serving to undermine the wages and well-being of American workers. Unfortunately, it is exactly this type of free trade that has been advocated by economists and businessmen and implemented by governments.

Side-by-side with developments in the realm of international trade, developments in international financial markets have mitigated against the pursuit of full employment policies. Here once again we see an interaction between independent market developments and unwise policy. The development of new electronic information and communication technologies has contributed to a shrinking of the globe and increasingly interlinked financial markets. Thus, wealth holders now have portfolios that contain financial assets from around the world, and reductions in transaction costs in financial markets have increased daily buying and selling. In addition, prices across financial markets are now more closely linked, and financial capital moves rapidly between countries in response to small differences in interest rates, as capital seeks the highest rate of return.

These developments have been encouraged by economic policies in many countries through the abolition of controls on international capital movements. Such controls served to restrict destabilizing movements of capital that undermined domestic economic policy. However, governments have been increasingly persuaded by economists, central bankers, and the leaders of the financial community that these restrictions mitigate against perfectly competitive markets and contribute to inefficiency. The removal of controls has promoted the emergence of global financial markets, and "hot" money now flows rapidly across borders to equalize interest rates. As a result, domestic monetary authorities in many small countries have lost control over domestic interest rates, and they have therefore lost the power to pursue expansionary policies through lower interest rates. Worse than that, there is now pressure to raise domestic interest rates to guard against the possibility of a sudden outflow of funds, thereby producing a system with an upward bias to interest rates. This is one of the reasons why interest rates have been so high over the last fifteen years.

Pressures for the institutionalization of deflationary bias have also been operative in dealings with less-developed nations. Here, the key institutions have been the International Monetary Fund (IMF) and the World Bank. The irony is that both of these institutions were founded to facilitate global economic expansion and development. As with central banks, these institutions draw their management from the ranks of bankers, while their staff economists are drawn exclusively from mainstream economics departments. These sociological features mean that these institutions have a deflationary policy bias that is driven by management preferences and the intellectual beliefs of their advisers.

Getting aid from these institutions, particularly the IMF, has therefore been made contingent on implementation of "financial reform" programs that involve disinflation, cutting welfare and government spending, deregulation, the abolition of capital controls, and the adoption of fixed exchange rates to anchor domestic prices. This list of reforms effectively serves to lock domestic monetary policy into a deflationary stance. As long as this goal is achieved, IMF programs are unilaterally declared a success, without regard to the induced problems of economic contraction and worsened income redistribution.

CONCLUSION: FIXING THE DISORDERED ECONOMY

Over the last twenty-five years, the process of creative destruction has promoted structural changes that have tilted the balance of power in favor of business over labor and promoted declining wages. At the same time, the economics of disinflation and fiscal austerity have come to dominate economic policy. In the realm of monetary policy, the argument is that the economy is handcuffed by a binding inflation constraint that compels an unemployment rate of between 6% and 7%. Though theoretically contested and empirically unsubstantiated, this argument has provided the necessary pretext for implementing deflationary policies favored by financial interests.

Having succeeded in implementing deflationary policy, supporters of business domination have now embarked on a second stage that seeks to repeal the New Deal by permanently shrinking government and eliminating government's role as provider of an effective social safety net for the young, the aged, the infirm, and the unemployed. At the same time, the U.S. economy is increasingly being locked into an international financial and trading system that facilitates the mobility of capital, and opens U.S. workers to wage competion from pauperized Third World workers. The net result of these developments will be to further diminish labor's power relative to business, thereby contributing to further declines in the wages of ordinary American workers.

The changes underway are accelerating the refashioning of the American economy. The transition from the Main Street capitalism of the Golden Age to the Mean Street capitalism of our leaden age has been taking place for twenty-five years. The longer this process goes on, the harder it becomes to reverse, because the new business practices and international linkages become more deeply entrenched. Reversing this transformation requires (1) addressing the imbalance in the distribution of power across business and labor, and (2) replacing the deflationary bias in economic policy with an expansionary tilt. Expansionary policy cannot work unless an appropriate economic structure is in place, so that restoring structural balance is a prerequisite for fixing the disordered economy. However, the continued dominance of the fiction of a natural economy has prevented this and led to fatalistic acceptance of the economics of business domination. Structural Keynesianism challenges this fatalism.

CHAPTER 4

The State of the American Dream

C HAPTER 3 provided some preliminary evidence on the downsizing of the American dream, as well as providing a sketch of the causes. This chapter documents the performance of the American economy in greater detail. In a manner analogous to that of a lawyer, the chapter assembles an array of evidence that reveals the adverse economic consequences of the shift from the Main Street capitalism of the pre-1973 era to the Mean Street capitalism of today.

The shift to Mean Street capitalism has manifested itself along four dimensions. First, the economy is growing more slowly than in the past. Second, the economy is running slacker and operating less efficiently than before. Third, there has been a significant worsening of income distribution, with wages of ordinary workers actually declining over the last twenty years. Fourth, workers are more economically insecure and subject to greater levels of stress. Slower, slacker, more unequal, and less secure are the hallmarks of the disordered economy. Economic booms may temporarily ameliorate these conditions, but once the boom is over, they reassert themselves.

GROWING MORE SLOWLY

Figure 4.1 shows how the levels of output per-worker and output per person in the U.S. economy have evolved over the period 1948–94.[1] In 1948, each employed worker produced $22,276 of output, and by 1994 this figure had grown to $43,425. Thus, if the economy were perfectly egalitarian, and all workers were paid an equal wage and owned an equal share of American business, then each would have had an income of $43,425 in 1994. Output per person has also increased over this period from $8,833 in 1948 to $20,508 in 1994. Thus, if the economy's output were divided equally among every man, woman, and child, each would have received an income of $20,508.

Figure 4.1 shows that output per-worker (which measures worker productivity) and output per person have both risen steadily. Moreover,

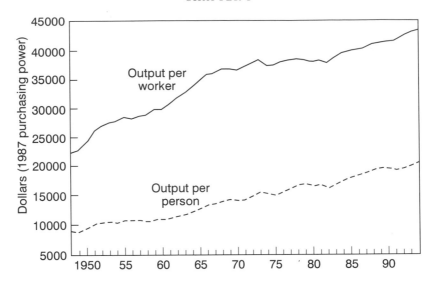

Fig. 4.1. Output per worker and output per person, 1948–94. *Source*: Author's calculations based on CITIBASE data.

this rise has continued in the period after 1973, the year that dates the end of the Golden Age. Figure 4.1 therefore reveals the tremendous and growing productivity of American workers, which is a major piece of good news.

It also helps resolve a basic misconception. All too often, it is claimed that America can no longer afford high wages, a quality system of public education, sound infrastructure, social security for the elderly, a system of universal health care, and a social safety net that provides a reasonable level of income protection. The data in Figure 4.1 firmly refute these claims. America has a larger national income, both in total and on a per-person basis, than ever before. If ordinary Americans feel that they cannot afford these possibilities, it is not because the economic pie is too small. Rather, it is because the pie is being divided in such a way that most Americans have been receiving a shrinking slice.

Though figure 4.1 contains this good news, it also hides bad news. figure 4.2 provides another plot of per-worker output, along with a plot of a hypothetical path of per-worker output based on the pre-1973 average growth rate. Between 1949 and 1973, per-worker output grew at an average annual rate of 2.2%, but the growth of per-worker output slowed to 0.6% in the period 1974–94. The steep broken line shows what output per worker would have been if productivity growth had continued at the

50

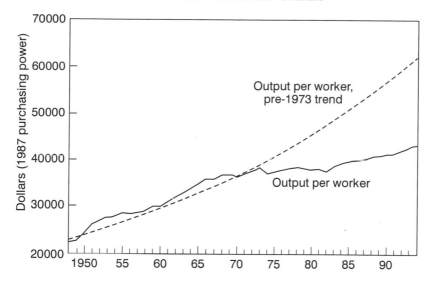

Fig. 4.2. Output per worker with pre-1973 trend, 1948–94. *Source*: Author's calculations based on CITIBASE data.

Golden Age rate of 2.2% per annum. In 1994 actual per-worker output was $43,425: if productivity had grown at its old rate, actual per worker output would have been $62,099. Thus, it would have been $18,673 (43%) higher. This is a staggering amount, and shows how slow growth gives rise to huge losses that cumulate over time owing to the power of compounding.

Slower productivity growth has slowed the expansion of national income, but at least it has been growing. However, when it comes to worker's wages this is not the case. Figure 4.3 shows how average hourly wages for production and nonsupervisory workers have evolved. Such workers represent 80% of all workers: they exclude management and professionals. Wages are stated in 1996 dollars. In 1959, the average hourly wage was $10.64. Wages then rose steadily and peaked in 1973 at $13.58 per hour. Since then, they have declined and in 1996 stood at $11.82. Comparing figures 4.1 and 4.3 reveals that though the economy has been growing, ordinary workers have not been sharing in this growth.

This is the central fact of the disordered economy, and it has not been corrected by the most recent boom. Even though the U.S. unemployment rate fell to a twenty-three year low of 4.9% in 1997, and the before-tax profit rate hit an all time high of 11.4 percent in 1996, wages have actually fallen over the current business cycle. In 1989, the average hourly

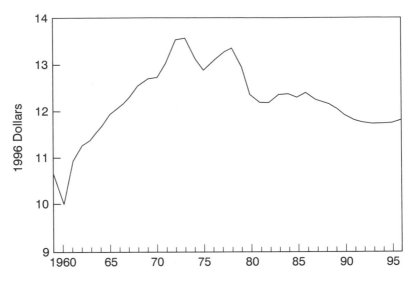

Fig. 4.3. Real average hourly wage of nonsupervisory workers. *Source*: Author's calculations based on CITIBASE data.

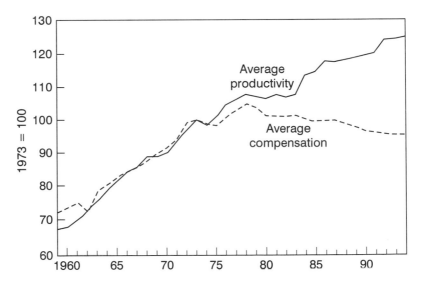

Fig. 4.4. Nonsupervisory average productivity and compensation. Data provided by Economic Policy Institute, Washington, D.C.

wage was $12.14: in 1996, it was $11.82. Economic booms, which can temporarily obscure much of the bad news, cannot obscure this.

There is no denying that average hourly wages have fallen. However, some assert that this is because employee benefits have risen. Figure 4.4 firmly scotches this argument. It shows average productivity of production and nonsupervisory workers and the typical compensation of such workers, where compensation is defined to include benefits.[2] Up until 1973, productivity and typical worker compensation moved closely together. In the mid-1970s, compensation started to fall behind but continued rising. Compensation peaked in 1978 (a little later than wages), and since then has fallen steadily. Figure 4.4 reveals a fundamental disconnect between compensation and productivity, the result of which is that ordinary workers have not been sharing in productivity growth. This is the most glaring symptom of the disordered economy.

RUNNING SLACKER

Not only is the economy growing more slowly with ordinary workers not sharing in that growth, it is also running slacker and less efficiently, in the sense of not using all available resources. Figure 4.5 shows the rate of manufacturing capacity utilization, which measures the extent to which the economy's machines and factories are being put to work. This series fluctuates with the business cycle: in booms, capacity utilization is high, in slumps it is low. Figure 4.5 shows a graph of manufacturing capacity utilization. In the period 1948–73, average manufacturing capacity utilization (MANCAPU1) was 83.6%; but in the period 1974–95, it fell to 80.4%. This reveals how our factories have been systematically underutilized and allowed to sit idle when they could have been put to work. The cost of such idleness is lost output and income.

Just as the economy's factories and machines are being underutilized, so too are American workers, as illustrated in figure 4.6, which shows the rate of unemployment. Like the rate of capacity utilization, the unemployment rate fluctuates with the business cycle: in booms it goes down, and in slumps it goes up. However, the critical fact is that the average rate of unemployment was 4.8% in the period 1948–73, but it jumped to 6.8% in the period 1974–94. This represents an increase of almost 50%. It means that more workers who want to work are now unable to find work, thereby wasting their productive skills and abilities. The lost output that these workers could have produced is not the only bad: higher rates of

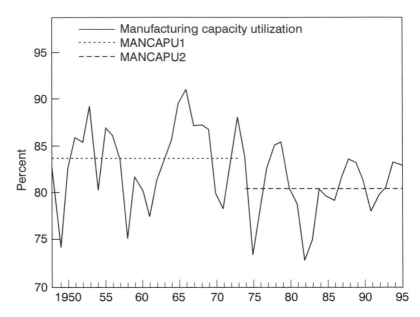

Fig. 4.5. Manufacturing capacity utilization, 1948–95. *Source*: Author's calculations based on CITIBASE data.

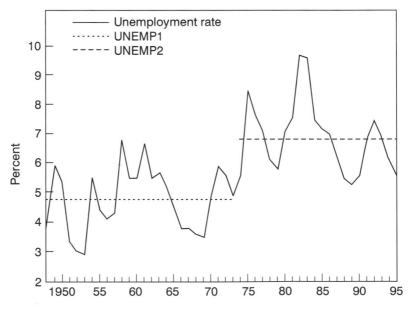

Fig. 4.6. Unemployment rate, 1948–96. *Source*: Author's calculations based on CITIBASE data.

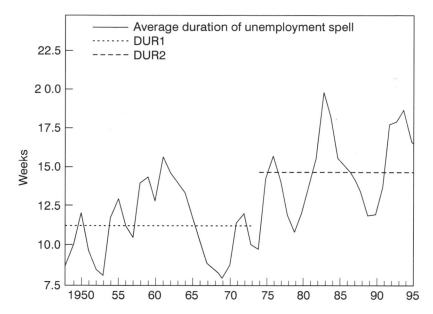

Fig. 4.7. Average duration of a spell of unemployment, 1948–95. *Source*: Author's calculations based on CITIBASE data.

unemployment reduce labor's bargaining power vis-à-vis business, and this helps explain why wages have declined and workers have not received their share of productivity growth.

This picture of worsened employment conditions is confirmed by a number of other pieces of evidence. Figure 4.7 shows the average duration (measured in weeks) that unemployed workers have been unemployed. In the period 1948–73, the average duration of a bout of unemployment was 11.2 weeks, but in the period 1974–95, it rose to 14.7 weeks. Thus, if a worker becomes unemployed, he or she can now expect to spend longer waiting to find a new job.

Figure 4.8 shows the extent of involuntary short time working by employed workers. In the period 1956–73, the average number of workers on involuntary short time was 3.5%: in the period 1974–95, this number rose to 4.6%. Thus, more workers are being forced to work less than they would like to and must live with reduced wage income.

Lastly, figure 4.9 shows an index of help wanted. In the period 1948–73, the average level of the index was 1.1; but in the period 1974–95, it has fallen to 0.8. This indicates that, on average there are now relatively fewer job vacancies at any time.

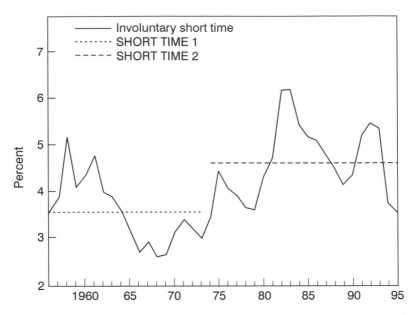

Fig. 4.8. Percentage of employed workers on involuntary short time. *Source*: Author's calculations based on CITIBASE data.

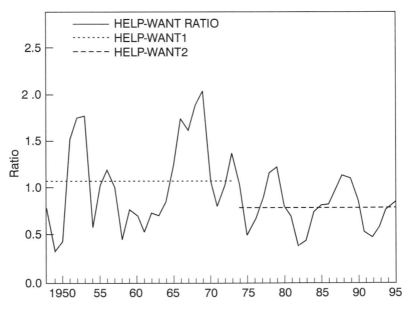

Fig. 4.9. Ratio of newspaper help-wanted ads to unemployed, 1948–95. *Source*: CITIBASE.

In sum, manufacturing capacity is being underused, more workers are
unemployed, workers are spending longer periods of time unemployed,
more workers are on involuntary part-time work, and there are fewer vacancies for unemployed workers. Taken together, these conditions show
how the economy is failing to use the available resources, be they machines or people. Though individual firms may be highly efficient, the
economy as a whole is running slacker and less efficiently. This is wasteful
and has also increased the vulnerability of labor, thereby contributing to
the undermining of labor's bargaining power relative to business.

BECOMING MORE UNEQUAL

Accompanying the slowdown in growth and the increase in the rate of
unemployment, has been an increase in the level of inequality. Figures 4.3
and 4.4 showed how average hourly wages and average compensation
have both fallen steadily since the mid-1970s. This fall has taken place
even though worker productivity has risen. Ordinary workers have been
cut out of productivity gains, which have accrued exclusively to profits
and persons at the top of the pay scale. The extreme example of this is
the increase in chief executive officer (CEO) pay, which has risen dramatically over the last twenty years. This is reflected in the CEO-worker pay
gap shown in table 4.1. Whereas CEO pay was forty-one times average
annual factory worker pay in 1960, it rose to a multiple of 157 in 1992.
The trend appears to show no sign of abating, and in 1996 the average
CEO was paid 212 times the earnings of an average factory worker.[3]
This multiple is way out of line with conditions in other countries. In
Germany, the average CEO is paid thirty times the average production
worker; in Japan, the average CEO is paid 20 times the average production worker.

CEO pay is the most visible manifestation of increasing inequality in
America. Table 4.2 compares the distribution of income in 1970 with that
in 1993. In 1970 the top 5% of households received 16.6% of total income; by 1993, this had risen to 20%, which means that their income
share increased 20.5%. The highest fifth of households saw their share of
income increase from 43.3% to 48.2%, an increase of 11%. Meanwhile the
middle class—which comprises the second, third, and fourth fifths—saw
its share decrease from 52.7% to 48.2%, a decline of 8.5%. Finally, the
lowest fifth of society saw its income share drop from 4.1% to 3.6%, a
12% decline.

TABLE 4.1

CEO–Worker Pay Gap (U.S. dollars, not adjusted for inflation)

	1960	1970	1980	1992
CEO	190,383	548,787	624,996	3,842,247
Factory Worker	4,665	6,933	15,008	24,411
CEO multiple of factory worker pay	41	79	42	157

Source: Business Week, April 26, 1993.

TABLE 4.2

U.S. Income Distribution by Quintile and
Highest Five Percent

Quintile	1970	1980	1993
Lowest Fifth	4.1	4.2	3.6
Second Fifth	10.8	10.2	9.1
Third Fifth	17.4	16.8	15.3
Fourth Fifth	24.5	24.8	23.8
Highest Fifth	43.3	44.1	48.2
Top 5%	16.6	16.5	20.0

Source: Dembo and Morehouse (1995).

Estimates of the distribution of income and wealth constructed by Professor Ed Wolff of New York University show that wealth is even more concentrated than income. Wolff's estimates of the distribution of wealth in 1992 are reported in table 4.3. This table reveals an extraordinary inequality in the distribution of wealth, which dwarfs that of income inequality. Ownership of wealth is analyzed by asset category, and decomposed by size of holdings. Thus, the top 1% of wealthy households own 49.5% of all stocks. Ownership of stocks is highly concentrated, with the top 10% owning 86.3% of all stocks. This means that the benefits of enhanced corporate profitability accrue to the few. Conservative analysts often like to claim that all Americans own stocks and that all therefore benefit from rising stock prices. However, owing to the degree of concentration of stock ownership, higher stock prices acheived by downsizing and lower wages render the vast majority of Americans net losers. Almost 100% of their income is derived from wages, and they own little stock; any capital gain on their holdings of stock is therefore swamped by the loss of

TABLE 4.3
Percentage of Total Assets Held by Wealthy Class, 1992

Asset Type	Top 1%	Next 9%	Bottom 90%
Assets Concentrated among the Wealthy			
Stocks	49.5	36.7	13.6
Bonds	62.4	28.9	8.7
Trusts	52.9	35.1	12.0
Business equity	61.6	29.5	8.9
Non-home real estate	45.9	37.1	12.3
Total for group	54.4	33.3	12.3
More Widely Held Assets			
Principal residence	9.0	27.1	63.9
Deposits*	22.4	37.3	40.3
Life insurance	10.0	35.1	54.9
Pension accounts†	16.4	45.9	37.7
Total for group	12.9	32.3	54.8

Source: Wolff 1996, cited in Mishel et al. 1997, p. 280.

* Includes demand deposits, savings and time deposits, money market funds, and certificates of deposit.

† IRAs, Keogh plans, 401(k) plans, the accumulated value of defined contribution pension plans, and other retirement accounts.

wage income. The notion that corporate America is owned by working families is a myth of fantastical proportions. It is also a useful myth.

In sum, the distribution of income and wealth clearly reveals two Americas: the top 20% and the rest. If the top 10% are viewed as representative of America, then America is indeed prospering. On the other hand, if the bottom 80% are viewed as representative of America, then the American economy is not delivering.

BECOMING MORE INSECURE

As economic growth has faltered and hourly wages have fallen, American workers also have become increasingly insecure. This increase in economic insecurity was vividly brought out in the week-long series on "The Downsizing of America" that the *New York Times* ran in March of 1996. The extent to which ordinary workers have been impacted is visible in a range of statistics. The *Times* reported that, since 1980, 75% of house-

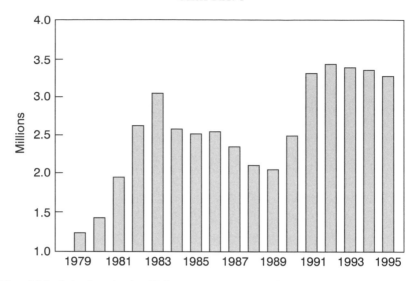

Fig. 4.10. Jobs lost in the U.S. economy, 1979–95. *Source: New York Times,* March 3, 1996, p. A27.

holds have had a close encounter with unemployment: a family member had lost a job in 33% of households, while 40% of households knew a relative or friend who had lost a job. One in ten adults acknowledged that a lost job had precipitated a major personal crisis in their lives.

The increased insecurity of workers is evident in the permanently higher rates of job loss. In the era of the Golden age, job losses tended to be concentrated in periods of economic recession but tapered off in periods of economic boom. In the new era of economic insecurity, job loss is a persistent threat that intimidates all working Americans. Moreover, the consequences of job loss are more severe owing to the higher average rates of unemployment. This increase in the rate of job loss is illustrated in figure 4.10.[4] In the recession years of 1981 and 1982, there were 1.94 million and 2.62 million job losses, respectively. In 1992, there were 3.43 million job losses; in 1993, there were 3.38 million; in 1994, there were an estimated 3.34 million; and in 1995, there were an estimated 3.26 million. These last four years were supposedly a period of economic recovery, yet job losses were almost 25% higher than they had been in the terrible recession year of 1982. This indicates just how much more insecure the labor market has become.

Not only is the rate of job loss up, but the cost of job loss has also increased. From 1981 to 1983, workers losing jobs suffered a weekly pay cut of $62 per week (measured in 1994 dollars); in 1994, laid-off workers suffered an average weekly pay cut of $85. A survey conducted in 1994 of full-time workers who lost jobs in 1991 or 1992 showed that 35% got new full-time jobs at equal or higher pay, 25% got full-time jobs at lower pay, 8% found only part-time work, while 8% became self-employed. The remaining 24% were still unemployed or had dropped out of the labor force.

The increase in economic insecurity that characterizes the disordered economy is captured in a telephone poll conducted by the *New York Times* in March 1996. The *Times* polled 1,265 adults from throughout the United States, where these persons were randomly selected from the 36,000 active residential telephone exchanges. Here are some of the results:

1. Fifteen percent were "very worried" that they or someone in their household would lose their job in the next twelve months; 31% were "somewhat worried."

2. Of all respondents, 9% felt "very insecure" economically, while 26% said they felt "somewhat insecure." For those already hit by layoffs, the situation was much worse: 29% said they were very insecure, while 26% said they were somewhat insecure.

3. Seventeen percent said that it was "very unlikely" that the next generation would have a better life than their parents, as measured by living standard, better home, and better education; 32% said it was "somewhat unlikely."

4. Fifteen percent of households reported that they had been forced to work reduced hours within the last three years; 19% said they had experienced a pay cut, while 7% said they had been forced to take a cut in both hours and pay.

5. Seventy-two percent thought that the problem of layoffs and loss of jobs was a "permanent problem."

6. Of respondents who were not already retired, 35% said they were very worried about whether they had enough saving for retirement; 42% said they were "somewhat worried."

The sense of losing ground was pervasive, with 53% of respondents feeling that they were not as well off as they had expected to be at this stage of their lives. Of those who called themselves middle class, 35% felt they were in danger of falling out of the middle class. Moreover, 53% of middle-class respondents worried that they or someone in their household might soon be laid off. These responses indicate just how threatened

American workers feel. Being paid less and living with greater economic insecurity are the twin forces that are downsizing the American dream.

This subjective reported sense of greater economic insecurity is supported by the data studied by economists.[5] In 1970, 40% of those living below the poverty line were children, and 19% were elderly. As of 1994, only 10% are elderly, and 38% are children.[6] The remaining 52% of the poor are working-age adults. Labor Department economist, Stephen Rose, reports that in the 1970s, 67% of men had a "strong attatchment" to their firm and had worked full-time for eight of the last ten years with the same firm.[7] Such strong attatchment fell to 52% in the 1980s. At the same time, weak attachment—that is, working for the same employer for less than three of the last ten years—rose from 12% to 24%. Higher employment turnover, presumably the result of layoffs rather than voluntary quitting, disrupts career paths and lowers average earnings.

Rose predicts that more and more families will have an encounter with the welfare system. Given current conditions, over the next ten years:

39% of families will be eligible for earned income tax credit (EITC) in at least one year in ten;

in any one year, about one in six families will be eligible for EITC;

two of five families with children will have one year or more in which they are eligible for EITC;

30% of families with male heads of households will have at least one year in which they are eligible for EITC, as will 46% of families with a female head.

This widespread decline in well-being is captured by consideration of the relation of the minimum wage to the poverty level. The minimum wage was introduced in 1938, when it was set at 46% of the official poverty level for a family of three. In 1968, the minimum wage peaked at 118% of the official poverty level for a family of three. Since then, it has fallen continuously, such that in 1995 it covered only 72% of the official poverty level. Professor Ed Wolff of New York University has calculated that, if the minimum wage had kept pace with inflation since 1965, then the current wages of 30% of American workers would fall below the minimum wage. In effect, nearly one of three American workers is currently working for a wage that would have been illegal thity years ago.[8] The bottom line is that there has been a generalization of the economic insecurity and poverty that was previously restricted to the unfortunate and unlucky members of society.

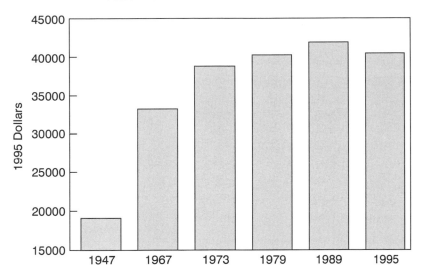

Fig. 4.11. Median family income, 1947–95. *Source*: Mishel et al. 1997, p. 44.

BECOMING MORE STRESSED

Not only are American workers becoming more economically insecure, but there is also evidence that they are working longer and becoming more stressed. These developments have been documented by Harvard economist Juliet Schor in her book, *The Overworked American: The Unexpected Decline of Leisure.*[9]

The increase in working hours involves many crosscurrents, and is linked with both social change and declining wages. As noted earlier, average hourly wages have been declining since the early 1970s. Real median family income, shown in figure 4.11, rose slightly during this period. It peaked in 1989 at $42,049 and has since fallen back to $40,611 in 1995.

However, the only reason that family income was maintained is the massive increase in labor force participation of married women. This increase in female labor force participation reflects a combination of social trends and families' economic straits. Put simply, jobs paying family wages have been disappearing, and sustaining a family now requires that both adults work. Having both work has sustained family income despite the decline in average hourly wages, but it has also produced greater stress: both must now do market and household work. The result has been a

TABLE 4.4
Market and Household Hours Worked by Labor-
Force Participants

	1969	1987	Change
Market Hours			
Men	2,054	2,152	98
Women	1,406	1,711	305
Household Hours			
Men	621	689	68
Women	1,268	1,123	−145
Total Hours			
Men	2,675	2,841	166
Women	2,674	2,834	160

Source: Schor (1991, p. 35).

squeeze on the amount of time that people have for themselves. More-over, the effective monetary benefits of labor force participation are lower because there are many costs to working. For families with young children, the largest expense is daycare; for all families, there is a loss of life quality associated with the decline in time for family and household work.

Not only have both family adults been compelled to work in order to sustain their living standards, but they have also been forced to work longer. This is captured in table 4.4, which shows market and household hours worked by both men and women. In the period 1969 to 1987, market hours worked by men increased by 98 hours—equivalent to 2.5 extra weeks at 40 hours per week. Womens' market hours increased by 305 hours, which is equivalent to 7.5 weeks. Household work by women decreased by 145 hours, while that of men increased by 68: the net result is that households lost 77 hours (approximately 2 weeks) of household work. With unchanged median family income, these numbers show that Americans are working longer just to maintain their current position, and the quality of family life is likely declining. A time squeeze has therefore accompanied the wage squeeze.

The increase in stress is also evident in the workplace environment. The *New York Times* survey referred to earlier found that 75% of those polled thought that companies were less loyal to their employees than ten years ago. Seventy percent said that people compete more at work, and 53% thought that there was an angrier mood at work: only 8% thought the mood was friendlier. The sense of losing a grip on life, and the sense of stress that goes with this, is also captured by the *Times* poll. Eighty-two percent of respondents said they would work longer if it might help them keep their jobs; 71% said they would take fewer vacation benefits; 53% said they would accept smaller benefits; 49% said they would challenge the boss less often, and 44% said they would accept a lower wage. Wage squeeze, time squeeze, and mental siege: this is the state of working America. Booms may temporarily alleviate economic insecurity and the fear of losing one's job, but the wage and time squeeze are permanent.

THE END OF ECONOMIC GROWTH?

Growing slower, running slacker, becoming more unequal and more stressed: these are the hallmarks of the disordered economy. They add up to declining well-being for ordinary Americans.

The slowdown in the rate of growth has received widespread attention from many economists.[10] This slowdown is of particular importance because of the power of compounding. This was illustrated in figure 4.2, which showed that output per worker would have been $18,673 higher if the rate of growth had been sustained at 2.2% per year over the period 1974–94.

Why has growth slowed? An important part of the answer lies in the fact that the economy has been running so much slacker, underutilizing its factories and operating with higher unemployment. These weaker economic conditions contribute to an explanation of both the slowdown in growth and the increase in inequality. High unemployment has weakened labor's bargaining power, thereby reducing wages. At the same time, excess capacity, combined with the weaker consumer demand resulting from lower wages, may have dampened the beneficial side of creative destruction that is the fountain of growth.

The above explanation of the growth slowdown contrasts with a number of other popular explanations. In a recent book, Jeff Madrick has elegantly argued that the decline of economic growth reflects the drying up of the external wellsprings of technical advance, and Americans will have to live with the fact that the economy has shifted permanently to a lower rate of growth.[11] Little can be done to restore the old higher growth rate, and the principal task is therefore one of adjusting the public's expectations such that they are consistent with the new lower growth rate.

Although it is clear and simple, this argument, has problems. First, it fails to explain why slow growth has been accompanied by worsened in-

Economic
Growth  Prosperity

Fig. 4.12. Economic growth as "manna from heaven."

come distribution and declining average wages: slower growth may imply slower growth of wages, but it does not imply a decline, nor does it imply a shift of income to the richest. Second, there appear to be no grounds for believing that we have entered a period of reduced technological innovation. Indeed, the spread of the new electronic communication, computing, and robotic technologies suggests the opposite. Third, the declining growth story treats the process of economic growth as if it were independent of the economy: in effect, the cause of economic growth is identified with manna from heaven. Inevitably, there are epochs in which growth is faster owing to the good fortune of external scientific discoveries that lend themselves to easy engineering for economic gain. However, growth is also generated through the incentives provided by robust economic conditions. Thus, growth and economic conditions interact in a positive self-reinforcing pattern, and bad economic policy can reduce growth by negatively affecting economic conditions.

These competing descriptions of the growth process are illustrated in figures 4.12 and 4.13. Figure 4.12 illustrates the manna-from-heaven approach, in which growth unidirectionally affects prosperity. Figure 4.13 shows the interdependent approach, in which there are positive feedbacks among economic growth, prosperity, and income distribution. Economic growth positively affects prosperity, and prosperity feeds back and positively affects growth by creating robust market conditions that provide an incentive to innovate. Prosperity (low unemployment) also positively affects income distribution, and improved income distribution feeds back and positively affects prosperity by strengthening demand for goods and services.

Such an account of the growth slowdown dovetails with the economic story provided in chapter 3. Much emphasis was placed on bargaining power, and how it is affected by the strength of unions and by economic conditions. Figure 4.13 shows that bargaining power directly affects the level of prosperity and indirectly affects growth. A more equal balance of power between business and labor equalizes income distribution, thereby enhancing prosperity, which in turn fosters faster growth.

Another popular explanantion for the slowdown in growth is that the period 1950–70 was a unique period of *Pax Americana*. World War II

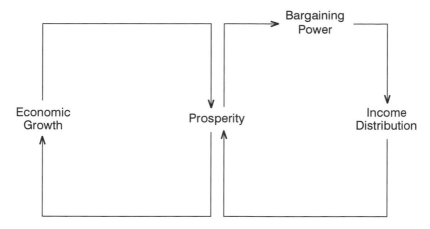

Fig. 4.13. Economic growth as an interdependent process produced within the economic system.

resulted in the destruction of America's industrial competitors, and America also benefited from the adoption of new production techniques introduced during the war. As a result, the United States emerged from World War II as the global industrial leader, and during the next twenty years enjoyed unparalleled economic supremacy. Moreover, not only had America's competitors been destroyed by the war, but they were also therefore forced to buy American products in order to rebuild. However, by 1970 this process of rebuilding was completed, and America had to compete with German and Japanese businesses that now had newer and better factories.

As with the manna-from-heaven hypothesis, the World War II hypothesis is also flawed. World War II undoubtedly benefited the American economy by promoting scientific innovation and improving techniques of mass production. The destruction wrought on America's industrial competitors also benefited major sectors of the American economy such as steel, machine tools, and industrial equipment. Thus, profits in these sectors were high, and with the help of unions, workers were able to capture some of these profits in the form of higher wages.

While clear and simple, there are problems with the "end of *Pax Americana*" argument. First, it is not clear why monopoly should have produced faster growth and innovation. Second, higher prices and higher profits caused by this temporary monopoly position reduced the purchasing power of wages for workers in the rest of the economy. The end of corporate America's monopoly power may therefore have actually benefited most workers. The increase in product market competition, resulting from the reemergence of Europe and Japan as industrial powers, lowered prices and increased the quality of goods. Though workers located in those industries that previously had monopoly power may have suffered as employment fell, workers in the rest of the economy actually benefited.

This is an example in which free trade worked to the benefit of average Americans. Europe consists of industrialized countries with wage structures and systems of social welfare and governance similar to those of America. As such, trade has not been based on pauperized wages or cost advantages conferred by the absence of environmental and safety regulation; instead, it has been based on product competition. This stands in sharp contrast with the impetus to free trade embodied in NAFTA and GATT. Here trade is not driven by product competition, but is instead driven by systems competition, predicated on pauperized wages and absence of welfare standards. Whereas product competition raises workers' standards of living by lowering prices and increasing quality, systems competition produces downward pressure on wages and social governance standards, to the detriment of worker well-being. This argument is explored in detail in chapter 9, which explains why ill-considered free trade can promote a race to the bottom.

Another explanation of the growth slowdown is the "deindustrialization of America" hypothesis. This hypothesis has greater legitimacy, even though deindustrialization has elements of both cause and effect. A well-known fact is that productivity growth is faster in manufacturing industry than services. This is because manufacturing uses machines and labor, and new machines can be introduced that increase output while reducing the use of labor. Such a process is more difficult in the service sector: the extreme case is the playing of a Mozart quartet, which will always require four musicians.

The decline in the share of manufacturing employment and the shift to service employment is shown in figure 4.14. This shift has lowered the overall rate of growth since manufacturing has become a smaller share of the total employment, and it has a higher rate of productivity growth.

One reason for this relative decline in manufacturing is the natural process of economic development. Thus, consumers tend to increase the proportion of their spending going to services (i.e, such things as restaurants, entertainment, and vacations) as they become richer. However, another important reason behind deindustrialization has been ill-advised economic policy. In the early 1980s the Federal Reserve drove up interest rates, causing the dollar to appreciate in foreign exchange markets. This

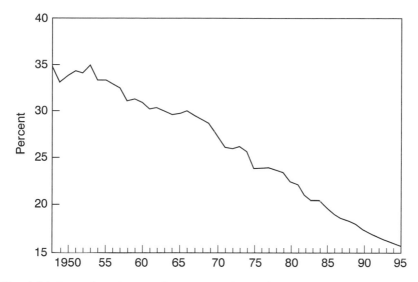

Fig. 4.14. Manufacturing employment as share of total, 1948–95. *Source*: Author's calculations based on CITIBASE data.

made American goods expensive relative to foreign goods and prompted a flood of imports that drove many American manufacturers out of business. It also prompted many American companies to shift production overseas where labor and others costs were cheaper. The result was a massive and permanent deindustrialization. Since then, the shift to free trade has provided a continuing incentive to move manufacturing production overseas, with lower tariffs compounding the advantage of lower overseas wages. The shift toward a service economy would have ocurred of its own accord, but policy has accelerated this shift and made it larger than necessary.

In sum, though there are valid reasons for believing that growth would have slowed of its own accord, there are also grounds for arguing that the slowdown has been worsened by the weaker economic conditions associated with business domination and the turn to deflationary policy. The forces that have made for a more unequal economy, have also made for a slower-growing economy. Ending business domination and reversing the policies that reinforce it are therefore the sine qua non for ending the dismantling of the American Dream.

CHAPTER 5

The Logic of Economic Power, Part I:
Diagnosing the Problem

CHAPTER 4 provided detailed evidence of the economic problems that has enveloped Main Street America over the last twenty-five years. At the economywide level, this decline has manifested itself in slower growth, greater inequality, and higher rates of unemployment. For ordinary people, it is has been felt in the form of stagnant wages, increased insecurity, and greater stress. This situation has now reached such a stage that even when the economy is in the midst of a business cycle boom, Main Street America remains in the doldrums.

A similar crisis has afflicted Canada and Western Europe. In those countries, rather than declining wages and increased inequality, the crisis has manifested itself in massively increased unemployment that hovers around 10% of the labor force. Their symptoms are slightly different, owing to different labor market institutions that have maintained the wage floor, but the causes of the malaise are the same.

This chapter presents a simple framework describing how the economy functions.[1] This framework is then used to explain the dismantling of prosperity and to identify policies that can help reverse this process. The description of the economy presented below complements the earlier description presented in chapter 2. That earlier description of the process of creative destruction dealt with how the economy evolves over time (i.e., the dynamic process of change). This description deals with the determination of economic activity (i.e., current conditions).

THE SKILLS-MISMATCH HYPOTHESIS: WHY IT'S WRONG

Before turning to my own argument, it is worth addressing the skills-mismatch hypothesis that is so often used to explain the plight of working America. The conventional wisdom explains the dismantling of prosperity in terms of technological change, which has produced a skills mismatch. This mismatch has lowered wages for those at the bottom of the income distribution, while increasing the incomes of workers with high cognitive skills at the top of the income distribution.

According to the skills-mismatch story, increased unemployment and stagnant wages are attributed to massive technological change that has caused loss of jobs and obsolescing of skills. Side-by-side with this, it is also claimed that these technological changes have created employment opportunities requiring new skills. As yet these opportunities have gone unfilled because of shortages in the supply of these skills. As a result, those with the right skills have found their wages bid up owing to increased demand, while those without have found their wages falling.

In the face of this sea change in technology, the received wisdom maintains that government can do little to remedy the situation, other than increase worker training expenditures so as to accelerate new skill acquisition. The claim is that the situation will ultimately improve, and society will once again enjoy full employment with even greater prosperity supported by the new more productive technologies.

This view of the jobs crisis is both benign and fatalistic: benign because it claims that things will get better, and fatalistic because there is little we can do about it. It has dominated public discussion. Worse still, it partakes of a "blaming the victim" mentality, in that unemployment and lower wages are due to workers' lack of education, skills, and accomplishment (in this, it is like the high-wage theory of unemployment that also blames workers for unemployment). If workers had chosen to go to college, then they too could have enjoyed rising incomes. The view is clearly stated in a 1993 *New York Times* article titled "Workers of the World, Get Smart," which quotes Labor Secretary Robert Reich "[There is a] mismatch between the skills Americans have and the skills the economy requires. . . . The long-term crisis in advanced industrial nations reflects in part a shift in the relative labor demand against less educated workers and those doing routine tasks and toward problem solving skills."[2] In another article the *Times* reports that "wages may be falling because many of the workers now entering the labor force are poorly educated and therefore have less value to employers."[3]

The skills-mismatch hypothesis has quickly become part of economic lore, and it is repeatedly bolstered by assertion. Yet, the reality is that the skills-mismatch story is flatly inconsistent with the facts (Howell 1997). The skills-mismatch story says that there has been a relative increase in the demand for skilled workers. The implication is that we should have seen a shift toward increased employment of skilled workers, and that this shift

71

should have begun when wages began to crumble. Yet, the fact is that patterns regarding the occupational skill mix of employment have been very stable. Among blue-collar workers, the ratio of skilled to unskilled workers has shown no change. Among white-collar workers, there has been a steady, slow upward trend in the ratio of skilled to unskilled workers, but this trend shows no change. That is, the trend is the same as it was in the fifties, sixties, and seventies: why then the sudden collapse in wages?

In another paper, Howell and Wieler (1996) noted that the new technologies often reduce skill requirements rather than increasing them.[4] Manufacturing plants that adopt new technologies do not appear to shift toward relatively greater use of skilled workers. The decline in wages has also affected the entire blue-collar wage distribution: failure to use computers cannot explain the wage decline of meat packers, truck drivers, and construction laborers. Indeed, wages of cashiers and sales clerks have declined, and these workers are some of the most intensive users of computers. At best, the skill hypothesis may explain the gains of college graduates, but it cannot explain the losses of the low-skilled.

The skills-mismatch hypothesis is often predicated on the increased use of computers. Computer investment surged in the 1980s, but it still remains a tiny fraction of total investment, and computers are a tiny fraction of the total capital stock in the economy. Blaming the collapse of wages on the absence of computer skills is similar to the snowball theory of avalanches. Moreover, the collapse in wages began in the 1970s, well before the surge in computer investment.

Howell and Weiler also examined data on the share of employment as constituted by high-skill white-collar, high-skill blue-collar, low-skill white-collar, and low-skill blue-collar. Only the low-skill white-collar employment share has fallen significantly, and women are heavily concentrated within this category; yet, women have been one of the few groups to experience any wage gains.

Ultimately, the skills-mismatch hypothesis is predicated on conventional demand-and-supply analysis. The argument is that the demand for low-skill workers has collapsed, and this has caused the price of low-skill labor (i.e., the wage) to fall. However, it is widely documented that the supply of low-skill labor has also been falling as the educational attainment of American workers has increased.[5] This reduction in supply therefore makes the conventional explanation of the wage collapse even more suspect because it should have worked to raise wages.

Gordon (1996) documented a series of other inconsistencies in the skills-mismatch hypothesis.[6] The biggest decline in low-skill earnings took place in the early 1980s, which was before computerization massively affected the work place. The gains to earnings of college graduates also appeared before computerization. Indeed, since the mid-1980s, earnings of college graduates have just been holding even. Davis and Topel (1993) noted that the meager growth of labor productivity outside of manufacturing is also inconsistent with the technological change–skills-mismatch hypothesis.[7] If skill-biased technical change has been so important, why has labor productivity growth been so slow? Howell and Wolff (1991) find little statistical correlation between skill demands and average hourly wages of nonsupervisory workers: this suggests that skills are not the dominant factor in setting hourly wages for these workers.[8] A similar conclusion is reached by Wieler (1994), who finds no evidence that changes in actual skill composition had any statistically significant relation to changes in industry earnings levels.[9]

In sum, there is a wide array of evidence that is grossly inconsistent with the technological change–skills-mismatch explanation of the collapse of hourly wages. Despite this inconsistency, it continues to be the received wisdom. According to conventional economics, workers are paid what they produce. Consequently, if workers are being paid less it must be because they are less productive owing to adverse skill shifts. This is argument by tautology. However, so powerful is the conventional wisdom that other candidate explanations are almost completely suppressed. This is illustrated in the proceedings of a conference on income inequality held by the Federal Reserve Bank of New York in January 1995. Of the ten papers presented, all advanced the skills-mismatch hypothesis.[10]

POWER AND THE DISTRIBUTION OF INCOME

In stark contrast to the skills-mismatch hypothesis, the thesis of this book is that there has been a devastating shift in the balance of power between capital and labor. This shift has favored capital and has resulted in wholesale redistribution of income from labor to capital; hence the increase in profits and executive pay.

Interestingly, both the skills-mismatch hypothesis and the balance-of-power hypothesis emphasize technological change—though the latter also emphasizes other factors. However, the implications of the two hypotheses are vastly different. The balance-of-power perspective maintains that the crisis is not self-correcting and that recent developments should be seen as part of a permanent decline in the economic well-being of ordinary Americans. Though the new technologies are indeed more productive, and therefore have the potential to enhance popular prosperity, they have also caused a permanent decline in the relative bargaining strength of labor.

According to this view, job training will do nothing to end the crisis. Worse than that, to the extent that it is accepted as a cure for our ills, it compounds the problem by maintaining a damaging economic status quo. Instead, remedying the crisis requires policies specifically designed to reverse this shift. This implies a major U-turn in policy, because existing policies have actively contributed to worsening the balance of power.

With regard to particulars, the thrust of the argument is that technological and political developments in Europe and North America have raised the mobility of both financial and physical capital. This increased mobility has enabled firms to reduce the share of wages in national income by increasing the threat of worker replacement: the reduced wage share has in turn diminished worker purchasing power, which has in turn generated an underlying fragility to overall spending in the economy. When investment spending by corporations is strong, demand for goods and services is strong. When investment spending peters out, however, the weak state of households means that demand quickly falls off. The combination of weak spending and mobile productive capital has resulted in the emergence of global excess capacities, underutilization of factories, and increased unemployment.

Moreover, this shift in the balance of economic power has not only been felt by workers; it has also been felt by national governments, whose powers of sovereignty have been increasingly jeopardized by the new powers of capital. In the period of the Golden Age, government had the upper hand in its dealings with business; now, the situation is increasingly reversed. Government lives in fear that business will move, and government is correspondingly shackled.

The Verities of the System

An essential ingredient for good policy analysis is a sound theoretical framework. Successful policy is not built on wishful thinking; rather, it is the product of clear-sighted analysis. For this reason, economic theory should always precede economic policy.

Given this, it is necessary to begin with a brief characterization of the economy as it really works. Such a characterization involves four axiomatic principles.

1. The levels of employment and output (GDP) depend on the level of demand for goods and services. Slack demand tends to lower output and employment; brisk demand tends to produce inflationary pressures.

2. The level of demand depends importantly on the distribution of income between wages and profits. High wages tend to stimulate demand owing to their effect on consumption. However, to the extent that higher wages reduce the profit rate, they can adversely affect investment spending, which reduces demand.

3. The distribution of income between wages and profits depends on bargaining between workers and firms. Conflict is an essential part of this bargain, because profits come at the expense of wages in bargaining between individual firms and workers. Moreover, the relative bargaining strengths of workers and firms depend importantly on the state of the economy, with increases in the rate of unemployment serving to weaken worker power. Worker power is also affected by the ease with which firms can replace existing workers and by labor legislation providing benefits for workers and protection against layoffs and other employer sanctions.

4. Firms are driven by the search for profits and will therefore shift their production to new sites if they can earn higher profits by doing so. This principle applies to both manufacturing and financial firms. Manufacturing firms shift the location of production in response to cost differences: financial firms manipulate the composition of their portfolios if they can earn higher yields (with unchanged risk) by doing so.

This characterization of the economy is illustrated in figure 5.1. At the center of the analysis lies the issue of bargaining power, which determines the distribution of income across wages and profits. Income distribution then affects the level of demand for goods and services, which in turn determines the level of economic activity. This affects employment conditions and the rate of unemployment, which feeds back on the distribution of bargaining power between firms and workers.

Not only is bargaining power determined by current conditions within the economy, it is also affected by structural factors that are independent of current economic conditions. These outside factors include the extent of capital mobility, which refers to the ease with which firms can shift the geographical site of their activities. They include the nature of technology, which affects how easy it is to replace workers. Ease of replacement is also affected by labor laws governing replacement. Bargaining power is affected by the extent of unionization, because collective action by workers

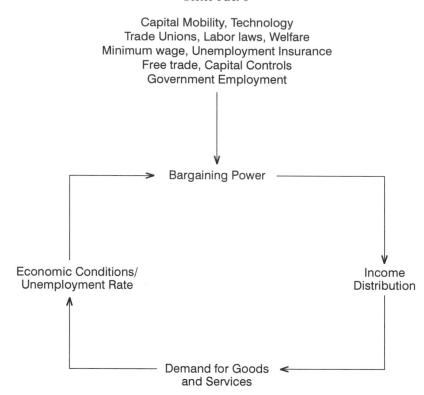

Fig. 5.1. The verities of the economic system: interaction among power, income distribution, and economic activity.

is far more powerful than individual action. Free trade is also relevant because the level of tariffs affects the relative profitability of overseas production, which affects firms' willingness to transfer production overseas. Lastly, government has an enormous affect on bargaining power through the provision of unemployment and welfare benefits, which provide workers with protection against the threat of layoffs. The level of government employment is also important because it offers alternative employment opportunities.

Firms engage in a perpetual search for profits, and this provides the fuel for conflict. Firms are constantly trying to reshape the bargaining outcome to their advantage, and they are therefore active agents of change. This is an aspect of the process of creative destruction that was examined in chapter 2. Thus, firms seek to develop new organizational forms and new technologies that increase their mobility and facilitate their ability to replace workers.

This type of innovation is illustrated by Volkswagen's plant of the future that is being built in Brazil.[11] This plant assigns major component suppliers space in the plant, and they then supply their own workers to add components to vehicles rolling down the assembly line. This arrangement transforms Volkswagen from a manufacturer into a contractor, who subcontracts out to other companies and oversees their work. The VW claim is that it will improve efficiency. The alternative interpretation is that it fragments the workforce, introduces many unions where previously there was one, and promotes the trend to squeezing subcontractors and employees. In this connection, it is noteworthy that the auto parts industry has never been as successfully unionized as the auto assembly industry. Introducing auto parts workers into the assembly process therefore undermines the assembly workers. In Brazil, the parts workers are paid approximately one-third of the amount paid to assembly workers.

Another way in which firms seek to affect structural change is through lobbying. Thus, they actively engage in the political process through powerful and well-funded lobbying. This lobbying is directed toward increasing their economic power, and the business sector has lobbied for free trade, for reductions of the minimum wage and unemployment benefits, and for reduction of the size of the government sector. In addition, the business sector has been a supporter of macroeconomic policies that have operated the economy with higher rates of unemployment. The stated justification is that this lowers inflation, but it also weakens workers' bargaining power.

Figure 5.1 illuminates the economic consequences of the shift in the balance of power in favor of business. It has served to redistribute income toward profits at the expense of wages, thereby lowering demand and raising unemployment. One of the most disturbing features is that economic policy has been substantially co-opted by business interests so as to further such shifts. The market-driven process of creative destruction tends to produce power shifts favorable to business because business has greater control over the direction of technological and organizational change. This built-in tendency has been aggravated by business's capture of policy. Thus, politics and policy, which have historically provided the counterbalance to unmitigated business ascendany, are now actively promoting this outcome. Restoring this traditional role of policy is therefore critical to the restoration of popular prosperity.

The Arithmetic of Transactions Costs

Within the above framework, the realized pattern of income distribution depends importantly on the ease with which firms can shift production and fire workers. This in turn depends on the costs of transactions. Such costs refer to costs that firms must incur in implementing different strategies. These costs are myriad in character. For purely financial dealings, they include costs such as brokerage fees, commissions, and official taxes and charges such as stamp duties. With regard to production location decisions, they include such costs as transportation (including shipping, breakage, and insurance) and costs of coordinating production across geographically dispersed locations. In the context of international trade, they also include tariffs, which are a cost incurred for transporting goods across country borders. Finally, with regard to replacement of workers, these costs include the value of production lost during the replacement period, costs related to training new workers, and subsequent reduced productivity that may come from having an alienated workforce.

Transactions costs are important because they have a major impact on the relative power of business. They affect firms' abilities to shift production or threaten employed workers with replacement by unemployed workers. To see how these costs affect economic outcomes, consider their impact on the working of financial markets. Suppose there are two types of investment of identical risk, yeilding returns of R_1 and R_2. If there are no financial transactions costs, then the law of arbitrage implies that market forces will equalize the two rates of return. The economic logic is that any time that R_1 does not equal R_2, there will be an incentive for wealth owners to rearrange their portfolios by selling the investment with the lower return, and buying the investment with the higher return.

Now suppose there are transactions costs of C associated with buying and selling investments (where these costs are expressed as a rate per dollar). In this case, the law of arbitrage implies that market forces will only ensure that the absolute difference between the two rates of return is less than the transactions cost. Instead of forcing the two rates of return to be equal, market forces will only ensure that there is a maximum gap between the two rates of return. If the rate differential is less than the transactions cost, it is not worth incurring the transaction cost to get the higher rate.

Exactly the same logic applies to manufacturing firms and their choice of production location. Suppose firms can site production in two possible locations: at one site they earn a profit rate of P_1, whereas at the other, they earn a rate of P_2. In the absence of transactions costs, market forces will tend to drive the profit rates toward equality. The mechanism for achieving this is the traditional market mechanism: as firms relocate to the site with the higher profit rate, they drive up wages and other costs at that site, thereby reducing the profit rate. Correspondingly, as they leave the other site, they drive down wages and costs at that site, thereby raising its profit rate.

However, if there are transactions costs associated with relocation, then market forces will only ensure that profit rate differential is less than the transactions costs. The economic logic is exactly the same as in the discussion of financial markets and portfolio investments. As long as the profit rate differential at the two sites is less than the transaction cost, it is not worth incurring the costs of relocation.

Finally, this arithmetic of transactions costs can be modified to understand a firm's decisions about replacing its existing labor force of "insider" workers with unemployed "outsider" workers. If there are no transactions costs, firms will replace insiders as long as outsiders are willing to work for less. If there are replacement costs, however, then firms may stick with more expensive insiders, because the wage savings from replacement do not cover the costs of replacement.

TRANSACTIONS COSTS, BARGAINING, AND INCOME DISTRIBUTION

What has this to do with the current economic crisis? Transactions costs have a critical affect on the firms' bargaining power, and they therefore affect the distribution of income. Though conventionally talked about in the politically neutral terms of supply and demand, the determination of wages involves a process that pits the power of firms against the power of workers: sometimes these workers are collectively organized in unions, but more often they are not. In this real world, transactions costs act as a protection for workers against firms.

In the first instance, firms faced a decision about the locus of production. For example should firms site production in the United States, or should they relocate to Indonesia where they can take advantage of plentiful cheap labor, minimal social insurance taxes, fewer pollution manadtes, and scant worker safety laws? Alternatively, should firms that operate in high labor-cost regions within the United States (such as the Northeast) or move to lower labor-cost regions (such as the Southeast)? In both cases, moving production potentially confers significant labor cost savings. These savings may not be sufficient because of transactions costs associated with the suspension of production. If these transactions costs fall below a threshold level, firms will relocate to take advantage of the labor-cost savings. At this stage, workers at existing plants will either become unemployed, or firms will be able to use the credible threat of moving to extract wage concessions. In either case, the net result is that wages are reduced and profits increased.

The same issues arise in connection with firms' threats to replace existing workers with unemployed workers as a means of winning wage concessions. Now it is the transactions costs associated with "replacement" that protect employed workers: these costs include production lost during the replacement period, worker retraining costs, and possible adverse labor productivity consequences that follow from having an alienated workforce. If these costs are sufficiently large, then replacement threats will not be credible, and firms will be unable to secure wage concessions. If, however, these costs fall below a critical threshold, such threats become credible. At this stage, existing workers must confront either being fired and replaced by cheaper labor or grant wage concessions. Once again, the net result is a redistribution of income from wages to profits.

These examples illustrate the critical influence of transactions costs in determining the distribution of income between wages and profits. Applied to the problem at hand, the underlying thesis is that, over the last twenty-five years, the size of transactions costs has declined tremendously. This has eroded worker's bargaining power, resulting in stagnation of wages and a shift in the distribution of income toward profits. In the United States, this redistributive process began to be visible in the 1970s, when real wage growth ceased; it then accelerated in the 1980s, aided by the laissez-faire atmosphere promoted by the Reagan-Bush administrations.

This redistribution of income has in turn had a depressing influence on the demand for output, because workers tend to spend a greater share of their income (i.e., save proportionately less) than do the wealthy. The result has been an ongoing deterioration in the robustness of business conditions. Though punctured by intermittent cyclical recoveries driven by increased consumer indebtedness and bouts of investment spending by firms, the overall trend has been persistently downward. Indeed, this process has fed into a vicious spiral wherein worsening income distribution has weakened demand for output and has thereby put further pressure on firms to reduce costs.

The Sources of Declining Transactions Costs

The sources of this underlying decrease in transactions costs are manifold. One source is technological advance. The conventional view represents such advances as if they were scientific manna from heaven. A bargaining power perspective views these advances as, in part, purposefully sought out by firms. Profit-seeking firms fully recognize the implications of transactions costs, and they recognize the benefits they reap from reducing such costs. They therefore direct part of their management research energies to finding ways to reduce these costs.

Among financial firms, the improvements in electronic communication and data processing have vastly reduced the costs of trading financial assets. The result has been quicker and cheaper adjustment of portfolios and an increased ability to shift financial wealth between countries. In manufacturing, transactions costs have fallen because of technological developments that have facilitated management of production across multiple distant locations. Thus, whereas the multinational corporation was previously an organizational form restricted to a few of the largest business enterprises, today it is widespread.

Another source of lowered transactions costs has been a decline in shipping costs. A major innovation in shipping has been containerization. The first container ship crossed the Atlantic in May 1966. Cheap to operate and easy to handle, containerization now accounts for almost 60% of seaborne trade measured by value. In the 1950s, port turnaround times were up to three weeks; today, they have been reduced to 24 hours. Before containerization, the cost of sea freight was 5% to 10% of the value of the consignment; now, it has been reduced to 1.5%. A $6,000 motorcycle can be shipped between continents for $85; a $1 can of beer can be shipped for $.01.[12]

This decline in shipping costs has facilitated production in regions and countries that are geographically distant from core markets. It has also promoted a system of national and international subcontracting, in which production is subcontracted around the world to the cheapest producer. The role of the lead firm is thereby reduced to that of coordinating production, and assembling the components supplied by subcontractors. The result is mobile production that fully exploits lowest labor costs, and increasingly pits worker against worker across different regions and countries.

Other technological innovations that have reduced transactions costs include applications of automation that have promoted the hiring of less

81

skilled workers. Such applications mean that workers can be trained faster and replaced more easily. Of course automation can be a two-edged sword, and there are also instances where it has raised necessary skill levels, albeit among a smaller workforce. Another innovation is improved monitoring technology, which has given management greater ability to observe workers. This has reduced workers' abilities to threaten noncooperation in response to wage stagnation.

Technological developments have undoubtedly contributed to substantial reductions in firms' transactions costs. However, another cause of reduced transactions costs has been government policy. In financial markets, the abolition of capital and exchange controls has facilitated the international movement of financial capital. Governments have also promoted the development of global securities trading in the hope of expanding employment in their own financial centers. In goods markets, governments have promoted free trade and reduced both tariffs and red tape obstructing the international movement of goods. This has lowered the effective cost of overseas production. The passage of NAFTA and the GATT show that this trend continues.

Another source of declining transactions costs has been the decline in trade unionism, combined with changes in labor markets. These developments have reduced the costs associated with the replacement strategy, so that workers have been unable to win any share of productivity growth and, in many instances, have actually had to make wage concessions. The reasons for the decline in union strength were discussed in chapter 3. The objective effect is that it has greatly increased the power of capital. Weaker unions mean that firms do not have to share the fruits of productivity growth with workers, and can even extract wage givebacks. Moreover, a diminished threat of unionism has meant that nonunion firms have been able to reduce the premium they previously paid their workers to prevent their workforce from becoming unionized. Finally, the popular misunderstanding of what unions do has caused a decline in social taboos against scabbing, which has weakened workers' strike threat as firms now find it easier to get replacement workers. This latter feature interacts with the state of the economy, in which permanently higher rates of unemployment have made jobs harder to come by, thereby making unemployed workers more willing to replace existing insider workers.

Lastly, there have been changes in labor-supply conditions with the emergence of such firms as Manpower, Inc., which is now the single biggest private employer in the United States. These firms provide a ready supply of workers who can be quickly and easily assembled to plug any labor shortages. Moreover, these temporary workers receive lower pay and no benefits, and their availability serves to keep the lid on wages and benefits. In effect, firms that supply temporary workers provide a form of labor inventory so that a ready source of labor is on hand to meet any emergency need.

The temporary-labor service industry has emerged in response to the demand from employers for such sources of labor. Its emergence is an example of organizational creative destruction and illustrates how organizational developments are driven by the needs of business. In 1996, workers placed by temporary agencies rose to 1.87% of average daily U.S. employment, up from 1.01% in 1991.[13]

A hidden impact of this new industry has been to reduce the bargaining power of workers. Temporaries give firms an additional source of labor supply with which to buffer variations in demand. Consequently, permanent workers are unable to win wage increases automatically when market conditions tighten. Temporaries also offer firms a protection against strikes and therefore implicitly weaken the strike threat.

Along with the availability of temporary contract workers, firms have also increased the use of part-time and directly hired temporary workers. Part-time work confers a benefit on individuals whose family arrangements are such that they do not want full-time work. Very often such persons are married and have a partner who brings home a full-time income. By increasing the supply of workers who do not require benefits, this arrangement undercuts the bargaining position of workers who are not part of a family unit with a second full income. Very often such workers are single women who are heads of a household. Meanwhile, directly hired temporary workers have served as a means of introducing two-tier pay systems. Such temporaries are not paid as a high a wage as permanent workers, nor do they get full benefits packages. They are therefore keen to become permanents, while also being resentful of the fact that permanents are paid more for doing the same job. This serves to divide the workforce, and puts permanents on notice that there are others who would readily take their places.[14]

The Impact on Government

Just as the reduction in transactions costs has hurt labor, it also has hurt government. In particular, it has reduced government's ability to raise revenue by taxing capital, and it has hurt government's ability to conduct national economic policy. The reduced ability to tax capital has amplified the effect of the crisis on ordinary Americans, because the burden of taxa-

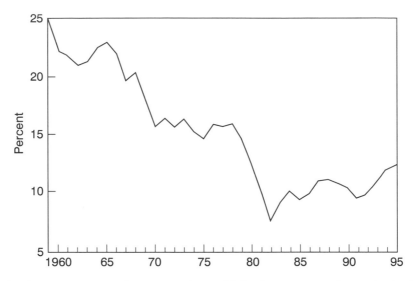

Fig. 5.2. Corporate profit taxes as a share of federal tax revenue. *Source*: Author's calculations based on CITIBASE data.

tion has increasingly been shifted onto households, as government has been forced to look for replacement sources of revenue. In this fashion, falling transactions costs have doubly hurt workers, first by contributing to stagnant wages, and then by contributing to higher tax burdens on their households. This reduction in corporate tax burdens is shown in figure 5.2. In 1959, corporate profit taxes represented 25% of government revenues; by 1995, they had fallen to 12.5% of government revenues.

The new power of corporations has affected every level of government, from Federal, to state, to municipal. The desire to create jobs in an era of unemployment, combined with the greater mobility of capital, has pitted government against government in an auction of business tax exemptions and subsidies designed to attract businesses. A recent example of this was the bidding war that took place in 1993 over the siting of Mercedes-Benz's proposed U.S auto-assembly factory. This auction, conducted between North Carolina and Alabama, was finally won by Alabama. The estimated tax concessions were $167,000 per job. There was always going to be just one Mercedes plant, and at the end of the day there is just one plant; however, Mercedes will be now paying permanently reduced taxes. Another example was the 1993 bargaining between United Technologies Corporation U.T.C.) and the state of Connecticut over tax exemptions: in that case U.T.C. used the threat of relocating production to either Georgia or Maine to win significant tax concessions. Yet another example,

TABLE 5.1

Incentives Given by State and Local Governments to Attract
Companies' Investment

Location	Year	Plant	Tax Concession per employee (U.S. dollars)
Portugal	1991	Auto Europa, Ford, VW	254,000
Alabama, U.S.	1993	Mercedes-Benz	163,000
South Carolina, U.S.	1994	BMW	108,000
Birmingham, U.K.	1995	Jaguar	129,000
Lorraine, France	1995	Mercedes-Benz, Swatch	57,000
South Wales, U.K.	1996	LG Electronics	47,000

Source: The Economist, February 1, 1997, p. 25.

again from 1993, concerns the Travelers Corporation which pitted Connecticut against New York state, and won tax concessions from Connecticut by threatening to leave.[15] Such auctions reduce total state revenues, and the shortfall either has to be made up by additional taxes on households or cuts in state government services and education.

Within the United States, which is a continental economy, this auction has been played by pitting state against state. In Europe, a similar auction has been played with country against country. An example of this process has been the competition between member countries of the European Economic Community over location of Japanese car plants, a competition that was frequently won in the 1980s by the United Kingdom, owing to the Thatcher government's willingness to provide huge tax concessions. Some examples of the auction-house frenzy for corporate investment projects are illustrated in table 5.1. The record goes to Portugal, which gave tax exemptions equal to $254,000 per employee to get Ford and Volkswagon to locate there.

Another way in which reduced transactions costs have affected government is their impact on government's ability to pursue sovereign economic policies. In market-oriented economies that allow international movements of financial capital, wealth holders will shift funds across countries so as to earn the highest rates of return (adjusted for risk differences). Such behavior produces pressures for equalization of cross-country interest rates.

Where there are transactions costs, this equalization will be incomplete (as discussed in connection with the arithmetic of transactions costs). From the standpoint of national economic policy, this is an enormous benefit becaause it potentially allows governments to pursue independent monetary and fiscal policies. In a world with no transactions costs, the law of arbitrage implies that interest rates across countries must be equal, preventing governments from controlling domestic interest rates. Instead, interest rates are determined by global financial markets. However, transactions costs permit cross-country differences in interest rates that do not warrant a response from financial arbitrageurs. Transactions costs therefore reduce the exposure and vulnerability of sovereign macroeconomic policy to international movements of financial capital. This is a theme that we shall return to in chapter 10.

Despite this clear benefit, governments around the world have bowed to the poltical pressures applied by business interests and relaxed controls on international flows of financial capital. In many countries, regulations governing these flows have been completely abolished. This elimination of controls, combined with the new electronic transfer technologies that have lowered trading costs, has enormously increased the scale of these flows. As a result, government economic policy is now hostage to the sentiments of financial markets. If financial capital dislikes the direction of economic policy, it can simply excercise a veto by selling domestic currency and bonds, thereby driving the exchange rate down and interest rates up.

Conclusion

To summarize, lower transactions costs have vastly increased the power of business relative to both labor and government. This power shift has contributed to the stagnation of wages, and it has also contributed to a shift in tax burdens from business onto households. The decrease in transactions costs has been driven by the process of creative destruction, which has spawned both technological and organizational change. It has also been fostered by sociological developments affecting attitudes to trade unions and by the capture of economic policy by business interests. Restoring the balance of power requires confronting these developments and implementing new policies designed to reverse these trends, as will be discussed in the next chapter.

✳ CHAPTER 6 ✳

The Logic of Economic Power, Part II:
Policies for Prosperity

A SIMPLE framework for understanding the determinants of economic prosperity was discussed in chapter 5. This framework can now be used to explain both the origins of the prosperity of the Golden Age (1945–73) and the causes of its demise, and to suggest policies for creating a new Golden Age.

THE END OF THE GOLDEN AGE

Figure 6.1 describes the functioning of the system and shows the loop connecting bargaining power, income distribution, the demand for goods and services, and employment conditions. Both bargaining power and the state of demand are affected by policy. Bargaining power depends on such structural factors as free trade and labor laws: the state of demand is influenced by monetary and fiscal policy. Underlying the end of the Golden Age has been a deterioration in labor's bargaining power relative to business and the emergence of increasingly fragile demand conditions.

The Golden Age can be understood as the fortuitous coincidence of favorable structural conditions and favorable demand conditions. On the structural side, the Great Depression transformed American labor markets. In its aftermath there had been a huge increase in the extent of unionization which continued into the 1950s. In 1953, 35.7% of the labor force was unionized, giving American workers an unprecedented level of clout that enabled them to win high wages.

New Deal legislation had also implemented a range of social insurance reforms that provided protections to workers. Moreover, terrified by the prospect of a return to mass unemployment and the political risks such a return posed to the very survival of free-market capitalism, governments were committed to full employment. This commitment was underwritten by the Keynesian revolution in economic theory that provided the know-how to achieve this goal. Demand management could now be used to keep the excesses of the business cycle at bay.

87

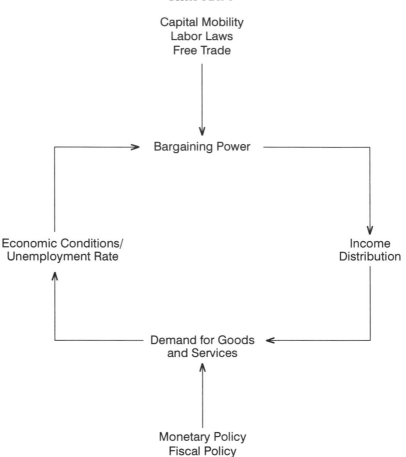

Fig. 6.1. Effect of monetary and fiscal policy on the demand for goods and services and the level of employment.

Lastly, most countries had strict controls on international movements of financial capital, and national financial markets were also relatively unintegrated. Countries therefore could follow independent economic policies consistent with their own needs. Interest rates were therefore set according to each country's employment needs, rather than in a globalized financial market.

Side-by-side with this favorable structure, the demand side of the economy was also healthy. During World War II, production had been devoted to the war effort, and there was little for households to buy. As a result, when the war ended, most households had considerable savings, little debt, and a large pent-up demand for consumer goods. The G.I. bill provided further underpinnings to this demand, paying for returning soldiers to go to college, and providing cheap mortgages to purchase homes. This in turn spurred a housing boom and increased the demand for consumer durables with which to furnish the new homes. It also spurred the development of suburbia, with its associated demand for roads and automobiles. Lastly, there was strong overseas demand for American products as Europe and Japan rebuilt their economies, and this demand was financed through Marshall Plan aid.

On top of this, there was a massive business investment boom, as firms sought to convert from war-time production to civilian production. This boom was further fueled by exploitation of war-time innovations, particularly in the aerospace industry, which were now put to civilian use. The government also contributed to demand by engaging in major infrastructure spending, as epitomized by the building of the interstate highway system. Finally, there was the advent of military Keynesianism, with the onset of the Cold War spurring massive peacetime defense spending for the first time in U.S. history. Though this spending may have detracted from the long-term health of the economy, in the initial phase, it was a boon to demand.

Favorable structural conditions and robust demand conditions therefore combined to set the U.S. economy on a trajectory of relatively full employment and robust growth. This trajectory was sustained by the growth of consumer credit, with higher incomes supporting higher borrowing, and higher borrowing supporting increased demand and further growth.

However, over time the structural conditions that supported this prosperity were gradually eroded by the developments described in the previous chapter. Keynesian economics, which was the dominant economic theory of the time, failed to identify this evolving condition. Though it provided profound insights into the determinants of demand, it lacked an understanding of the role of structural conditions in determining bargaining power and the distribution of income. Indeed, class conflict and the problem of income distribution were entirely absent from Keynesian theory. This absence was fully in keeping with 1950s culture, for the Cold War imposed a denial of the significance of class and conflict in the economic process.

The gradual deterioration in the structural conditions supporting prosperity were obscured in the late 1960s by the Vietnam war mobilization, which contributed to the maintenance of strong demand conditions.

However, this cover was stripped aside by the oil shock of 1973, which revealed the contested nature of the system. The period after the first oil shock rendered visible the new mobility of capital, as American business began to exploit the divide between the Rust Belt and the Sun Belt. Thus, Rust Belt firms increasingly began to migrate to the Sun Belt to obtain lower wages and escape the pressures of unionization.

The oil shock also ignited a burst of cost inflation, and this fed into a wage–price spiral driven by the struggle between business and labor as to who was to bear the burden of higher oil prices. This acceleration in inflation ultimately prompted the Federal Reserve to adopt restrictionary monetary policies that raised interest rates and unemployment. In the late 1970s, inflation was declared public enemy number one, and this provided the cloak for the Federal Reserve to increasingly side with financial interests. Since then, controlling inflation rather than ensuring robust employment conditions has been the Federal Reserve's goal.

With hindsight, the cessation of wage growth and the rise in the rate of unemployment that followed the oil shock reveal the 1970s to have been a turning point. In the 1980s, the full force of the wage squeeze and the dominance of business was felt. The mild recession of 1980 combined with the Reagan recession of 1981–2, which was the deepest economic downturn since the Great Depression, marked the inauguration of the new era. Since then, business has been ascendant, and the result has been a wholesale redistribution of income toward executive pay and profits and away from working-family wages.

THE PROBLEM OF CAPITAL MOBILITY: WHAT IS TO BE DONE?

Behind the wage squeeze lies the deterioration in labor's bargaining position, caused by the decline in firms' costs of replacing workers and the increase in the mobility of production. This decline has been driven by both technological innovations and officially sanctioned economic policies, and it has increased the power of capital relative to both labor and government. The result has been a worsening of the distribution of income and a shift in the distribution of tax burdens.

The decline in bargaining power is a principal cause of the wage stagnation and economic insecurity that afflicts the industrialized world. This raises important questions concerning the appropriate policy stance to transactions costs, globalization of markets, and capital mobility. Unfortunately, the existing policy agenda is constructed exclusively on the basis of conventional economics, which unilaterally asserts that lower transactions costs, increased globalization, and increased capital mobility are beneficial.

The conventional approach to transactions costs is that they represent a friction that inhibits competition and the realization of gains from trade. Consequently, conventional theory suggests that policy should aim at eliminating such costs. However, as argued above, these costs have important implications for both the distribution of income and governments' ability to tax capital and conduct sovereign economic policy. These considerations are neglected by orthodox theory. Since conventional theory dominates economic policy making, this has encouraged policymakers to push for reductions in transactions costs wherever possible. This push is reflected in the elimination of controls on the international movement of financial capital, the encouragement of multinational production, and the encouragement of free trade in goods and sevices. It is also visible in official attitudes toward labor markets, in which unions and minimum-wage regulations are seen as frictions that impede market efficiency. The assumption is that there is such a thing as a natural labor market and that eliminating unions and minimum wages is the way to restore the natural market.

The notion of a natural market denies the role of bargaining power in determining market outcomes. In doing so, it suppresses transactions costs as an important strategic variable. Once market outcomes are viewed as the product of a bargaining process, transactions costs acquire major significance for the distribution of income. This compels a reassessment of policy. The question then becomes, what is the best policy toward transactions costs? Should policy always be directed toward eliminating frictions, or should policy sometimes actually encourage them? In any event, elimination of frictions will seldom be distributionally neutral, as it will almost always alter the balance of power among market participants to some degree.

A good point of departure for addressing this question is to distinguish between domestic and international transactions. Prima facie, reduction of transactions costs within the domestic economy would appear to be a good. For instance, reducing transportation costs reduces resources used in transporting goods, thereby freeing them for use in some other beneficial activity. Similarly, increasing the mobility of production can potentially move employment to relatively depressed areas, thereby bringing prosperity to those areas.

It should also be noted that, although reduced transactions costs bring benefits, they may also have significant negative consequences. In particular, increased ease in shifting production around the economy increases the bargaining power of capital because firms can effectively pit workers from different regions in a competition for jobs. Indeed, in the period since the 1973 oil shock, this has been a significant feature of the U.S. economic scene. Thus, workers from the Sun Belt have increasingly been pitted in an implicit contest with workers from the Rust Belt, and firms have used this contest to extract wage concessions.

On balance, an integrated national market would appear to be beneficial, because it allows consumers to reap the benefits of lower prices associated with large-scale production and competition among producers. Rather than ensuring an appropriate distribution of income by limiting the scale and extent of competition among firms, it is better to do so by setting a floor to the labor market and removing wages from the field of competition. This can be acheived by adequate minimum wages and unemployment benefits, combined with restrictions on firms' rights to replace workers. Competition can then be restricted to product competition among firms on price and quality, rather than cost competition based on cutting wages.

One important area in which transactions-cost policy could make a difference concerns mandated employer contributions on behalf of workers. A recent adverse development that is part of the wider move to subcontracting is the replacement of full-time workers with part-time and contract workers. Firms have an economic incentive to avoid costs such as health insurance contributions and pension contributions. A transactions-cost approach to policy would counteract this incentive by requiring that firms pay contributions on all workers including part-time and contract workers.

Another adverse development has been the massive increase in overtime work, so that American workers are working longer than ever, at a time when unemployment and underemployment are up. Indeed, there are many informal indications that much of this overtime work is involuntary, with workers facing a choice of work longer or be replaced. In this instance, firms have an incentive to avoid hiring additional workers so as to avoid additional pension and health insurance costs. A transactions-cost policy for reversing this trend would require that overtime hours be

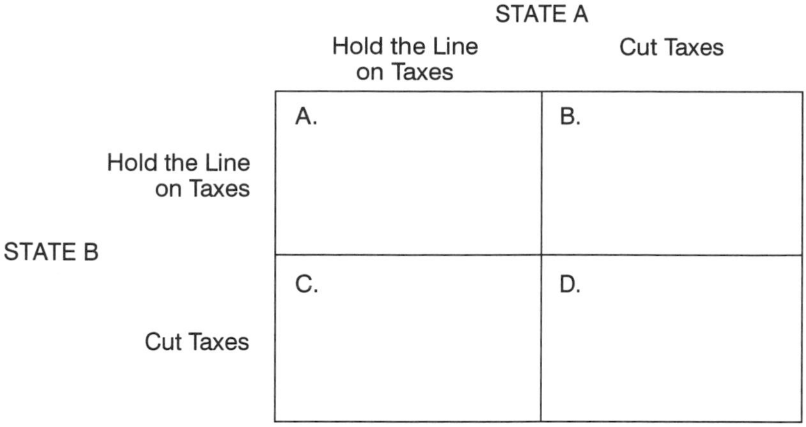

STATE A

	Hold the Line on Taxes	Cut Taxes
STATE B Hold the Line on Taxes	A.	B.
Cut Taxes	C.	D.

Fig. 6.2. The tax auction frenzy as an example of the prisoner's dilemma.

considered analogous to the hiring of a new worker, so that firms would have to start making fresh contributions on all time over forty hours. Whether or not one agrees with the specifics of these particular proposals, what is clear is that transactions costs matter. Economic policy needs to address the implications of transactions costs by recognizing the consequences of their erosion and by reflecting on where they might be usefully bolstered to secure desired outcomes.

A second policy area concerns the coordination of state government tax policy. There is an urgent need to put an end to the auction of corporate tax exemptions intended to attract new jobs. For the government sector considered as a whole, this is a zero-sum game: the only winner is the corporate sector, which pays lower taxes. Thus, states that participate in these tax auctions simply siphon jobs from other states, and lower overall state tax revenues. Rectifying this problem calls for greater coordination of taxation policie across states.

The problem of tax auctions partakes of the prisoner's dilemma illustrated in figure 6.2. There are two states: state A and state B. Each state may either hold the line on taxes or cut taxes to attract new business. Holding the line (Box A) yields maximum tax revenue for the two states as a group and has no effect on overall jobs. However, each state has an incentive to break ranks by trying to attract business covertly and thereby make itself better off. If it alone cuts taxes, then it gets the jobs, and it gets all the tax revenues associated with the jobs. However, given this incentive, all states break ranks and all cut taxes (Box D). Consequently, all are made worse off since tax revenues are reduced and jobs are unchanged. The only beneficiary is business, which ends up avoiding paying lower taxes. To be concrete, there was always going to be one Mercedes-Benz plant in the United States, and at the end of the day, there still is. However, the tax auction between Alabama and North Carolina resulted in Mercedes-Benz's winning enormous tax concessions.

This problem of investment credit tax auctions has afflicted state government within the United States. As shown in chapter 5, it is a problem that increasingly afflicts national governments as well. Governments are increasingly trying to poach corporations and wealthy citizens by making their tax laws relatively more favorable. These actions reflect the workings of individually rational self-interest. When all are guided in this fashion, the outcome is socially suboptimal. The only way to achieve the socially optimal outcome is to put in place binding agreements that stop states from breaking ranks. This is an instance of designing the economy to promote prosperity.

A third area for transactions-cost policy concerns the maintenance of sovereign economic policy. Here, taxes can be used to counter the effect of declining transactions costs in financial markets. Such taxes are commonly referred to as *Tobin taxes,* after the economist James Tobin who first proposed them. Their purpose is to reduce asset and currency market speculation and reduce flows of hot money that undermine national economic policy. The logic is that placing a small tax on such dealings would make it unprofitable for speculators to daily shift billions of dollars in response to rumors and political sentiments. In this fashion, the Tobin tax can be used to counter some of the adverse effects of declining transactions costs.

The Tobin tax places a small friction in the working of international currency markets. It is quite possible that this friction is insufficient, or that speculation will continue in overseas financial markets. In this case, tougher direct controls on the flow of international hot money may be needed. This is paricularly true for European economies, which have been subject to persistent and frequent currency crises. The frequency of these crises has increased since the 1970s, when many countries abolished controls on movement of financial capital. It may well be time to restore such controls. One possible scheme is that operated by the Chilean government, under which inflows of international money into the Chilean economy are obliged to commit to a minimum residence period of one year. This effectively filters out purely speculative money.

LEVELING THE LABOR-MARKET PLAYING FIELD

The shift in the balance of power between labor and capital is central to understanding the stagnation of wages and the explosion of income inequality. A crucial element in this shift is the decline of unions.[1] A significant cause of this decline is the toothless state of labor law, which gives corporations every incentive to intimidate workers who would like to belong to unions even though such intimidation violates fundamental legal rights of workers.

The Wagner Act of 1935 (section 7) clearly states that workers have the right to join unions: "Employees shall have the right to self-organization, to form, join, or assist labor organizations, to bargain collectively through representatives of their own choosing, and to engage in other concerted activities for the purpose of collective bargaining or other mutual aid or protection." Yet, these rights have been hollowed out by a corporate offensive against unions.

This corporate offensive is based on the axiom that "Justice delayed, is justice denied." The strategy is to generate as much delay as possible through delayed National Labor Relations Board (NLRB) hearings, delayed meetings, delayed elections, appeals, appeals of appeals, and stalled negotiations.

Side-by-side, there is underlying pressure on workers who want to join unions. Workplaces are filled with antiunion material, and management wages a twenty-four-hour public-relations campaign against unions. Meanwhile, unions have no access to challenge management's claims about unions. One in twenty workers who seek to organize a union are discharged according to Professor Paul Weiler of Harvard University.[2] Indeed, the odds may be much higher when one considers discharges among those who are initially active in starting a unionization campaign.

The corporate offensive is visible in corporate practice. Bronfenbrenner reports that 70% of firms now use management consultants in their anti-union election campaigns; an additional 15% use an outside law firm.[3] An article titled "Yes, We Allow No Solicitation Today" in the journal *Personnel,* advises the following: "The National Labor Relations Act allows management to inform employees about its opinions regarding employees' decision to join a union. . . . The steps that management can take to prevent workers from seeking out union representation include developing an open-door policy for employee communication, establishing two-way

95

communication, implementing a no-solicitation policy, and restricting the types of notices workers are allowed to post on bulletin boards."[4] An article in *Personnel Journal* titled "Maintain a Union-Free Status" advises that a "Company faced with the possibility of a trade union organizing its employees should, within the limits of the law, actively oppose the attempt. A company is guaranteed the right to present its views, arguments, and opinions opposing the union. . . . A company may present to its employees statements referring to the general downward trend in trade union membership, that union membership does not guarantee employment, and that a company is required only to bargain in good faith and is not required to accept any union demands."[5]

The combination of corporate opposition, delay, and intimidation is critical. Data shows that the union win rate in elections drops off sharply with delay between filing for an election and the conduct of the election. If an election is held in the first month after filing an election petition with the NLRB, unions win 56.7% of the time; if the election is delayed six months, unions only win 46.6% of the time.[6]

The corporate offensive is visible in the changed character of elections. In 1962, 46% of all NLRB elections were conducted as consent elections. In 1991, only 1% of elections were conducted under consent conditions. Stipulated elections take longer to complete than do consent elections and give corporations the opportunity to intimidate workers. In 1962, 60% of elections were conducted during the election petition filing month or the following month. In 1976, it was down to 39%; in 1991, it had fallen to 34%.

In many instances, unions feel compelled to withdraw petition filings. In 1970, the withdrawl rate was 22%; in 1980 it was 24%, and by 1990 it was 31%. The rising extent of withdrawals reflects the scale of the corporate offensive. Union organizers are realists, and they will not seek an election until well over 50% of the workforce have checked petition cards. This far exceeds the NLRB's official requirement that 30% check cards. Despite these precautions, employers are able to intimidate workers in the interval between card checking and conduct of the election.

The ability of firms to defeat unionization efforts reflects the tilted playing field. As Richard Bensinger, Director of the AFL-CIO Organizing Institute, put it: "During every union campaign, workers are bombarded with speeches and one-on-one arm twisting by supervisors in an attempt to get them to vote against the union." Meanwhile, employers require workers to attend antiunion meetings on company time, and union organizers are barred from company property and have no access to workers during working hours. These restrictions are not the result of the National Labor Relations Act, but the result of courts' overturning NLRB decisions on appeal by corporations. Justice Clarence Thomas, in his first decision (*Lechmere*, Inc. vs. NLRB) authored for the majority on the Supreme Court, allowed that employers were permitted to deny union organizers access to portions of company premises to which even the general public has access, such as shopping center parking lots. Under these conditions, it is small wonder that the right to organize has been hollowed out and that unions have declined.

The American dream is paying the price of this hollowing out. Union strength was critical to the advance of the American dream in the era after World War II. In 1953, 35.7% of all workers belonged to unions. With so many organized, unions secured for working families a slice of America's expanding productivity. Moreover, nonunion workers benefited too, because employers raised wages to reduce workers' incentive to unionize. As noted in chapter 3, the social compact of this era was not founded on corporate generosity: it was founded on a level labor-market playing field. As that playing field has tilted in favor of business, business has withdrawn from that social compact. The solution is clear: the playing field must once again be leveled.

The legal principles guaranteeing the right to organize and bargain collectively already exist. What is needed is legal reform that makes this right effective. The incentive for corporations to frustrate the purpose of the law is just too great. Plain-vanilla Chicago School approach to the economics of crime says that raising the costs of breaking the law by giving the law teeth is the way to change things. Union supporters are frequently dismissed; the only penalty against these illegal discharges is reinstatement with back pay, long after the election is over. Employer threats during organizing drives, such as plant closure, are unfair labor practices. However, the only penalty is that the employer post a notice, long after the election is over, that it will not do this again. If the union lost, it can also appeal for a fresh election. By then, union sympathizers have quit or been fired, remaining workers have been intimidated, and new hires have been carefully screened to weed out prospective union sympathizers.

Raising the penalties associated with unfair labor practices would go a long way toward ending such abuses. Where firms have been found to violate the law, monetary penalties should be substantial. Where violation is intentional, top management should be held personally accountable. Workers who are unfairly dismissed should not only be entitled to back pay, but should also be entitled to compensatory damages for psychological distress. Intentional violation is a form of managerial crime and should be treated as such. CEOs claim credit for corporate performance, and this is their justification for massive CEO pay. CEOs should also be held personally responsible for unfair labor practices. If CEOs can personally benefit from the good they purportedly accomplish, commonsense symmetry says that they should be responsible for the bad.

Legal reform will go a long way toward fixing the problem, but unions also need to educate the public regarding the necessity of unions. Though intuitively sympathizing with unions, the public's intellectual attitude toward unions is grounded in the philosophy of economic naturalism, whereby unions are viewed as a distortion to natural markets. This leads the public to believe that a natural labor market can be recovered by diminishing the power of unions. The reality is that it merely creates a market in which business dominates labor.

Interestingly, the notion of natural markets is not applied to large corporations. These are massive pools of financial capital governed by the protections and provisions of corporate law. Corporations are clearly unnatural, yet we view them as a design worth having because they enhance economic productivity and performance. The bottom line is that the philosophy of economic naturalism is at odds with the reality of our economy, and it is interpreted tendentiously to discredit those institutions that help level the playing field for workers and their families.

Free Trade

The question of free trade has recently been at the forefront of the policy debate in the United States, and it will be discussed further chapter 9. Some preliminary comments are in order. In the new globalized economy, getting trade policy right is essential if the overall policy vision is to be sustainable.

Clearly domestic factors have played an important role in the worsening of income distribution, but so, too, have the growth of international trade and multinational production. This growth has increased the threat to American workers posed by the abundance of cheap foreign labor, and this threat neccesitates a reexamination of trade policy.

From the standpoint of orthodox theory, increased international trade is an unambiguous good. Consequently, declining international transactions costs and increased multinational production are both seen as sources of major gain. Orthodox economists have therefore persistently pushed for free trade and the elimination of all tariffs, and these policies have reinforced the secular reduction in international transactions costs.

This conventional approach to trade draws no distinctions between types of trading partner. Instead, all trade is viewed as good, and the greater the diversity of the trading partners, the greater the benefits to trade. Thus, Americans supposedly have the most to gain from trading with countries like China, Mexico, and the Phillipines. Nothing could be further from the truth. Instead, the benefits to trade depend importantly on the trading partner. Without doubt, trade can be enormously beneficial, generating greater product diversity, lower prices attributable to economies of scale associated with larger markets, lower prices attributable to climatic and natural resource advantages in the production of certain commodities (e.g., Colombia will always produce coffee cheaper than the United States), and lower prices from increased market competition.

However, trade ceases to be a good when it rests exclusively on wage differentials. Instead, it becomes an implicit instrument for battering down wages and increasing profits. These considerations force a reconsideration of trade policy. Free trade is desirable where countries have similar wage structures, employee protection laws; and environmental protection laws; where countries differ in these regards, we need to be much more cautious. Free trade predicated exclusively on wage competition is entirely unacceptable and represents a major threat to mass prosperity in America and Wetern Europe.

In light of the above, trade policy must distinguish between trade liberalizations with high employment–high wage (northern) economies, and surplus labor–low wage (southern) economies. Where there are conditions of domestic monopoly or where countries have a natural advantage in the production of goods, free trade is desirable. Thus, it makes no sense for the United States to try to produce coffee when Colombia has a natural climatic advantage. When the only reason for trade is cost advantages predicated on poverty-level wages, and lack of obligations regarding pollution abatement, worker safety standards, health costs, and provision for social security, then free trade is unacceptable.

Under such conditions, trade will ultimately promote a decline in the wages of American workers as companies either transfer production overseas, or use the prospect of doing so to extract wage concessions. Moreover, to the extent that the U.S. system of worker protections becomes viewed as a source of cost disadvantage and job loss, this will unleash political pressures for its repeal. In the realm of free trade, the law of one price becomes a mechanism for enforcing the lowest common standard.

Given this, free trade is appropriate where the requisite criteria are satisfied. For instance, the acronym NAFTA should have stood for North Atlantic Free Trade Agreement. However, if the criteria are not met, countries should be subject to a social tariff designed to compensate for their exploitative economic conditions. As conditions in countries improve, this tariff can be lowered so that it can be used as an incentive mechanism for governments in underdeveloped countries to advance the welfare interests of workers. Moreover, the tariff proceeds could be used to provide grants to developing countries for purchases of U.S. exports, thereby helping both U.S. workers and underdeveloped countries.

POLICIES FOR FULL-EMPLOYMENT

As noted in chapter 5, the rate of unemployment is important for determining bargaining outcomes and the distribution of income. Unemployment in turn depends on the level of demand for goods and services, which is itself affected by government monetary and fiscal policy. *Monetary policy* refers to the government's control over interest rates and the money supply, excercised through the central bank (the Federal Reserve in the United States). *Fiscal policy* refers to the government's control over taxes and its own spending. This effect of monetary and fiscal policy is illustrated in figure 6.1.

In the period of the Golden Age, government was committed to full employment as a policy goal, and monetary and fiscal policy were directed toward this end. In the period since the end of the Golden Age, there has been a steady retreat from the commitment. Once viewed as an unquestioned goal of public policy, full employment has now become increasingly viewed as a special-interest policy designed to help those who cannot compete under the rigors of the market place. How this retreat has come about is examined in detail in chapters 7 and 8. The immediate significance is that committing monetary and fiscal policy to full employment is another necessary step in reversing the wage squeeze.

This shift in policy direction has meant that both monetary and fiscal policy have been increasingly run for the benefit of Wall Street rather than Main Street. With regard to monetary policy this has been reflected in an obsession with inflation. This obsession was clearly visible in the Federal Reserve's setting of interest rates during the first half of 1994. Thus, just as a real jobs recovery started to pick up steam, the Fed tightened monetary policy and raised interest rates six times over the course of the year. As a result short-term rates moved from just over 3% to almost 6%. This policy was pursued in the absence of any substantive indications of accelerated inflation, and even though the costs of unemployment are large and clear, whereas the costs of inflation are hard to identify.

The good news is that, despite the Fed's actions, the current economic recovery has continued and unemployment has fallen. The bad news is that the reduction in unemployment has been smaller and slower than it would have been, and the recovery has been more fragile. This has contributed to continuing uncertainty over jobs, which has kept a tight lid on wage growth. Indeed, despite the supposed boom, average hourly wages have still not recovered to the level of the last business cycle peak: in 1989, they were $12.14 per hour; in 1996, they were $11.82 per hour.

Just as monetary policy has been increasingly run for the benefit of Wall Street, so, too, has fiscal policy. However, here the capture has been less complete. Thus, reshaping fiscal policy for the benefit of Main Street America should prove easier. Paramount in this reshaping is the necessity of squarely confronting the issue of income distribution and government's relation to income distribution. Income distribution profoundly influences the robustness of economic activity, and hence government should be concerned with it independently of any concerns with social equity or fairness. These latter concerns provide additional grounds for government action on income distribution.

Given this, how should government use fiscal policy to intervene in securing an appropriate domestic income distribution? First, there is the use of the power of taxation. Thus, income taxes should be broadly progressive, meaning that higher-income groups should bear a slightly higher tax rate than lower-income groups. Moreover, the income tax should distinguish between earned and unearned income. Progressive taxation of earned income helps rectify some of the adverse market-based developments that have favored executive and professional pay over the pay of other workers; progressive taxation of unearned income helps rectify the adverse changes that have favored profits over wages. There should also be reasonable limits to deductions such as mortgage interest and limits to tax-free pension-fund contributions. The original intent of the mortgage deduction was the creation of a home-owning democracy and not the provision of tax subsidies for owners of half-million-dollar homes. Likewise, tax-free pension-fund contributions were designed to encourage reasonable provision for old age, not as a means of conferring tax-free savings on the highly paid who already have plenty of disposable income.

101

CHAPTER 6

THE ECONOMY AS A "CORRIDOR": POLICY EFFECTIVENESS
AND ECONOMIC STRUCTURE

The use of monetary and fiscal policy to achieve full employment are the
hallmarks of Keynesian economics. However, it is vital to recognize that
these instruments of policy are only effective in an appropriate economic
environment. This is the lesson of structural Keynesianism outlined in
chapter 1. In the period 1945–1973, the structure of the economy was
such that this was the case. The success of the Keynesian economic policy
revolution therefore rested on a new understanding of the significance
of monetary and fiscal policy, combined with a favorable economic
structure.

The importance of structure was not well understood, and, as the
economic structure deteriorated in the period after 1973, so too did the
feasibility and efficacy of Keynesian demand-management policies. Therefore, restoring the viability of demand-management policies requires the
restoration of an appropriate economic structure. In the absence of this,
Keynesian policies are unlikely to be able to permanently restore aggregate
demand. Instead, their sustained application is likely to produce rising
government deficits and debt, persistent trade deficits, and financial turmoil resulting from capital flight. These are the hallmarks of the last
twenty years, and they have prompted a retreat from the policies of demand management. Rather than retreat, the appropriate response should
have been to refashion the system so as to restore the feasibility and effectiveness of demand management.

Such considerations link with the observation in chapter 1 that capitalist economies come in a range of forms, and the real problem lies in
fashioning the form that works best for the average person. The metaphor
of a corridor can be used to describe the economic system.[7] The walls of
the corridor are analogous to the institutions, laws, and regulations that
constrain economic activity, and economic activity takes place within the
corridor. The goal of policy should be twofold. Structural policy should
see to it that the corridor is designed such that it is wide enough and
pointed in the right direction: demand-management policy should ensure
an appropriate level of economic activity within the corridor.

Further reflection reveals that the situation is even more complicated.
The walls of the corridor constrain the activities and choices of business.
Because these constraints are binding, business has an incentive to try and
get around them. This is where the process of creative destruction enters,

because business will seek to introduce innovations that mitigate the constraints of the corridor. Thus, if unchanged, over time the corridor is likely to become increasingly ineffective at guiding economic activity. The increase in capital mobility, the decline in transactions costs, and the increase in the power of business relative to government and labor correspond to a gradual erosion of the corridor. This reveals that policy design must be an ongoing process that responds to developments brought about by the process of creative destruction.

Restoring prosperity requires rebuilding the corridors governing economic activity and seeing that they are again pointed in a direction that promotes social well-being. This is what is meant by restoring structural conditions favorable to Keynesian demand-management policies. Unfortunately, conventional economics, which dominates the counsels of economic policy making, has actively sought to demolish the existing corridors. The policies of orthodoxy have therefore exacerbated an already difficult situation, and these policies threaten to entrench deep structural changes in the domestic and international economy that will be difficult and perhaps impossible to reverse.

The Triumph of Wall Street: Finance
and the Federal Reserve

CHAPTERS 5 and 6 emphasized the role of economic policy in contributing to the dismantling of prosperity. Economic policy is important because of the impact of laws and regulations on business' transactions costs, which in turn affects the bargaining power of business. A second way in which policy matters is through its effect on demand for output, which then affects employment conditions. Figure 7.1 shows the now-familiar diagram detailing these channels of influence.

In the period of the Golden Age, policymakers were committed to running the economy with low unemployment. However, in the late 1970s there was an abrupt policy U-turn, and inflation was suddenly public enemy number one. This policy U-turn was spearheaded by the Federal Reserve.

The Fed's shift of priorities represents a return to the more traditional stance of central bankers, among whom there is a long-standing history of opposition to inflation. This opposition is justified under the rhetoric of sound money, and no distinction is drawn between stable rates of low inflation and massive hyperinflation associated with economic and political instability. All inflation is viewed as a disease, and it is an article of faith that low inflation inevitably results in hyperinflation. Though there is absolutely no evidence supporting this belief, the disease metaphor has proved persuasive, and zero-inflation is now the sanctioned goal of policy.

The argument developed in this chapter is that it is not danger to society's economic health that motivates central bankers' opposition to inflation; rather, it is their own political and economic self-interest. The predisposition against inflation reflects the sociological origins of central bankers, who are usually drawn from the ranks of financiers. Inflation is anathema to this group because it erodes the value of financial assets. Today, the Federal Reserve is firmly under the control of financial interests, and it is engaged in a crusade against inflation that disregards the consequences for unemployment and the distribution of income.

This shift in Federal Reserve policy can only be understood by reference to the deeper intellectual and political forces that have shaped the current

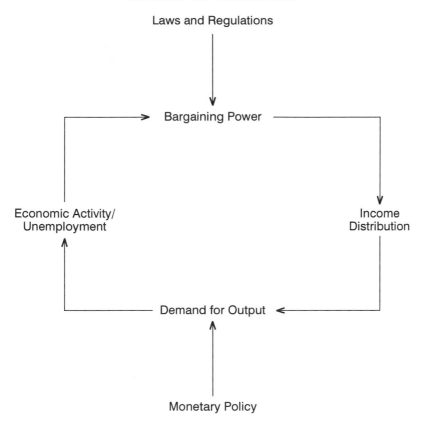

Fig. 7.1. The economic system and the influence of government regulation and monetary policy.

policy climate. The argument developed below is that the Federal Reserve has committed itself to monetary policy with a deflationary bias. This policy shift has also occurred in Western Europe and Canada. Moreover, in all countries, there is an emerging policy agenda that seeks to institutionalize this committment permanently by making central banks completely independent and thereby freeing them of public accountability. Because central bankers tend to be drawn from the ranks of financiers, such independence will effectively institutionalize a deflationary policy bias.

Explaining these developments involves a complicated train of thought that shows how conservative economic theory has been used to justify deflationary policy and shows that deflationary policy furthers the economic interests of Wall Street and finance capital. This is the subject matter of the current chapter.

THE ORIGINS OF DEFLATIONARY POLICY BIAS

Evidence regarding the dominance of zero-inflation policy is now abundantly available. For instance, E. Gerald Corrigan, the former President of the influential Federal Reserve Bank of New York, writes in the 1992 Annual report:

> [E]ven today, with the outlook for inflation seeming to be so benign, we must remain vigilant and we must staunchly resist those voices that would suggest that a "little more" inflation may not be all that bad, especially if it brings a lot more growth. . . .The battle against inflation is never over and the very minute that a society declares victory in that battle is likely to be the very minute that the seeds of the next round of inflation are sown, with all of their painful and inevitable consequences for the future. . . .(M)onetary policy and the effort to control inflation rightly stand at the center of the trilogy [of central banking activities and responsibilities].[1]

These comments were written at the height of the last recession, and they are representative of the thinking of the Federal Reserve in general. They might just as easily have come from Alan Greenspan, the current Chairman of the Federal Reserve.

Across the the ranks of the Federal Reserve system, there is now a widespread official consensus that the Fed's preeminent goal should be zero inflation, that inflation is bad for society's economic well-being, and that zero inflation should be pursued independent of its effect on unemployment. Indeed, since the underlying theoretical belief is that inflation has no effect on economic activity, the Fed claims that systematic pursuit of a zero-inflation target cannot cause unemployment. This is a wonderful tautological line of defense against critics of the Fed who blame it for higher unemployment.

The dominance of deflationary bias within the counsels of the Federal Reserve is the result of a theoretical counterrevolution in economics that has gone under the banner of "new classical" macroeconomics. The economics profession used to view mild inflation as an economic lubricant that greased the wheels of adjustment in labor markets, thereby reducing unemployment.[2] However, new classical macroeconomics has accomplished an intellectual transformation that has rendered inflation an unmitigated evil with no palliative effect on unemployment. Today, it is

106

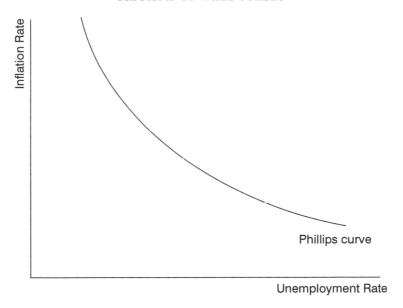

Fig. 7.2. The Phillips curve showing the trade-off between inflation and unemployment.

the assumptions and policy prescriptions of this new paradigm that provide the rationale for the Federal Reserve's pursuit of deflationary monetary policy.

How did this transformation come about? The 1960s marked the high-water point of Keynesian economic policy. During this decade there was a widespread belief that monetary and fiscal policy could be successfully used to permanently achieve full employment. However, even then economists were aware that higher rates of employment automatically involved accepting a little more inflation. This was the inescapable trade-off between inflation and unemployment that was made famous by the "Phillips curve" (fig. 7.2). According to the logic of the Phillips curve, any attempt to reduce unemployment will involve a leftward movement along the curve and will increase inflation.

Beginning in the late 1960s, and continuing through the 1970s, U.S. inflation began to worsen. This worsening was the result of a combination of multiple events, including excessive demand pressure from the Vietnam war mobilization, social conflict in society that spilled over into economic conflict over income distribution, the 1972 world commodity price explosion caused by a worldwide economic boom, a decline in the trend

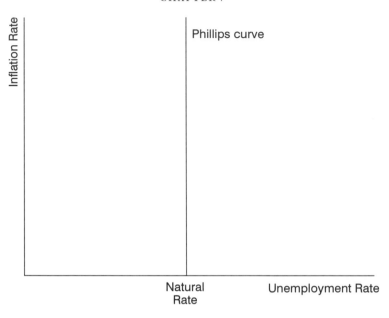

Fig. 7.3. The new classical vertical Phillips curve showing that unemployment is fixed at the natural rate, and that there is no trade-off between inflation and unemployment.

rate of productivity growth, and three successive oil price shocks in 1973, 1976, and 1979. However, rather than supplementing existing inflation theory with a multicausal theory of inflation, the economics profession adopted a novel monocausal theory known as the "natural rate" of unemployment.

The argument behind natural-rate theory is that if unemployment falls below its natural rate, inflation will increase and accelerate as long as unemployment remains below that rate.[3] Because ever higher and accelerating rates of inflation are unacceptable, the policy message flowing from natural-rate theory is clear: the unemployment rate should not be allowed to fall below its natural rate. As a result, economic policy is rigidly bound by an inflation constraint that is determined by the natural rate of unemployment.

According to new classical natural-rate theory, the Phillips curve is vertical and fixed at the natural rate of unemployment (fig. 7.3). There is no inflation-unemployment trade-off, and the Fed cannot affect the rate of unemployment; all it can do is control the rate of inflation. Any attempt to lower the unemployment rate below the natural rate will just cause a movement up the vertical Phillips curve and increase inflation. Given the claim of a binding inflation constraint, the best thing that the Fed can do is aim for zero inflation. If we are going to end up at the natural rate anyway, it is best to end up there with zero inflation.

Consequences of the Triumph of Natural-Rate Theory

Introduced by Edmund Phelps (1967) and Milton Friedman (1968), the theory of the natural rate was initially confined to laissez-faire academic economists and conservative think tanks.[4] Since then, it has spread into the highest counsels of economic policy making. This spread is captured in the *Economic Report of the President,* a document drafted each year by the President's Council of Economic Advisers.[5] In 1970, the report declared 3.8% unemployment as the definition of full employment, and used 3.8% unemployment as the basis for computing the economy's maximum "potential output." In the 1979 *Economic Report* the official definition of full employment was revised to 5.1% (1979, pp. 72–74). By 1983, the triumph of natural-rate theory was so complete, that the new term "inflation threshold unemployment rate" (1983, p. 37) was introduced, and this new inflation threshold unemployment rate was declared to "probably lie(s) between 6 and 7 percent" (1983, p. 37).

The intellectual arguments for the natural-rate hypothesis have been bolstered by its rhetorical adoption of the natural metaphor, which implies that anything other than the natural rate is "unnatural." If the natural rate were identified with rates of 1% or 2% unemployment, adoption of the theory would be of little significance. However, once the natural rate is defined as 6% to 7% unemployment, its adoption implies significantly higher unemployment with huge and unnecessary social and economic costs.

Worse than that, by adopting the language of free markets and perfect competition, natural-rate theory subtly entraps policy makers into the belief that the actual rate is the natural rate. Thus, as economic performance has faltered over the last two decades, this has led to the notion of a rising natural rate. In the face of persistently rising unemployment, policymakers have been enjoined to do nothing. The defense is that actual unemployment is the outcome of the natural working of the free market, and trying to reduce unemployment would only contribute to higher inflation.

The argument that the actual rate is the natural rate protects the Fed from having to intervene to bring down unemployment. However, natural-rate economics is even more insidious. Thus, supporters of the natural rate argue that inflation is an evil that must always be eliminated, and this then justifies the Fed undertaking an activist anti-inflation policy. The policy U-turn is complete; from having been previously engaged in activist employment policy, the Fed is now enaged in activist anti-inflation policy.

This commitment to activist anti-inflation policy has had dire consequences for working Americans. Inflation can be the temporary result of an economic boom produced entirely by private-sector forces, or it can be the result of conflict between business and workers over wages and the distribution of income. Mild inflation is often an indication that workers have some bargaining strength and may even have the upper hand. Yet, it is at exactly this stage that the Fed now intervenes owing to its anti-inflation commitment, and this intervention raises interest rates and unemployment. Thus, far from being neutral, the Fed's anti-inflation policy implies siding with business in the ever-present conflict between labor and capital over distribution of the fruits of economic activity. Just as the Golden Age policy goal of low unemployment meant implicitly siding with labor, the Fed's current policy of zero inflation means implicitly siding with business. Of course, natural-rate rhetoric means that the policy of zero inflation is never presented in this light, and the public does not recognize its consequences. In this fashion, natural-rate theory serves as the perfect cloak for a pro-business policy stance.

MONETARY POLICY AS SURROGATE INCOMES POLICY

The Federal Reserve's belief in natural-rate theory, combined with its obsessive fears about inflation, have served to lock monetary policy into a permanently contractionary mode. This is illustrated in figure 7.4, which shows the short-term level of real interest rates, measured as the three-month treasury bill rate minus the Consumer Price Index inflation rate. The average real interest rate for the period 1948–73 was 0.88%; the average for the period 1974–79 was −1.31%; the average for the period 1980–95 was 2.73%. This is a 200% increase over the Golden Age, and it has resulted in the economy operating with persistently more unemployment

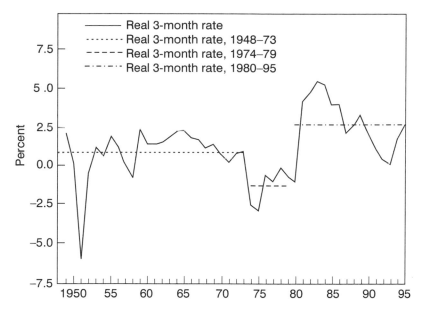

Fig. 7.4. Real three-month interest rate and period averages. *Source*: Author's calculations based on CITIBASE data.

than necessary. As a result, American workers have been placed in a more defensive position, and this helps explain why wages have stagnated over the last fifteen years.

Under the guise of conducting anti-inflation policy, the Fed has kept real interest rates at a permanently higher level, and it has been willing to further raise rates whenever there is a hint of robustness in labor markets. In effect, the Federal Reserve has been using monetary policy as a form of surrogate incomes policy, and this surrogate policy has been tilted against wages in favor of profits.

The Fed's surrogate incomes policy has been vividly evident over the course of the current business cycle. Toward the end of 1993, almost two years after the last recession was supposed to have ended, the economy began to experience significant job creation. With the unemployment rate falling from 6.8% to 6.4% during the last quarter of 1993 and the job market showing evidence of a long-awaited recovery, the Federal Reserve proceeded to respond by doubling short-term interest rates in the space of a year. Beginning in January 1994, the Federal Reserve raised the federal funds six times over the course of the year so that the federal funds rate rose from 3% in January 1994 to 5.9% in February 1995. The nominal justification for these rate hikes was that the economy was approaching the natural rate of unemployment, and inflation was about to take off. However, there was no evidence to this effect other than speculative assertion, and despite continued modest job growth, inflation subsequently fell in 1995 and 1996 from its 1994 level.

The Fed's surrogate incomes policy was again evident at the beginning of 1997 when the federal funds rate was raised from 5.25% to 5.5%. Though there was again no evidence of an acceleration in inflation, the Fed claimed that an acceleration was imminent. In the absence of evidence, the Fed now resorts to the defense that monetary policy must be forward looking and preemptive with regard to inflation, and this gives it a license to do anything.

The most explicit evidence regarding the Federal Reserve's surrogate incomes policy comes from testimony that Chairman Greenspan gave before the Senate Budget Committee on January 21, 1997. In this testimony, Greenspan announced:

> As I see it, heightened job insecurity explains a significant part of the restraint on compensation and the consequent muted price inflation. . . . The continued reluctance of workers to leave their jobs to seek other employment as the labor market has tightened provides further evidence of such concern, as does the tendency toward longer labor union contracts. . . .The low level of work stoppages of recent years also attests to concern about job security.

> [However] we must recognize that . . . suppressed wage cost growth as a consequence of job insecurity can be carried only so far. At some point in the future, the trade-off of subdued wage growth for job security has to come to an end. . . .[E]ven if the level of real wages remains permanently lower as a result of the experience of the past few years, the relatively modest wage gains we've seen are a transitional rather than a lasting phenomenon. The unknown is how long the transition will last. Indeed, the recent pick-up in some measures of wages suggests that the transition may already be coming to an end.

Such testimony leaves little doubt that the Fed's goal is to hold the lid on wages, and it is willing to run the economy with higher rates of unemployment and greater job insecurity if necessary.

In effect, the Fed has unilaterally taken on the role of regulating the distribution of income and seeks to do so in a manner favorable to business. This stance is evident in the most recent business cycle, during which profits have reached record levels. The 1996 before-tax profit rate was 11.39%; the previous peak was 11.29% in 1966. The massive scale of the increase in profit rates can be seen by comparing current profit rates with those obtaining at the peak of the last business cycle in 1988. In that year, the before-tax profit rate was 7.29%. Thus, there has been a 50% increase in profit rates over the space of eight years.

The Fed has felt no need to step on the brakes when profit incomes have been growing. Indeed, since rising profits are good for investment spending, they have been deemed a good to be encouraged. It is only when labor incomes have started to show indications of rising that the Fed has felt the need to step on the economic brakes. By arguing that rising capital incomes are good for the economy, while rising labor incomes are inflationary, the Fed has constructed a position that justifies using monetary policy to further profit growth but restrict the economy whenever there is any prospective indication of wage growth.

Chapter 3 showed how the growth of real wages (i.e., purchasing power wages) depends on the growth of dollar wages and the rate of price inflation. This relation is reproduced in equation (7.1). The Fed is now committed to holding dollar wage growth equal to the rate of inflation,

$$\text{Real wage growth} = \text{growth of dollar wages} - \text{inflation} \qquad (7.1)$$

and this policy effectively locks American workers into stagnant wages. This in turn means that all the benefits of productivity growth are accruing to profits.

The increase in capital mobility combined with the decline in unions would have produced a shift in income distribution toward profit anyway. However, the Fed's policy stance over the last eighteen years has exacer bated this shift, and the Fed remains vigilant in the interest of business through its conduct of surrogate incomes policy.

Inflation is a matter of rising prices. Stagnant real wages refers to a situation in which prices rise faster than dollar wages, thereby causing the purchasing power of wages to fall. We are currently in an era of very low inflation, bordering on deflation (falling prices). However, real wages are stagnant, and prices are rising faster than dollar wages. Unfortunately, the public mistakenly labels such a situation one of excessive inflation. This has helped the Fed by giving public support to the goal of lowering inflation. However, the reality is that inflation is not the problem; the problem is stagnant wages, and the Fed has contributed to this.

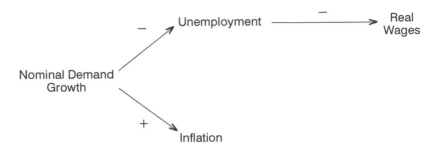

Fig. 7.5. The mechanics of demand-pull inflation; − = decrease; + = increase.

THE VERITIES OF INFLATION

The theory of the natural rate now dominates the mainstream of the economics profession, and since the counsels of the Federal Reserve are exclusively drawn from this mainstream, such thinking also dominates the Federal Reserve. The intellectual capture of the economics profession and the Federal Reserve explains how anti-inflation policy has come to be the officially sanctioned credo of monetary policy. Perhaps what is most surprising is that this intellectual revolution has been accomplished despite lack of persuasive evidence. Thus, statistical work on the effects of monetary policy consistently reveals that systematic monetary policy impacts output and unemployment.[6] This finding is completely inconsistent with natural-rate theory, which argues that monetary policy cannot affect output and employment and only affects inflation. Moreover, this work has been explicitly conducted on the theoretical grounds defined by new classical macroeconomics and using the empirical methodology developed by new classical macroeconomists.

Whereas new classical macroeconomics adopts a monocausal approach to inflation, the reality is that inflation is multicausal. A significant distinction is that between "demand-pull" and "cost-push" inflation. The mechanics of demand-pull inflation are shown in figure 7.5. The driving mechanism is the growth of nominal demand which decreases (−) unemployment and increases (+) inflation, thereby generating a Phillips curve. The reduction in unemployment in turn raises real wages. The theoretical rationale for this inflation-unemployment relationship is that, in a multisector economy, faster demand growth raises inflation in sectors

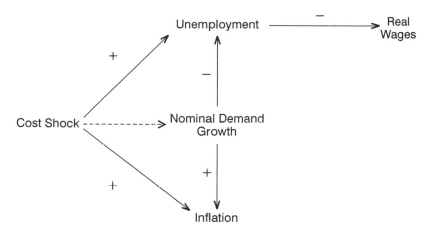

Fig. 7.6. The mechanics of cost-push inflation; − = decrease; + = increase.

with full employment, but reduces unemployment in depressed sectors. This is the theoretical foundation of the Phillips curve trade-off illustrated in figure 7.2.[7]

The mechanics of cost-push inflation are shown in figure 7.6, and rest on a price-wage spiral caused by conflict between business and labor over the distribution of income. Such conflict may be caused by domestic economic disturbances, or it may be caused by shocks from outside the economy such as an increase in oil prices or imported goods prices. This then triggers a struggle over which party is to bear the burden of the shock. The initiating cost shock (such as an increase in oil prices) increases (+) both inflation and unemployment, and the inflation is self-sustaining as the price increase feeds into wages, which then feedback into costs and prices.

How a cost-push inflation plays out depends very much on how the central bank responds. If it holds the line on interest rates and expands nominal demand, this mitigates unemployment but further increases inflation. If the central bank raises interest rates, this increases unemployment and reduces inflation. This second response is tantamount to siding with business, because it raises unemployment and lowers real wages. This reveals how central bank inflation policy is never politically neutral.

The existence of these patterns has been repeatedly confirmed in well-specified economic models. The inflation-unemployment trade-off is confirmed in estimates of the Phillips curve provided by Gordon (1988),

Rissman (1993), and Palley (1997a), while the existence of a relationship between real wages and unemployment is confirmed in estimates of the wage curve provided by Blanchflower and Oswald (1994).[8] This wage-curve relationship shows that real wages fall as unemployment increases.

THE POLITICAL ECONOMY OF ECONOMIC POLICY MAKING

Whereas the theory of the natural rate has provided the surface justification for the implementation of deflationary monetary policy, understanding the reality of deflationary policy requires the adoption of a political economy perspective. Keynesian economics eschewed such an approach to policy questions and instead adopted the idealized notion of a "benevolent" policymaker who always acted in the national interest. The assumption of a commonly shared national interest can be labeled the "big happy family" approach. Unfortunately, this approach denies and obscures the conflictual dimensions to economic activity and economic policy making: it is not for nothing that we have trade unions and political parties.

The new classical macroeconomics, associated with the conservative revolution in economics, has attacked the "big happy family" view of economic policy making. In principle, this represents an advance since the big happy family is clearly inaccurate. However, rather than introducing conflict, new classical macroeconomics adopts an antigovernment approach that views government as the villain. The public continues to be described as one big happy family with a commonly shared national interest, but it is frustrated in achieving its goals by government, which is self-interested and therefore undermines the national interest. These differences between the Keynesian and new classical approaches to the political economy of policy making are shown in figure 7.7.

When applied to the theory of inflation and unemployment, new classical macroeconomics views inflation as caused by the Federal Reserve pushing the economy beyond the natural rate of unemployment in order to generate more output and tax revenues. Since the natural rate of unemployment represents the amount that the public actually wants to work and produce, the Fed is effectively working against the public's best interest. The policy prescription is clear: the Fed must be forced to stick to the natural rate and follow a zero-inflation policy. In this fashion, new classical macroeconomics claims that the Fed's high unemployment anti-inflation policies are actually in the best interests of working Americans.

116

POLICYMAKER

	Benevolent	Self-Seeking
Unified "Happy Family"	Keynesian	New classical
PUBLIC		
Divided		Structural Keynesian

Fig. 7.7. Different theoretical constructions of the political economy of policy making.

This antigovernment characterization of the inflation problem is part of a long history of antigovernment thinking in economics. In the modern era, the leader of the attack on government has been Milton Friedman who, early in his career, argued that the Federal Reserve caused the Great Depression of the 1930s. Thus, the worst economic downturn in the history of capitalism was not the result of anything internal to the economic system; rather, it was the result of misguided policy on the part of the Federal Reserve.

Friedman's monetarist attack on government rested on its proclivity to create macroeconomic instability: the focus was government's capacity to conduct economic policy. In particular, monetarists argued that there are long and variable lags in the implementation of policy, and these lags mean that policy can be destabilizing.

Whereas governments' capacity and judgment were the basis of the monetarist critique, new classical macroeconomics questions government's motives. The central assumption of the new paradigm is that there exists a divide between us and government. New classical macroeconomics therefore discards the notion of a benevolent public policymaker and replaces it with a political economy that retains a unified public interest but introduces a self-interested government.

This antigovernment stance derives from an even earlier attack on government predicated on the theory of bureaucratic and governmental failure.[9] Bureaucratic-failure theory emphasizes incentives regarding different choices and behaviors. It was initially used as an argument against government interventions to correct market failures related to environmental pollution and inadequate provision of public goods such as defense. The bureaucratic-failure theorists acknowledged that the market tended to overpollute because business treated the environment as free and therefore used it without regard to environmental consequence. They also acknowledged that the market cannot provide defense because everyone would have an incentive to get a free ride, and not pay his share. However, given that, they argued against government attempts to correct these problems (except notably defense) because bureaucrats had their own private interests and would not act in the national interest. They also argued that bureaucrats might be bought off by special interests (i.e., through lobbying) and again not follow national interests. Either way, the implication was to keep government out of the picture as much as possible because the cure was worse than the problem.

This view of political economy and government is the one that now dominates the economics profession and economics textbooks, and it has spread throughout society. Through such teaching, doctoral students in economics are socialized into an antigovernment predisposition. More importantly, so, too, are the hundreds of thousands of undergraduates and M.B.A. students who each year take economics courses. Because economics has become a prerequisite for a career in business, law, or government, we are producing an elite who are educated to adopt an antigovernment stance, and construct our political problems in terms of an "us" versus "government" divide. Inevitably, this view has percolated throughout American society, and it is now the dominant construction of American political economy.

New classical political economy borrows from bureaucratic-failure theory and casts government as the enemy, while retaining a unified "happy family" public interest. The reality is that, not only is there no benevolent public policymaker, but there is also no unified public interest. Instead, the economy is riven by different economic interests, the clearest manifestation of which is the conflict between business and labor over the distribution of income. This economic conflict in turn is represented in the political process through the existence of political parties. However, political parties also represent more than just the narrowly economic, and they also pursue the selfish interest of politicians. This situation is illustrated in figure 7.7 by the lower right-hand box labeled "Structural Keynesian."

The upshot of this situation is that different economic interests compete to control the policymaker. The policy choices of policymakers are determined within the political environment and primarily reflect the preferences of the group that currently has political dominance. Within this world, there is no divide between "us" and "government": rather, government is "us"—or at least government is the representative of the winners of the political process as constituted by the electoral and lobbying process.[10]

This structural Keynesian approach to economic policy recognizes that the domain of economic policy making is a "contested terrain."[11] It contrasts with both the Keynesian "benevolent policymaker" approach, and the new classical "us versus government" approach. The most frequent construction of the contested terrain view has been in terms of a divide between labor and capital. However, this representation can be refined by distinguishing among labor, industrial capital, and financial capital.[12] Introducing a distinction between industrial and financial capital then adds a significant dimension that is important for understanding the turn to deflationary policy.

THE POLITICAL ECONOMY OF DEFLATIONARY MONETARY POLICY

We are now in a position to provide a structural Keynesian account of the emergence of deflationary monetary policy. Economic policymakers face a Phillips curve trade-off between inflation and unemployment such as that illustrated in figure 7.2. The exact shape of this trade-off is determined by the structural particulars of each economy, but the logic is clear: if policymakers want to reduce unemployment, then they will have to tolerate a little more inflation.

Given the possibilities determined by the Phillips curve, labor would prefer the economy to operate in a region with low unemployment and higher inflation, corresponding to the far-left region of the Phillips curve. Low rates of unemployment increase labor's welfare by increasing the availability of jobs, reducing the insecurity of unemployment, and by raising real wages. This latter effect arises because labor is in a position to bargain for more.

Industrial capital's preferred region of economic activity is characterized by moderate unemployment and moderate inflation, corresponding to the middle region of the Phillips curve. When unemployment is too low, profits are depressed because labor is too strong. When unemployment is too high, profits are depressed because consumption demand is

119

weak. Consequently, industrial capital's profits are maximized when unemployment is moderate.

Lastly, finance capital's preferred region of economic activity is characterized by low inflation and high unemployment, corresponding to the far right region of the Phillips curve. Finance capital strongly dislikes inflation because it erodes the value of financial assets, and finance capital is therefore willing to tolerate more unemployment to offset this danger. However, even finance capital has an aversion to extreme rates of unemployment as this gives rise to increased rates of default and bankruptcy.

In addition, there is another reason why finance capital prefers the low inflation–high employment region. Achieving such an outcome requires tight monetary policy and higher interest rates. Once in place, this results in large transfers of income from borrowers to lenders, so that finance capital benefits. Working families lack financial wealth, and they therefore must borrow to pay for purchases of homes, education, cars, and consumer durables. High interest rates mean higher debt-service payments, so that their incomes are effectively reduced, while the income of finance capital is increased. Through this channel, the Federal Reserve profoundly affects the distribution of income.

In which region the Fed chooses to operate the economy depends on the configuration of political power. If labor is the dominant political force, the Fed will push the economy toward the region of low unemployment and higher inflation. If industrial capital is dominant, the economy will be pushed toward the region of moderate unemployment and moderate inflation. Lastly, if finance capital is dominant, the Fed will tend to operate in the region with low inflation and high unemployment.

In this light, the current triumph of zero-inflation policy within the Federal Reserve can be interpreted as a reflection of the political triumph of financial capital in the wider political process. Policy also will be biased toward low inflation and high unemployment—the region preferred by finance capital—when bureaucratic failure matters and Federal Reserve policy is influenced by the private concerns of its officers. This is because central bankers are usually drawn from the financial community and therefore share finance capital's preference for low inflation.

Because finance capital has a stronger interest in low inflation and high unemployment than does industrial capital, these two groups can sometimes part ways. Indeed, this consideration helps explain why a number of leading industrial capitalists supported President Clinton in the 1992 election. This group included John Scully, then CEO of Apple Computer, and the late Michael Walsh, then CEO of Tenneco. The same consideration is also present in other countries. For instance, in the United Kingdom, the Confederation of British Industry has frequently opposed hardline Conservative economic policy that has raised interest rates and unemployment in Britain. More recently, many British industrialists supported the British Labor Party under Tony Blair in the May 1997 election. Their thinking was that Blair would pursue a more expansionary policy, which would be good for profits.

Central Bank Independence and the Institutionalization of Deflationary Policy Bias

When viewed from the above perspective, natural-rate theory and its accompanying notion of a binding inflation constraint are revealed as a Trojan horse that has been used to capture economic policy. The reality behind the shift to deflationary monetary policy is that it has served to advance the interests of finance and industrial capital at the expense of labor. The pursuit of zero inflation and the willingness to accept high unemployment rates reflect the triumph of Wall Street, and Federal Reserve policy is now largely determined by the dictates of finance capital. A similar policy shift has also taken place in almost every major industrialized country, albeit this shift has been more politically contested in Europe than in North America.

At this stage, an emerging new agenda seeks to permanently institutionalize this triumph by making central banks independent of political control. Such a development would render the conduct of monetary policy free from any public accountability or control. Central bank independence, which is advocated by new classical economists, represents a means of institutionalizing Wall Street's triumph because central bankers are largely drawn from the ranks of financiers, and they therefore tend to favor the interests of finance. Democratically controlled central banks constantly struggle against this bankers' bias. The granting of central bank independence would institutionalize this bias by insulating the bank and disenfranchising outsiders in the making of monetary policy. The game plan is clear: natural-rate theory has provided the justification for zero-inflation monetary policy; central bank independence promises to institutionalize it.

This is not a figment of paranoid liberal imagination: rather, the process is already underway. However, it has received little public attention because it involves dry and technical economic issues. Italy, New Zealand, and Australia have already inaugurated independent central banking. Most importantly, the issue of central bank independence has repeatedly asserted itself in discussions within the European Community regarding the creation of a European currency. Thus, at this important time of re-designing Europe's monetary institutions, the conservative theories promulgated by the mainstream of the economics profession threaten to provide the tool for undermining the European tradition of strong demo-cratic control over the instruments of economic policy making.

In the United States, the Federal Reserve is already quasi-independent. Within the American setting, the new theory of central bank indepen-dence is being used to ward off those critics who have called for greater accountability and public control. The new theories therefore reinforce the Fed's existing autonomy. In this connection, it should be noted that neither the President nor Congress has the right to instruct the Fed re-garding the conduct of monetary policy. Moreover, neither Fed Gover-nors nor the Fed Chairman are subject to dismissal by either the Congress or the President. Fed decision making is highly secretive, and and the Fed's exemption from public accountability is compounded by a tendency among the financial press to lionize the Fed and its chairman, while pre-senting criticism of the Fed as "whining."

REFORMING THE FEDERAL RESERVE BANK, OR DID YOU KNOW THAT THE FED WAS OWNED BY CITICORP?

The tendency of central bankers to favor finance capital is reinforced within the United States by the institutional structure of the Federal Re-serve. To most people's amazement, the Federal Reserve Bank is not a government agency but is in fact privately owned by the commercial banks that are members of the Federal Reserve system. The name Federal Re-serve gives the impression of a government agency, but in fact the Fed is a private corporation whose stockholders are private commercial banks. In effect, the Federal Reserve is a bankers' club.

These private banks profoundly influence the Fed. In addition to the Board of Governors which is located in Washington, D.C., twelve re-gional Federal Reserve Banks are located in Boston, New York, Philadel-phia, Richmond, Atlanta, Dallas, Denver, St. Louis, Kansas City, Chicago, Minnesota, and San Francisco. The twelve district banks are locally owned and controlled. The President of each of these banks is appointed by its board of directors, of which one third are from the regional banking community and one third are from the regional business community. In this fashion, finance and industry control the regional Federal Reserve banks.

The Board of Governors, which has overall responsibility for the Federal Reserve System, consists of seven members, nominated by the President of the United States and confirmed by the U.S. Senate. However, these seven have fourteen-year terms and cannot be dismissed except for criminal behavior or gross incompetence. Thus, any sitting President can only expect to appoint two or three governors.

Interest rates and the direction of monetary policy are set by the Federal Open Market Committee (FOMC), comprising twelve members, seven of whom are from the Board of Governors, and five of whom are presidents of the regional Federal banks. The fact that five are regional Presidents gives the financial community enormous direct influence over Federal Reserve policy. Moreover, members of the Board of Governors also tend to be drawn from the financial community, thereby reinforcing this influence. Consequently, the institutional structure of the Fed imbues monetary policy with a bias that favors the bond market and works against families and small business.

CHANGING DIRECTION: AMERICA NEEDS A FAMILY-FRIENDLY FEDERAL RESERVE

Monetary policy and interest rates vitally affect the economic well-being of American families. Interest rates affect families' cost of living by impacting payments on variable-rate mortgages and consumer debt. They affect the ability of working families to own their own homes, which is an essential part of the American dream. Interest rates also affect job opportunities by impacting the level of economic activity: higher rates lower activity, which means fewer jobs. Moreover, this affects wages, because a robust economy means that employers must pay a little more to get and retain workers. It also means that employers may be forced to share some of the fruits of productivity growth with workers. Finally, interest rates likely affect the rate of economic growth. Lower interest rates encourage investment, whereas higher economic activity means that factories are using all their capacity, which acts as an incentive to build more capacity.

For all of these reasons, monetary policy profoundly affects the well-being of American families. It should therefore be conducted in a fashion that puts families first. Yet, far from this, the Federal Reserve actually conducts monetary policy with an almost total disregard for the interests of American families. Though deeply affected by monetary policy, the American family has no place at the table. A change of direction is needed.

It is not enough to trail behind the Fed constantly trying to persuade it, on technical grounds, not to raise rates. What is needed is a change of mentality that has the Fed place American families first. The Federal Reserve Reform Act of 1977 explicitly requires the Fed "to promote effectively the goals of maximum employment, stable prices and moderate long-term interest rates." However, the Fed has abandoned these responsibilities, and now focuses on only price stability. Its defense is the doctrine of the natural rate of unemployment (alias NAIRU) which maintains that the Fed cannot permanently lower the unemployment rate and the only thing it can really control is the inflation rate.

The Fed must relinquish its obsession with inflation and abandon the notion of a natural rate of unemployment. In its place, it must adopt a pragmatic monetary policy that consistently prods the economy toward higher employment, subject to maintaining a reasonable rate of inflation. Accomplishing this requires that employment and growth be given greater weight in its decision making. There is always a danger that inflation may accelerate when one pushes for full employment and growth. However, the Fed currently weights this risk excessively. The Fed can always tighten controls if inflation reaches an unacceptable level.

The above goal of getting the Fed to change its outlook can be complemented by a second agenda directed to reform of the Federal Reserve. The Federal Reserve is marked by profound institutional bias that works in favor of Wall Street and against working families and small business. Institutional reform could help reverse this bias. Such reform should focus on Federal Reserve appointments and their term and calendar. Thus, regional Federal Reserve Presidents and members of the Fed's Board of Governors should be nominated by the President, subjected to Senate confirmation, and serve four-year staggered terms. This simple measure would eliminate any proprietary influence of commercial banks over monetary policy, while staggered terms would prevent presidential packing.

The procedure for appointing the Fed Chairman should remain unchanged, as should his term. However, the calendar of appointment should coincide with the inauguration of the President of the United States. This would eliminate pressures such as occurred in 1996, when Chairman Greenspan's reappointment before the presidential election gave President Clinton a strong incentive to placate Wall Street by staying with Mr. Greenspan.

Lastly, the President and the Congress should expand the breadth of representation at the Fed. Others besides bankers and economists have the capabilities and the judgment to serve responsibly and effectively as governors of the Federal Reserve. Their skills and point of view are needed if the well-being of American families is to be the center of monetary policy.

From New Deal to Raw Deal:
The Attack on Government

CHAPTER 7 described how monetary policy has been captured by financial interests, and how this capture has given monetary policy a deflationary bias. The new stance of monetary policy contrasts with the expansionary stance of the Golden Age, and the change is visible in the much higher level of real interest rates that has prevailed over the last fifteen years. Monetary policy now works for the benefit of bondholders. The cover for this new stance is provided by the theory of the natural rate of unemployment, which maintains that monetary policy is handcuffed by a binding employment constraint.

Along with the capture of monetary policy, there has been an attack on government. This assault is two-pronged. First, it seeks to take government out of labor markets by reducing the scale and scope of the social safety net: the goal is to undermine the wage floor. Second, it seeks to end activist fiscal policy, which has government using its tax and spending powers to affect income distribution and the level of employment. Here, the goal is to put an end to government's attempts to equalize income distribution and achieve stable high levels of employment.

The push to shrink the social safety net and neutralize fiscal policy represents an attempt to roll back the New Deal. At the beginning of this century, Theodore Roosevelt gave America the Square Deal: its focus was regulating the power of corporate America and guarding against monopoly. In mid-century, Franklin Roosevelt bequeathed the New Deal, and Harry Truman gave America the Fair Deal. The goals were full employment, high wages, and income security; together, the New Deal and the Fair Deal constituted a combination that democratized the American Dream. The 1980s saw the inauguration of the Raw Deal, the goal of which has been the restoration of nineteenth-century laissez-faire economics.

UNDERMINING THE WAGE FLOOR: TAKING GOVERNMENT OUT OF THE LABOR MARKET

One prong of the attack on government aims to take government out of the labor market by reducing the scale and scope of the social safety net. This process has links with the push for deregulation that started in the 1970s. Deregulation was initially confined to consumer product markets, but its logic is now being applied in labor markets. The original purpose of deregulation was to put prices in competition. Applied to labor markets, its purpose is to put wages in competition by making workers compete with one another in a new environment that is stripped of government supports for workers and their families.

As with the attack on unions described in chapter 3, the belief is that there exists a natural market, and the social safety net is a distortion of this market; hence, the justification for repealing it. However, removing the safety net will not create a natural market; it will only create a market where workers are vulnerable and business strong.

The significance of these supports is illustrated in figure 8.1. Government is important to the labor market, owing to its impact on the relative bargaining strength of workers and firms. This impact operates through many channels, including laws governing the right to collective bargaining and the right to form unions free from employer intimidation; protections against employer lockouts and unfair dismissal; and protections against employers bargaining in bad faith as a means of seeking permanent replacement of existing workers.

Another channel is the minimum wage, which sets a floor to market wages. The system of unemployment insurance and welfare also affects labor market outcomes by ensuring that unemployed and laid-off workers are not destitute. Lastly, labor market outcomes are affected by fair labor standards and occupational health and safety laws that limit working hours, ensure that working conditions are safe, and require that workers are appropriately trained and protected against the hazards that go with particular jobs.

The reason why this system of government oversight and regulation of labor markets matters is that it increases the bargaining power of workers vis-à-vis firms. Such measures limit the ability of firms to replace existing workers with unemployed workers, while also giving workers means of support that mitigate the threat of unemployment. By setting wage floors,

127

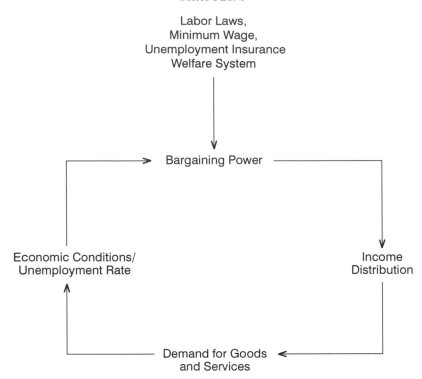

Fig. 8.1. The significance of the social safety net and government labor-market involvement for labor-market bargaining.

minimum wage laws and welfare entitlements prevent the forces of wage competition from fully exploiting the relative vulnerability of working families. Workplace safety protections and limitations on hours restrict the ways in which firms can place workers in competition with one another, while training requirements raise the cost to firms of firing experienced workers.

In terms of the analysis of the logic of economic power in chapter 5, the system of government oversight and regulation of labor markets raises firms' transactions costs, while also raising the value of workers' alternative options. The net result has been to increase worker bargaining strength, thereby raising wages and improving the distribution of income.

The implications of taking government out of labor markets are clear: workers lose, while business gains. The Raw Deal promotes such an agenda. Figure 8.2 shows the falling value of the minimum wage and average hourly wages. Between 1955 and 1969, the minimum wage rose by

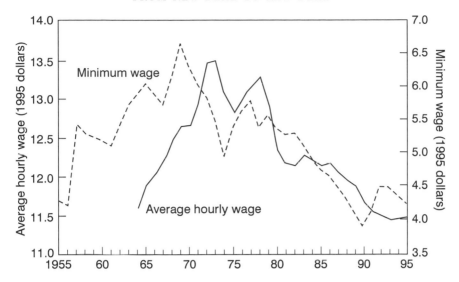

Fig. 8.2. Real value of the minimum wage and average hourly wage, 1955–95. *Source*: Author's calculation based on *Statistical Abstract*, 1993, table 675, deflated by Consumer Price Index, and CITIBASE.

almost 56% from $4.27 per hour (in 1995 spending power) to $6.65. Between 1969 and 1995 the minimum wage fell back to $4.25 per hour, below the 1955 level. The minimum wage contributes to setting the "wage floor." When the minimum wage was increasing throughout the 1950s and 1960s, so too were average hourly wages: when the minimum wage started falling after 1969, average hourly wages started to decline shortly thereafter. In 1950, a full-time worker earning the minimum wage would have earned 80% of the poverty level income for a family of three. In 1968, the same worker would have earned 118%. By 1995, full-time working at the minimum wage would have earned only 72% of the poverty level income for a family of three.[1] Though an increase in the minimum wage was legislated in 1996, this increase does not come close to restoring the minimum wage to its earlier levels. Moreover, it came as part of the welfare reform package that reduced welfare protections. Consequently, the policy of putting wages in competition remains intact.

A similar picture emerges from consideration of welfare payments made through Aid to Families with Dependent Children (AFDC). Figure 8.3 charts average hourly wages and the purchasing power of average monthly AFDC payments (measured in 1995 purchasing power). In 1955, average

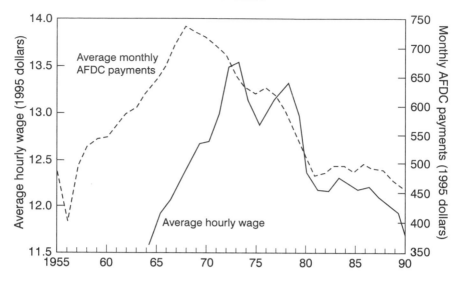

Fig. 8.3. Real value of monthly AFDC payments, average hourly wage, 1955–90. *Source*: Author's calculation based on data provided by D. M. Gordon and CITIBASE.

monthly AFDC payments were $486.34, and they rose to $738.14 by 1968, a 52% increase. By 1990, they had fallen back to $457.18. As with the minimum wage, this was below the 1955 level. AFDC payments also contribute to establishing the wage floor. When AFDC payments were rising, average hourly wages also rose: when they started to fall, average hourly wages started falling shortly thereafter. The minimum wage and welfare both act to support market wages, and eroding these two supports has contributed to the erosion of average hourly wages.

A 1996 report by the House Ways and Means Committee shows that states have not increased benefits nearly enough to keep up with inflation. As of January 1996, the maximum cash assistance within the forty-eight contiguous states for a family of three ranged from $120 a month in Mississippi, to $703 in Suffolk County, New York. In the median state (the one exactly in the middle), the payment was up from $184 in 1970 to $389. However, adjusted for inflation, the payment had actually declined 51%. The decline was 43% in Connecticut, 59% in Illinois, 47% in Massachusetts and Michigan, 65% in New Jersey, 48% in New York City, 60% in Pennsylvania, and 68% in Texas.[2] These findings make a mockery of the claim that rising welfare payments have been the cause of America's rising poverty. However, they do support the claim that undercutting support for workers has contributed to declining wages and increased income inequality.

The declining value of welfare payments has been continuing apace for twenty-five years. The recent 1996 welfare legislation adds a new dimension by removing lifetime entitlement and replacing it with a five-year entitlement. It also seeks to replace welfare with workfare by requiring welfare recipients to work for their benefits. There are already indications that state and local governments will use this new requirement to replace low-skilled unionized public-sector employees with welfare recipients. This concern emerged in New York city during the 1996 contract negotiations with the transit workers. Workfare therefore potentially represents the thin edge of a wedge undermining public-sector wages and unions.

Mishel and Schmitt (1996) have examined the wage and employment implications of the recent welfare reform legislation.[3] If those currently on welfare are to be absorbed into the ranks of the employed, as is the goal stated by Congress, then wages of low-wage workers (defined as the bottom 30%) will have to fall 11.9%. Wages for low-wage workers in states with large welfare populations will have to fall even more. In California, a 17.8% decline is needed; in New York, the decline is 17.1%. Workfare therefore threatens to exacerbate the trend toward putting wages in competition by reducing welfare benefits and increasing the supply of low-wage workers who have no alternative means of support. Anecdotal evidence to this effect is now starting to accumulate rapidly.[4]

Another area where the wage foor has been undercut is unemployment insurance (UI). Here, there has been a long-term decline in recipiency rates. The wage-replacement rate has remained steady, with UI replacing roughly 40% of wages. The duration of receipt has also remained steady at approximately twenty-four weeks. What has changed, however, is the percentage of unemployed persons receiving UI. This change is captured in figure 8.4. The UI recipiency rate was 75% of total unemployed in 1975; by 1995, it had fallen to 36%. In effect, changing the rules regarding qualification for UI has excluded more and more unemployed persons. Qualifying for UI has become increasingly dependent on a history of high-wage stable employment, whereas the economy has been producing more low-wage and contingent jobs. Hence, the increased exclusion rate.

The forces promoting the above developments are multiple. The push to put wages in competition rests on superficial similarity with the arguments that have driven the push for deregulation in the trucking, airlines,

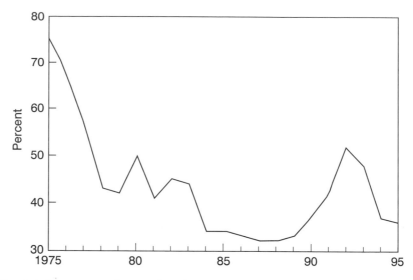

Fig. 8.4. Percentage of unemployed receiving unemployment insurance. *Source*:
U.S. Department of Labor, Unemployment Insurance Service.

banking, communications, and the electric utilities industries. In those
industries, the goal has been to put prices in competition and improve
efficiency, but the benefits appear somewhat ambiguous.[5] In labor markets, the issue is not one of improving productive efficiency or getting
firms to lower profit margins. Rather, it is a matter of putting workers in
competition with each other in order to drive down wages and shift the
distribution of income in favor of profits.

A second push for taking government out of labor markets comes from
supply-side economics (see below). The supply-side argument is that government intervention has destroyed the incentive to work and has promoted an outbreak of shirking by both rich and poor. To get the rich to
work, we need to increase incentives by cutting taxes. Similarly, to get the
poor to work, we need to increase incentives by cutting benefits. To para-
phrase John Kenneth Galbraith, the logic of supply-side economics is that
the rich are not working hard enough because they are not being paid
enough, while the poor are not working hard enough because they are
being paid too much.[6] However, the reality is that the purchasing power
of both the minimum wage and welfare payments have been falling, and
this is inconsistent with the supplysider's shirking hypothesis.

"Reform" is the rhetoric that surrounds discussions of welfare; "repeal"
is the true subtext. Real reform would involve providing support and

training for welfare recipients, while also ensuring the availability of jobs that pay at least the minimum wage and do not involve displacing existing low-wage workers. However, the true goal is to accelerate the process of putting wages in competition, while also saving on government outlays so as to enable further upper-end income-tax cuts that get the underpaid rich to work harder.

Handcuffing Fiscal Policy: The Saving-Shortage Hypothesis

Taking government out of labor markets and putting wages back in competition is one goal of the attack on government. The other is handcuffing fiscal policy by limiting government's ability to use its powers of taxation and spending. Figure 8.5 illustrates how fiscal policy impacts the economic system through its effect on the level of demand. Government purchases of goods and services directly increase demand, while transfer payments (such as social security) put income in households' pockets, thereby enabling them to spend more. Conversely, taxation takes income out of households' pockets. This illustrates how government can affect the distribution of income by taking from some households and giving to others. Lastly, corporate tax policy affects corporate investment spending on plant and machinery, and this also affects demand.

The centerpiece of the attack on fiscal policy is the saving–shortage hypothesis." The claim is that the U.S. economy suffers from a shortage of saving as a result of excessive government spending and excessive consumption by households. This shortage has supposedly restrained the level of investment and capital formation. As such, it poses a dire threat to future American prosperity, because investment and capital formation are the backbone of a rising standard of living. Remedying this situation therefore calls for cutting both private consumption and government spending.

The saving-shortage hypothesis asserts that saving causes investment. That is, if we increased saving, then we would increase investment in plant and equipment. However, the empirical evidence is that investment causes saving. Thus, firms first undertake spending on plant and equipment, and, once this spending takes place, it gets counted as saving in the form of capital accumulation. Consequently policies of austerity aimed at cutting consumption and government spending will not increase investment and growth. Indeed, they may actually reduce investment because

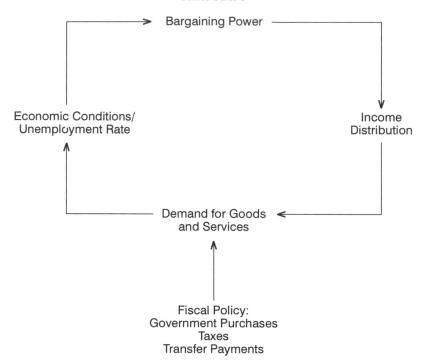

Fig. 8.5. Significance of government fiscal policy, based on government purchases, taxation, and transfer payments, for the level of demand for goods and services.

such policies reduce consumer demand so that firms no longer need to build additional productive capacity.

The fact that investment causes saving is deeply misunderstood by both the public and the economics profession because of a confusion between financial saving and real saving. *Financial saving* represents the accumulation of money assets, and it is accomplished by households not spending all their money income on consumption; reducing consumption does indeed increase financial saving. *Real saving* represents the accumlation of buildings, plant, and machinery that can be used to produce output in the future. Real saving is brought about by firms undertaking investment spending. Hence, investment causes real saving, and it is investment and real saving that are important for future prosperity. Attempts to increase financial saving may actually backfire with regard to investment and real saving by reducing demand for output, and eliminating firms' need for additional production capacity.

TABLE 8.1

Gross Investment and Its Components, as Shares of Gross
Domestic Product

Share of GDP	1955.1–1979.4	1980.1–1995.2	Change
Fixed investment	15.46	15.62	0.16
Producer equipment	6.51	7.35	0.84
Business structures	3.92	4.00	0.08
Residential structures	5.03	4.26	−0.77

Source: CITIBASE and author's calculations.

The key claim of the saving-shortage hypothesis is that there is a significant shortage of saving within the U.S. economy, and this has in turn reduced investment spending. However, examination of the data on investment spending show that this is not the case. At a casual level, the saving-shortage hypothesis is confounded by the run up in stock prices and the Dow Jones index. Wall Street is awash in cash as a result of retirement saving by households, and this has driven up stock prices to record highs. Firms are also awash with cash and have been using their surplus cash to repurchase their equity at record rates. These are not the signs of a saving shortage.

Table 8.1 displays data on the average gross domestic product (GDP) share of gross investment and its contributory components, for the period 1955.1–1979.4 and 1980.1–1995.2.[7] The later subperiod corresponds to the period of the supposed saving shortage. However, the average share of GDP devoted to fixed investment actually rose slightly from 15.45% to 15.62% in this period. Fixed investment can be divided into three components: producer equipment, business structures, and residential structures. Producer equipment represents business spending on machinery, and it is vital to the process of economic growth. Yet, this category of investment spending also increased, averaging 7.35% of GDP in the second subperiod, compared with 6.51% in the first subperiod. Spending on business structures as a share of GDP was essentially unchanged, whereas residential structures spending fell slightly.

Table 8.1 shows the relative constancy of the share of GDP devoted to fixed investment. Given this, why has the saving-shortage hypothesis gained such widespread acceptance? Its internal logic recommends shrinking government and reducing the burden of taxes on profits and interest income. Thus, the saving-shortage hypothesis serves as a Trojan horse promoting a political agenda aimed at shifting the distribution of income in favor of upper-income groups and diminishing the economic role of government. This Trojan horse character becomes evident when we examine its specific policy recommendations for households, business, and governments.

BLAMING HOUSEHOLDS

The saving-shortage hypothesis maintains that households are not saving enough. The obverse of this is that households are consuming too much and have been engaged in a consumption binge. Robert Blecker (1990) has provided comprehensive empirical evidence rejecting the consumption-binge hypothesis, but despite this it has still gained widespread acceptance. The consumption-binge hypothesis contributes to the creation of a political climate justifying policies of austerity. In effect, it represents households as undisciplined and indulgent, and as having failed to exercise appropriate restraint on consumption spending. The slow growth of income that has afflicted most U.S. households can then be blamed on their own improvidence, while policies of austerity that seek to increase national saving can be argued to be in households' best interest.

Whereas the consumption-binge hypothesis serves to create a climate justifying policies of austerity, the saving-shortage hypothesis gives direction to these policies; in this fashion, the two complement each other. Because shortage of savings is the problem, policy should be directed to increasing saving. This justifies replacing income taxes with consumption taxes. The argument is that such taxes increase the cost of consumption today and therefore encourage households to postpone consumption and save more.

Whereas income taxes tend to be progressive, consumption taxes are regressive and fall disproportionately on lower-income groups. The regressivity of consumption taxes, be they excise taxes or value-added taxes, has been documented by Anderson (1989). His findings are summarized in tables 8.2 and 8.3, which show tax burdens as a percentage of income. Excise and value-added taxes fall more heavily on lower-income groups because they spend a larger share of their income. This contrasts with the current income tax, under which marginal rates of taxation rise with income so that higher-income households pay proportionately more. Indeed, even a flat tax with a fixed exemption is progressive because a greater proportion of poorer households' income is covered by the exemption. In

TABLE 8.2

The Effect of a Value-Added Tax (VAT) on 1986 Income and Expenditure (U.S. dollars)

	Lowest 20%	*Second 20%*	*Third 20%*	*Fourth 20%*	*Highest 20%*
After-tax income	3,665	10,371	18,143	28,753	54,868
Average annual expenditures	10,923	13,073	18,240	23,570	37,889
5% VAT	546	654	912	1,179	1,894
VAT as percent of income	14.9%	6.3%	5.0%	4.1%	3.5%
Average annual expenditures minus food	8,864	10,668	15,231	19,802	32,411
5% VAT with food exemption	443	533	762	990	1,621
VAT as percent of income	12.1%	5.1%	4.2%	3.4%	5.0%

Source: Anderson (1989, p. 24).

sum, the adoption of a system of consumption taxes as advocated by pro-ponents of the saving-shortage hypothesis would amount to a tax increase on lower-income households and a tax cut for upper-income households.

The claimed saving shortage has also prompted calls for exempting div-idend and interest income from taxation. The argument is that dividends and interest provide the incentive to save, and making them tax exempt would encourage further saving. In fact, economic theory suggests that saving could equally decrease, while empirical evidence shows saving to be unresponsive to interest rates. Such exemptions would clearly provide a significant tax cut for upper-income households, because the private own-ership of stocks and bonds is heavily skewed toward the top 10% of upper-income households (table 4.3). This concentration is particularly marked with regard to holdings of stocks, bonds, trusts, business equity, and non-home real estate, which are the principal asset categories that earn interest and profits.

Another policy suggestion that follows from the saving-shortage hy-pothesis is reduction of the capital gains tax rate. The argument is that such a reduction would also increase the overall return to saving and therefore encourage saving. As with dividend and interest tax exemptions, there are theoretical and empirical objections. However, it is again clear that capital gains tax reductions would provide a tax cut heavily concen-trated among upper-income households because these households own the vast majority of stocks and bonds on which capital gains have accrued.

137

TABLE 8.3
Effective Tax Rates for 1988 (joint return, one dependent)

Adjusted Gross Income (U.S. Dollars)	Actual Tax Rate (percent)	Actual as % of the Average Tax Rate
0–10,000	0	0
10–20,000	4.3	32.1
20–30,000	8.3	61.9
30–50,000	11.0	82.1
50–100,000	16.0	119.4
100–200,000	21.8	162.7
200–500,000	25.0	186.6
500–1,000,000	26.8	200.0
1,000,000 +	26.6	198.5
Average	13.4	

Source: Andersen (1989, p. 14).

Lastly, the saving-shortage hypothesis promotes a view whereby increased inequality of income distribution is seen as a good thing rather than a cause for worry, because higher-income households tend to save more out of each additional dollar of income than do low-income households. Consequently, shifts in the distribution of income toward upper-income households increase total saving, to the benefit of all. This is the economic rationale of "trickle down" theory, which John Kenneth Galbraith has labeled "horse and sparrow" economics: feed enough oats to the horse, and some will pass through on to the road to feed the sparrow.

In sum, the consumption-binge hypothesis blames American households for stagnating real wages and low income growth, and argues for policies of economic austerity. Its twin, the saving-shortage hypothesis, has been used to advance an agenda that seeks to cut taxes on upper-income groups and redistribute income toward these groups.

In the early 1980s, supply-side economics and the Laffer curve provided the rationalization for redistributing income toward the wealthy. The logic of supply-side economics was that the rich were not working hard enough because they were not being paid enough, whereas the poor were not working hard enough because they were being paid too much.[8] The saving-shortage hypothesis is the 1990s analogue of supply-side economics and embodies a similar perverse logic. Now, the rich are not saving enough because they are not being paid enough, whereas the poor are consuming too much because they are being paid excessively.

In the 1980s, most economists rejected supply-side economics and saw it for what it was, namely, an attempt to redistribute income. However, many liberal economists have bought into the saving-shortage hypothesis (see, e.g., Friedman 1988) even though an agenda of upward redistribution of income lies at its core. The history of supply-side economics suggests that the tax policies advocated by proponents of the saving-shortage hypothesis are unlikely to increase saving, but they will result in significant tax cuts for upper-income households and a worsening of income inequality. Moreover, to the extent that tax cuts increase the government deficit, they may actually decrease national saving.

The Government Deficit and the Attack on Government

Throughout the 1980s and 1990s, the federal government has persistently run budget deficits, and this has provided fertile ground for attacking government. By exploiting simple analogies with ordinary households, conservative critics have been able to claim that government has been squandering the nation's seed capital

The saving-shortage hypothesis plays an important role in the conservative argument, because deficits are accounted for as negative saving by the government, so that government is notionally reducing national saving. Because a shortage of national saving supposedly constrains investment and capital accumulation, the government is implicitly responsible for slowing economic growth. In this fashion, the saving-shortage hypothesis casts government as part of the problem.

Not only is government cast as part of the problem, but the saving-shortage hypothesis then recommends fixing the problem by cutting taxes for the rich, cutting government spending, and cutting benefits for the poor. In this policy prescription, the saving-shortage hypothesis finds a sympathetic echo in supply-side economics, which argues for lower income taxes on the rich to increase entrepreneurial effort and reduced benefits for the poor to get them to work harder.

The saving-shortage hypothesis and supply-side economics represent two prongs of the attack on government. Supply-siders want to cut taxes on the rich and cut benefits for the poor to increase effort. The savings-shortage school wants to cut taxes on the rich to increase savings. It also wants to balance the budget to increase savings, and since taxes are to be cut (which increases the deficit), government spending must be re-

139

duced. In this fashion, the saving-shortage hypothesis implicitly promotes an agenda that seeks to shrink government and its involvement in the economy.

However, the reality is that the saving-shortage attack on government rests on a combination of faulty measurement of the deficit and misunderstanding of the economic effects of the deficit. The deficit is overstated owing to incorrect accounting, while government spending and the deficit only constrain capital accumulation when the economy is at full employment. The substantive foundation of the saving-shortage hypothesis is political and ideological.

Chapter 7 examined how the attack on activist monetary policy and the push for independent central banks is driven by a long-standing anti-government tradition in economics. This same tradition informs the anti-government character of the saving-shortage hypothesis and its attack on activist fiscal policy. In the 1960s, Milton Friedman and the monetarists attacked government countercyclical stabilization policy and argued that such policy was destabilizing. Friedman argued that mistaken contractionary policy by the Federal Reserve had actually been the principal cause of the Great Depression: "The fact is that the Great Depression, like most other periods of severe unemployment, was produced by government mismanagement rather than by inherent instability of the private economy (Friedman 1962, p. 38)." This view informed his critique of Keynesian macroeconomic stabilization policy. His formal argument was that attempts to stabilize the economy were counterproductive owing to long and variable lags in the implementation process.[9] This meant that government would likely be stepping on the brake just as the economy was slowing down, and stepping on the gas just as it was speeding up.

Behind these technical objections to stabilization policy lay a profound philosophical opposition to government. Thus, Friedman argued that government and the New Deal had been counterproductive with regard to the entire cause of social progress.

> The greater part of the new ventures undertaken by government in the past few decades have failed to acheive their objectives. The United States has continued to progress; its citizens have become better fed, better clothed, better housed, and better transported; class and social distinctions have narrowed; minority groups have become less disadvantaged; popular culture has advanced by leaps and bounds. All this has has been the product of the initiative and drive of individuals cooperating through the free market. Government measures have hampered

140

not helped this development. We have been able to afford and surmount these measures only because of the extraordinary fecundity of the market. The invisible hand has been more potent for progress than the visible hand for retrogression" (Friedman 1962, pp. 199–200).

The saving-shortage hypothesis draws on this antigovernment tradition. Its principle argument is "crowding-out" theory. Crowding-out theory maintains that government spending displaces private investment spending. This is an old argument that dates back to the Great Depression. In the 1930s, it was referred to as the "Treasury view" because the British Treasury opposed suggestions for public works programs on the grounds that government spending on such programs would displace an equal amount of private-sector investment spending. The Treasury maintained its stance despite mass unemployment and underutilization of factory capacity, which meant resources were idly sitting by and going to waste.

In modern economics, higher interest rates represent the formal mechanism through which crowding-out operates. The claim is that increased government spending drives up interest rates, thereby reducing private investment spending. The exact details of why interest rates rise differ by school of thought, but the policy recommendation is the same: namely, reduce government spending and benefit payments. In this fashion, crowding-out theory provides support for the political agenda of shrinking government.

The saving-shortage hypothesis casts government as part of the problem. It justifies this characterization by reference to the negative effects of government deficits on national saving, and crowding-out effects of government spending on private investment. However, this characterization suffers from profound problems which include inadequate theoretical logic, mismeasurement of the deficit, and misrepresentation of the character of government spending.

Economic Logic. The theoretical logic of crowding-out is extremely doubtful. First, because the Federal Reserve can use monetary policy to hold down interest rates there is no automatic need for interest rates to rise because of government spending. Indeed, chapter 7 showed how the Federal Reserve has been responsible for the rise in real interest rates.

Second, investment is not constrained by saving; rather, investment causes saving. Once firms have completed investment expenditures on buildings and machines, these expenditures then get counted as saving.

This means that an increase in the government deficit need have no adverse effect on investment. Indeed, increased government spending may actually increase investment spending through its positive effect on output. Government spending adds to demand and stimulates economic activity, which may encourage firms to build more productive capacity.[10]

The one occasion when deficits and government spending crowd out investment is when the economy is at full employment. In this event, the economy no longer has spare capacity and workers with which to produce extra output. If firms want to invest (i.e., buy machines and buildings), no resources are available to produce the additional machines and buildings. At this stage, cutting government spending can make resources available. If the government reduces the amount of output it buys or reduces the number of persons it employs, this releases manufacturing capacity and people to produce investment goods (buildings and machines). In these circumstances, government spending and deficits crowd out investment. However, the problem for proponents of the saving-shortage hypothesis is that the United States economy has not been at full employment these last twenty years.

Mismeasurement of the Deficit. With regard to "measurement" issues, Robert Eisner (1986) has noted that the deficit is significantly overstated because of the effect of inflation in reducing the national debt. Inflation reduces the value of debts. Financial markets recognize this, and interest rates therefore rise in inflationary times to compensate for this erosion. In effect, higher interest rates compensate lenders for loan principal erosion and are tantamount to an early repayment of loans. From an accounting standpoint, this means that the portion of interest rates attributable to inflation should be treated as loan repayment rather than spending. Such repayments represent government saving and should be accounted for as such.[11] Failure to do so therefore overstates the deficit and understates national saving.

A second criticism made by Eisner is that much government spending represents public investment spending on infrastructure such as roads, airports, and public buildings. There is also a case for treating part of education and health spending as investment in human capital. However, the national income accounts treat all government spending as consumption, thereby misrepresenting its character and giving government the air of profligacy. If these expenditures are accounted for correctly, the publicly recorded government deficit no longer provides a measure of government "dissaving," and national saving is again understated. The current accounting proceedings for recording government outlays therefore over-state the deficit, promote the hoax of a saving shortage, and encourage people to blame government.

Misrepresentation of Government Spending. The above failure to treat government infrastructure expenditures as public investment obscures the role of public capital in promoting economic growth. Public investment in infrastructure capital makes a significant positive contribution to the economy. It earns a high rate of return, both in terms of increasing the productivity of private business, and in terms of improved quality of life. Thus, better school facilities improve education, which raises worker pro-ductivity as well as improving the nation's citizenry. Similarly, better high-ways help business, while also making travel safer and saving on automo-bile wear and tear. This high rate of return to public investment has been documented by Aschauer (1991) and Munnell (1990). Proponents of the saving-shortage hypothesis, who point to the government deficit as reason for reducing government spending, may actually be reducing national in-vestment and saving.

WHY IT MATTERS: UNDERSTANDING CURRENT BUDGETARY POLICY

The saving-shortage hypothesis is beset with theoretical difficulties, and its arguments are built on faulty measures of government saving. How-ever, it is not an arcane theoretical controversy. Rather, it has critical pol-icy implications. Once hooked by its putative logic, one is compelled to adopt a political agenda that seeks to shrink government and redistribute income upward.

This agenda is evident in its policies for eliminating the government budget deficit. The government budget deficit is given by:

$$\text{Government deficit} = \text{tax revenues} - \text{government purchases} - \text{transfer payments}$$

Deficit reduction can be acheived either by increasing tax revenues or de-creasing government purchases and transfer payments (e.g., social security and welfare).

Proponents of the saving-shortage hypothesis argue for cutting pur-chases and transfer payments. They also argue for tax reductions so as to increase the private incentive to produce and save. Transfer payments tend

143

TABLE 8.4
Average Income Distribution by Household, 1986

Income by Definition	Lowest Fifth	Second Fifth	Third Fifth	Fourth Fifth	Top Fifth
Distribution of Income in Dollars					
Market income	1,563	11,734	23,391	37,064	81,813
After-tax income	1,445	10,749	20,218	31,149	64,352
Net income	6,805	15,258	23,186	33,213	66,107
Net change	5,242	3,524	−205	−3,851	−15,706
Distribution of Income in Percent					
Market income	1.0	7.6	15.1	23.9	52.5
After-tax income	1.1	8.4	15.8	24.4	50.3
Net income	4.7	10.6	16.0	23.0	45.7
Net change	3.7	3.0	0.9	−0.9	−6.8

Source: Bureau of the Census, Current Population Reports, ser. P-60, no. 164-RD-1, *Measuring the Effect of Benefits and Taxes on Income and Poverty: 1986*, December 1988, pp. 18–19, table 2.

to be relatively more skewed toward those at the bottom of the income distribution and are the most important way in which the Federal government helps equalize the distribution of income. Contrastingly, tax reductions are of value to those with income and are therefore of correspondingly greater value to upper-income households where the distribution of income is concentrated.

Table 8.4 contains data from a 1986 study by the Census Bureau, which shows how government helps equalize income distribution. *Market income* refers to income generated in the private sector; *after-tax income* is income net of all federal, state and social security taxes; *net income* is after-tax income plus all federal cash and noncash benefits. The table reveals how the income tax is mildly progressive because it increases the percentage share of income of those at the bottom. More importantly, it shows how transfer payments are heavily concentrated among lowest-income groups, so that cutting them reduces the deficit while minimally affecting upper-income groups.

Such considerations reveal how the 1996 welfare reform legislation is consistent with the political agenda underlying the saving-shortage hypothesis. By reducing welfare, it reduces transfers and reduces the deficit. At the same time, it implements the second stage of supply-side economics. The first stage was getting the rich to work harder by paying them more (i.e., cutting their taxes). However, the poor are still not working hard enough because they are being paid too much. The second stage therefore reduces welfare, which directly reduces the incomes of the poor. It will also likely lower wages for low-income workers by forcing welfare recipients to take work at any wage (Mishel and Schmitt 1996).

Lastly, just as the saving-shortage hypothesis promotes a view favoring tax cuts and reductions in government purchases and transfers, it also has a proclivity to exempt tax expenditures. Tax expenditures refer to tax deductions and allowances. In effect, there are two ways of spending tax revenues. One is to collect taxes, and then spend the revenues in the form of purchases and transfer payments; the other is to forgive agents their tax obligations. The de facto impact of tax expenditures is to increase the budget deficit. This impact is obscured because tax expenditures are not visible as an explicit expenditure. At the same time, the benefits of tax expenditures tend to accrue heavily to upper-income groups as they have the income against which deductions can be applied. Consequently, tax expenditures serve to redistribute income to these groups.

Even though tax expenditures increase the deficit, supply-siders and saving-shortage proponents tend to exempt them and even argue for their extension. The argument is that since tax expenditures accrue disproportionately to upper-income groups who have a high marginal propensity to save, cutting them would reduce private saving.

Such reasoning also favors extensive tax deductions for corporations (alias corporate welfare) in the form of accelerated depreciation allowances. Here, the logic is that total private saving consists of household saving and corporate saving, with the latter being financed by profits. To the extent that corporate tax expenditures increase corporate profits, it can be argued that they increase corporate saving. It is also true that ownership of corporations (i.e., stock ownership) is heavily concentrated among upper-income groups, so that increased profits resulting from corporate welfare accrue largely to this group.

BLAMING GOVERNMENT FOR
THE TRADE DEFICIT

A third focal point of the saving shortage hypothesis is the trade deficit. The trade balance corresponds to the gap between exports and imports, and can be interpreted as net foreign saving. If there is a trade surplus, the United States is building up claims on the rest of the world: if there is a trade deficit, the rest of the world is building up claims against the United States.

145

Over the last fifteen years, the United States has run large and persistent trade deficits so that net foreign saving has been negative. The saving-shortage hypothesis attributes these deficits to insufficient saving, and argues that they would have been lower if private and government saving had been higher. The claim is that there is a fixed amount of national income, and if government increases spending so that total spending exceeds national income, than this excess has to be imported. In this fashion, the government deficit causes the trade deficit.

Such reasoning appears logical and watertight, However, there is a critical unflagged assumption, which is that there is a fixed amount of income. If the economy has unemployment and unused industrial capacity, then the economy has the means to produce more output. This means that extra government spending can be satisfied by increased domestic production. National income is fixed only if the economy is at full employment and industrial capacity is fully utilized. Only then will increased government spending cause a one-for-one increase in imports. Over the last twenty years, the United States economy has not been at full employment, and this is the critical flaw in the twin-deficits argument.

With regard to policy, the trade deficit has been used to push two complementary agendas. In the early 1980s, the trade deficit was used to promote the notion of a competitiveness crisis, which was invoked to push for a new lean and mean workplace. Thus, the competitiveness crisis provided the window of entry for such developments as downsizing, subcontracting and outsourcing, and the replacement of permanent staff with temporary workers. In addition, the competitiveness crisis was also used to launch an attack on regulation of the workplace and environment, the argument being that these mandates made American industry uncompetitive internationally. In this fashion, the competitiveness crisis provided the justification for an assault on wages, work conditions, and worker protections.

Initially invoked in connection with the competitiveness crisis, the trade deficit has subsequently been invoked to attack government. Here, the vehicle has been the "twin deficits" version of the saving-shortage hypothesis, which maintains that the government deficit is responsible for the trade deficit (i.e., negative foreign saving). Proponents of the twin-deficits hypothesis therefore argue for reducing the government deficit, so as to reduce the trade deficit. In this regard, it is a variation of the saving-shortage hypothesis and shares the same political agenda of shrinking government and reducing transfer payments.

As with the debate over the relation between private saving and invest-

146

ment, the twin-deficits hypothesis raises issues concerning counting of the trade deficit, and issues of causation. Issues of counting arise because a significant portion of international trade (approximately 40%) involves intracompany trade.[12] Because the United States has the most extensive multinational production network, intracompany trade is relatively more concentrated among American entities. For instance, Nike is an American company that has extensive shoe manufacturing operations in Indonesia, and shoes from those plants are imported into the United States. Such transactions raise questions regarding the significance of the trade deficit. Rather than revealing a shortage of saving, it may simply be the artifact of transfer-pricing decisions that have multinationals allocate profits to countries where profit taxes are lowest.

With regard to causality, the twin-deficits hypothesis dogmatically asserts that the government deficit is the cause of the trade deficit. This is tantamount to saying that every dollar of government spending directly causes an additional dollar of imports. No economic model has ever come close to producing this type of finding. Despite this, the twin-deficits hypothesis is able to survive because it is also true that government spending does increase imports owing to its positive impact on economic activity. Consequently, a cut in the government deficit would indeed reduce the trade deficit. However, this reduction would be the result of lower aggregate demand, increased unemployment, and depressed economic activity, which together reduce prosperity and cause consumers to spend less on imports.

An alternative account of the emergence of structural trade imbalance is in terms of a combination of ill-guided monetary policy and problems in specific industrial sectors. The shift to permanent trade-deficit status occurred in the early 1980s, when the Federal Reserve adopted its current policy of high interest rates. This caused the dollar to begin a five-year appreciation (see fig. 8.6) that rendered large segments of American industry uncompetitive and provided an incentive to accelerate the transfer of manufacturing operations overseas. It also provided the opportunity for imports to gain a permanent beachhead in the American market.

A second element in the emergence of a structural trade deficit concerns the energy and automobile sectors, which account for almost the entire trade deficit in (fig. 8.7). These sector-specific deficits are the result of failed energy policy and problems particular to the auto industry. The conclusion is that the trade deficit is not the result of the government deficit; the proof is the fact that it has continued despite government moving into surplus.

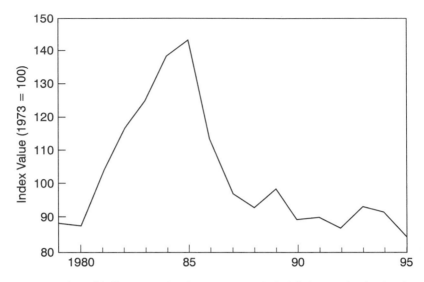

Fig. 8.6. Index of dollar versus G-10 currencies, 1979–95. *Source*: Author's calculations based on CITIBASE data.

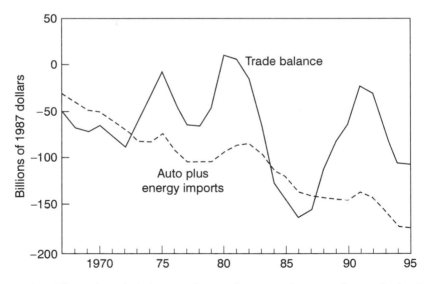

Fig. 8.7. The U.S. trade balance and auto plus energy imports. *Source*: Author's calculations based on CITIBASE data.

Just as the twin-deficits hypothesis misdiagnoses the causes of the trade deficit, so, too, it misunderstands the economic consequences. The focus of the twin-deficits hypothesis is foreign wealth accumulation, and it pays no regard to issues of employment because it assumes full employment. The reality is that the trade deficit is the result of a combination of production being shifted overseas to take advantage of cheap foreign labor, international uncompetitiveness in particular sectors, and an overvalued exchange rate. In each of these instances, employment suffers, and this calls for policy interventions in the form of a lower exchange rate and possibly trade regulation.

The trade deficit is one of the most difficult issues to understand, not least because it quickly becomes engulfed in issues of nationalism. The deficit does mean that the United States is building up obligations to the rest of the world. However, foreigners will in due course seek to spend these debts, and that will be good for the U.S. economy. In sum, the twin-deficits hypothesis seeks to use the trade deficit as a reason to cut back government spending; the competitiveness crisis hypothesis seeks to use it to downsize the workplace in the spirit of lean and mean. Both are wrong regarding the cause of the deficit; both push the agenda of the Raw Deal.

THE BALANCED-BUDGET AMENDMENT

No discussion of the attempt to handcuff fiscal policy and shrink government would be complete without a discussion of the balanced budget amendment (BBA).[13] The saving-shortage hypothesis, the consumption-binge hypothesis, supply-side economics, crowding-out theory, and the twin-deficits hypothesis provide the theoretical ammunition for the attack on government. The BBA is the institutional mechanism for locking in the Raw Deal. It bears the same relation to fiscal policy that central bank independence has to monetary policy: both seek to entrench the dominance of business interests institutionally.

Not only does the BBA lock in the Raw Deal, but it does so using a misleading indicator of federal fiscal integrity. In effect, it seeks to balance a deeply flawed accounting measure. Earlier, it was noted that the federal budget fails to distinguish between operating and capital expenditures on public investment. This failure to distinguish these expenditures is at odds with accepted accounting practice. The result is to overstate spending and give government an air of profligacy.

149

Second, the budget incorrectly accounts for the effects of inflation. As noted earlier, a proper treatment of interest on the national debt whould treat that portion of interest attributable to inflation as loan repayment rather than expenditures. In 1996, inflation was 3%, and the publicly held portion of the national debt was $3.6 trillion. Appropriate treatment of inflation would have reduced the 1996 deficit by $108 billion, so that the federal budget would have been in balance.

Passage of a BBA would likely have a range of deleterious effects, including possibly causing a recession in the initial implementation period and aggravating the swings of the business cycle thereafter. The BBA would also likely lower the economy's growth rate as well as cause a return of old-style financial crises.

Implementation Effects: Risking a Recession. In the first instance, there would be negative "implementation" effects. The federal budget is in deficit, so conforming to the amendment would require significant spending cuts. Aside from the political problem of getting agreement on what spending would be cut, there is a danger of such cuts causing a recession. Spending cuts would generate a large negative demand shock, and this could be sufficient to tip the economy into recession.

Destabilization Effects: Aggravating the Business Cycle. In addition to negative implementation effects, a BBA would aggravate the business cycle and turn mild recessions into severe economic downturns and possibly worse. One widely recognized source of destabilization concerns the conduct of fiscal policy. Recessions cause tax revenues to fall and welfare spending to rise, so that government either would have to cut spending or raise taxes to maintain budget balance; thereby lowering demand and aggravating recessions. An analogous logic applies for booms: tax revenues go up, so that government would increase spending to balance the budget. This would increase demand and aggravate inflationary pressures.

Less widely recognized are the destabilizing implications for monetary policy. To offset the destabilizing character of fiscal policy, the Federal Reserve would be obliged to move interest rates up and down like a yo-yo. In recessions, it would have to lower interest rates further; in booms, it would have to raise them further. Such interest-rate volatility would hinder business planning and likely lower investment spending.

Moreover, financial markets would come to expect interest rates to rise significantly after recessions. To avoid incurring losses, financial investors would not bid down rates on longer-term bonds in recessions, and the economy could get stuck in recessions with high long-term rates. In effect, the economy could get locked into a self-fulfilling high-interest-rate trap in which expectations of future high interest rates keep current interest rates high.

Keynesian economists emphasize the destabilizing demand effects of the BBA. Supply-siders emphasize the destabilizing effect of volatile tax rates. Paradoxically, both agree that the BBA is destabilizing. Under a BBA, the government would lower tax rates in booms and increase them in recessions so as to maintain budget balance. This would make tax rates more volatile. For supply-siders, optimal tax policy calls for constant tax rates, which help business planning. The BBA produces the opposite result.

Growth Effects: Public Investment and America's Third Deficit. The BBA would also have adverse growth effects. Over time, the economy is growing as a result of the effects of technological innovation, investment, education, and population growth. This growth manifests itself in higher national income. If passed, the BBA would require government to run a zero deficit, and the national debt would cease growing. The publicly held share of the national debt currently stands at 50% of GDP. Over time, with national income growing and the debt constant, this percentage would steadily fall.

In an economy with no growth, budget balance requires a zero deficit, this being the only way to stop the debt/GDP ratio from exploding. In a growing economy, the debt must also grow to stop the debt/GDP ratio from going to zero. This implies that a growing economy should run deficits. The meaning of budget balance depends on whether the economy is static or growing; this subtle point has been lost in the BBA hysteria.

If government is unable to borrow, this will negatively impact public investment, which will in turn hurt growth. When private-sector business wants to expand, it does so by bank borrowing or by selling equity on Wall Street. This provides the finance to buy the plant and machinery necessary for growth. Thus, business is not forced to rely exclusively on its existing profits. If it were, start-up companies that have no profits could never get going. Instead, business borrows to finance expansion and then uses the

151

resulting profits to redeem its debt. In a growing economy, this is an un-ending process, and it means that the total amount of business debt is always increasing.

The same logic applies to the government, which is in the business of being U.S.A., Inc. Government helps the economy grow by expanding the highway network, which facilitates commerce; by funding education, which educates our children and generates technical advances and higher productivity; and by providing the infrastucture that supports business operations. By growing the economy, these expenditures generate the tax revenue to pay back the initial borrowing. In effect, U.S.A., Inc. is just like private business, and needs to be able to borrow if the economy is to grow at its maximum rate.

The BBA prevents government from borrowing to finance public in-vestment. Instead, such projects will have to be financed out of current revenues or by tax increases. Whatever they are, politicians are not stupid. They know that taxes are unpopular and hurt the voters who pay them today. They also know that the benefits from capital spending accrue to the future, and the future does not vote today. The logic is clear: the BBA establishes an unambiguous incentive to cut back on public investment spending, with adverse consequences for economic growth and the qual-ity of life.

America's low rate of public investment has been termed "America's third deficit" (i.e., in addition to the budget and trade deficits). Public investment has a high rate of return, both in terms of improved quality of life, and in terms of increased business productivity. The existing low rates of public investment have been blamed for much of the post-1973 slow-down in economic growth. By further lowering such spending, a BBA would compound this problem.

Reduced public investment is also at odds with the problems posed by the graying of America and the need to fund social security. The putative problem is that twenty years hence, baby-boom demographics will pro-duce a surge in retirement, and the nation will have to devote much of its resources to supporting this elderly population. Far-sighted policy should anticipate this scenario by ensuring that the needed resources are in place. Unfortunately, one cannot build the needed factories today since they will be outmoded by then.

However, public infrastructure is extremely long-lived and offers a means of anticipating these needs. The nation is still benefiting from the interstate highway system and airports that were built in the 1950s.

Though many schools buildings are deteriorating and require improvement, they were built over sixty years ago. Thus, they have been long-lasting, and new schools can be equally so. Public infrastructure investment is one of the best ways to prepare for the aging of America, yet this is exactly what the BBA will inhibit.

Financial Instability Effects: Restoring Old-Style Financial Crises. The late Hyman Minsky argued that another serious effect of a BBA would be its impact on financial markets. Government bonds occupy an important place in private portfolios. They are safe and earn a reasonable rate of return while the markets in which they are traded are healthy. The BBA would put an end to new supplies of government bonds. For financial institutions, particularly banks, this would have serious consequences. Banks park their excess liquidity in government bonds because they are both safe and earn a return: when they have excess liquidity, they buy bonds; when they are short of liquidity, they sell bonds. In this fashion, government bonds help the financial system buffer business demands for credit.

If the supply of government bonds were to dry up, banks would look for other financial assets in which to park their liquidity. They would likely start increasing their holdings of corporate bonds. However, such bonds are risky, and their prices can fall in economic downturns owing to increased bankruptcy risk. Consequently, such a portfolio shift would inject more risk into the financial system. In the 1980s, the savings and loan (S&L) crisis cost the American taxpayer $500 billion, the banking system nearly went belly up, and the Federal Deposit Insurance Corporation was close to insolvent. The system just managed to weather that storm: there is a risk that future storms may be unmanageable if government bonds, which are the bedrock of the financial system, are replaced by corporate bonds in private portfolios.

Lastly, the BBA would effectively put an end to the Federal Reserve's ability to have the money supply grow, and for the Federal Reserve to conduct monetary policy. As the economy grows, there is a need for the money supply to grow in order to finance the increased level of transacting. The Fed grows the money supply by buying government bonds from banks and households and paying for these bonds with money. If there were no budget deficit, then households would have no government bonds, and the Fed would be unable to grow the money supply. The result would be a deflationary stagnation.

153

The BBA Is Bad Policy.   For all of the above reasons, the BBA risks seriously harming the long-term health of the American economy. Economic theory, both Keynesian and supply-side, provides no support for it. In 1996, over one thousand economists, including eleven Nobel Prize winners, signed a statement declaring it to be bad for America. In his commencement address at Yale University on June 11, 1962, President Kennedy spoke about fiscal policy and the national debt.

> The great enemy of the truth is very often not the lie—deliberate, contrived and dishonest—but the myth—persistent, persuasive, and unrealistic. Too often we hold fast to the cliches of our forebears. We subject all facts to a prefabricated set of interpretations. We enjoy the comfort of opinion without the discomfort of thought. . . .
>
> There are myths also about our public debt. It is widely supposed that this debt is growing at a dangerously rapid rate. In fact, both the debt per person and the debt as a proportion of gross national product have declined sharply since the Second World War . . . debts, public and private, are neither good nor bad, in and of themselves. Borrowing can lead to overextension and collapse—but it can also lead to expansion and strength. There is no single, simple slogan in this field that we can trust.

Conclusion

Government is currently under attack. This attack represents an attempt to repeal the Square Deal, the New Deal, and the Fair Deal, which together provided the basis of the American dream in the twentieth century. The goal is to institute a Raw Deal that undercuts the wage floor in labor markets, eliminates government's role in ensuring a fair distribution of income, and handcuffs fiscal policy so that it cannot be used to manage demand and ensure full employment.

The claim is that government-sponsored interventions in labor markets are a distortion of "natural" markets and should therefore be eliminated. Side-by-side, it is claimed that there is a shortage of saving that has reduced investment and capital accumulation and, in turn, lowered growth. Moreover, the structure of taxes supposedly discourages enterprise while encouraging shirking. Eliminating government interventions, cutting taxes, and cutting government spending are the proposed solutions, and these solutions are to be institutionalized through a balanced-budget amendment.

The reality is that these policies are an attempt to turn the clock back to the nineteenth century. In doing so, they will destroy the American dream and will bring back the deep business cycles of that bygone era. There is no such thing as a natural market: undercutting the wage floor will simply create a labor market in which business dominates labor, and will increase profits at the expense of wages. Meanwhile, cutting government spending, cutting benefit payments, and cutting upper-income tax rates will shift income from the poor and the middle to the rich. This is the true face of the Raw Deal.

Free Trade and the Race to the Bottom

A CENTRAL theme in this book has been the relationship between the increase in business power and the dismantling of prosperity. The sources of this increased power are multiple, and this has served to obscure what has been going on. However, one instance where the public has grasped the connection between power and wages is free trade. On this issue, there has been consistent popular opposition against business-sponsored policies promoting globalized free trade.[1]

The bottom line is that workers know, through their experience and common sense, that free trade can expose them to the winds of job losses and lower wages. Though free trade may also lower prices, its effect on employment security and wages can be sufficiently severe that, at the end of the day, workers are worse off. For these reasons, trade policy is too important to get wrong.

Despite massive popular opposition, both the North American Free Trade Agreement (NAFTA) and the General Agreement on Tariffs and Trade (GATT) were passed by the Congress. Their passage reflects the political and economic dominance of business. These measures constitute the foundation for the establishment of a pro-business international trading structure that will apply into the twenty-first century. This process of institutionalization is not so advanced that it cannot be sensibly reformed. However, the longer we wait, the more entrenched it will become.

For these reasons, debate over the consequences of free trade is of vital import. Yet, despite this evident importance, the monolithic probusiness character of conventional economics has prevented a sensibly nuanced debate from developing. Mainstream economists simply chant their mantra of free trade and label as "protectionist" all who want a subtler approach to trade.

This response reflects the ideological character of conventional trade theory, the basis of which is derived exclusively from laissez-faire economic theory. It is noteworthy that the political debate over NAFTA was much more contested than the debate among economists. The latter was characterized by almost uniform support for NAFTA. If the economist's guiding principle of the rational pursuit of self-interest is to be believed, the extent of opposition to NAFTA should itself have been sufficient to cast doubt on the claim that the agreement would benefit the public.

FREE TRADE AS SYSTEMS COMPETITION

The monopolization of the trade debate by free-trade theorists has had enormous ramifications for policy. The theoretical model underlying economists' rosy prognostications about free trade assumes full employment and has workers being paid an amount equal to their contribution to the value of production. These assumptions contrast with a structural Keynesian view in which unemployment is the rule and wages depend on conditions of power underlying the wage bargain. Depending on which perspective is right, there are enormously different consequences to free trade. If the bargaining-power approach is correct, reliance on orthodox analysis will produce misguided and damaging policy.

Behind these two perspectives lie fundamentally different views of the way international trade works. The orthodox view can be labeled the "market competition" approach, while the bargaining-power view can be labeled the "systems competition" approach. Orthodox economists treat international trade as if it were just an extension of domestic trade, the sole difference being that goods cross international borders. If domestic trade is beneficial because it increases competition and variety, then international trade must also be beneficial.[2]

However, there is a huge difference between domestic and international trade that is overlooked in the orthodox story. "Domestic" trade takes place within a common economic and social system. "International" trade often (though not always) takes place across different systems. Thus, whereas German–American trade takes place within an essentially shared system, Mexican–American trade takes place across very different systems.

These differences in system significantly affect the pattern of production costs and confer a competitive advantage on firms in one country. Thus, to stay competitive, firms in the country with higher systems costs will have to lower costs by such measures as cutting wages, worker benefits, and expenditures on worker safety and the environment. In this fashion, international trade implicitly pits system against system, and it ultimately serves to export the system with lower costs. Where one country's lower costs are the result of superior productive efficiency, all is well and good. However, where lower costs are the result of pauperized wages, oppressed workers, and an absence of concern for social and environmental well-being, the result is disastorous. In this case, systems competition becomes the law of the lowest standard, because it forces countries with high standards to lower them in order to stay competitive.

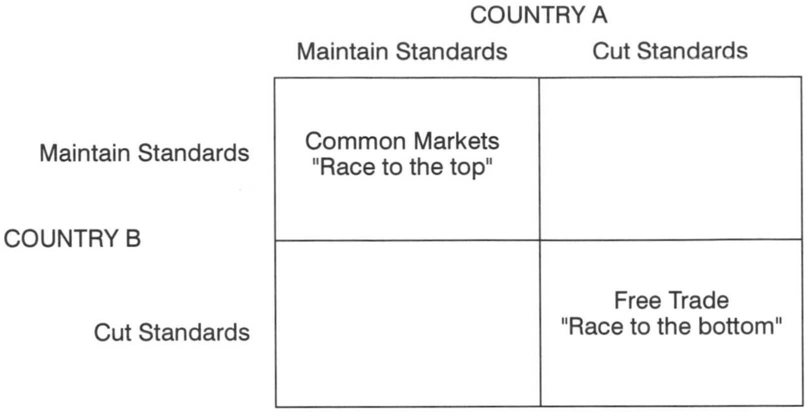

COUNTRY A

	Maintain Standards	Cut Standards
Maintain Standards	Common Markets "Race to the top"	
Cut Standards		Free Trade "Race to the bottom"

COUNTRY B

Fig. 9.1. Systems competition as a prisoner's dilemma problem.

This problem of systems competition is another example of the prisoner's dilemma (fig. 9.1). There are two countries, A and B. Each country can either maintain standards or cut standards. The social optimum is for both to maintain standards, in which case there is trade with fair work conditions and well-paid employment. However, each country faces an incentive to cut standards a little so as to gain a competitive advantage over its rival. The result is that both countries cut standards, resulting in a race to the bottom.

As always, the only way out of the prisoner's dilemma is some form of institutional arrangement that gets both countries to adopt the socially optimal outcome, which is why the international trading system needs to be appropriately regulated. Free trade is not the answer; nor is protectionism. The answer is a globally enforced trade charter that prevents a race to the bottom and turns international trade into a race to the top. Such an approach corresponds to a common-markets approach, which is discussed below.

How Important Is Trade?

Before delving into a formal analysis of the trade question, it is worth asking, how important is trade? Many conventional economists maintain that trade is simply too small to have a significant effect on the economy. After all only, 17% of U.S. employment is in manufacturing, whereas the rest is in the "nontraded" (i.e., service and government) sectors of the

TABLE 9.1
International Trade Characteristics

	1970	1990
U.S. exports plus imports as percent of GDP	12	22
Percent of U.S. imports that come from LDCs	14	35
Percent of European Union imports from LDCs	5	12
Percent of LDC exports that are manufactured goods	1955 = 5%	1992 = 58%

Source: Freeman (1995).

economy. Parenthetically, it should also be noted that these same economists also make the somewhat inconsistent claim that free trade will bring major economic benefits.

It is clear that trade has been steadily and rapidly growing in importance (table 9.1). Trade has increased as a percentage of GDP, and trade with less-developed countries (LDCs) has increased in both the United States and Europe. Moreover, there has been a big shift toward importing manufactured goods rather than primary commodities from LDCs.

Total trade flows are clearly large and significant. However, trade flows with LDCs are smaller. That said, in a bargaining-power framework, trade may be small compared to the economy, yet still exert significant leverage at the margin. This leverage can have a large impact on wages and income distribution. If business wants wage and benefit concessions, it is not necessary to close plants and shift production abroad; all that is needed is the "credible threat" of movement. In this case, workers will be forced into making concessions to keep their jobs. The threat of importing production is sufficient, and actual imports may never materialize. This does not mean that trade is insignificant.

Wood (1995) also argued that the threat of imports from foreign producers has gotten domestic producers to adopt defensive innovations to prevent imports. This defensive response has taken the form of increasing the extent of automation and the capital intensity of production. As a result, workers are fired. In the process, they suffer a wage cut because these jobs are in the higher-paying manufacturing sector.

Trade with developing countries is also increasingly concentrated in manufacturing, and this gives trade a significance over and above that captured by measuring trade as a percentage of GDP. First, manufacturing has traditionally been the center of high-paying jobs and has provided a lead to the rest of the economy regarding the setting of wages. Trade therefore has a direct effect on manufacturing wages and an indirect effect on wages in the rest of the economy. Second, manufacturing has traditionally been a heavily unionized sector, and unions are good for wages in both unionized and nonunionized firms. To the extent that trade shrinks the manufacturing sector, it also shrinks unions, and in doing so contributes a second blow against wages.

In 1983, 19.1 million workers were in manufacturing, constituting 28% of total employment. Of these, 5.3 million were unionized, making for a union density of 30% in manufacturing. In 1996, 19.7 million workers were in manufacturing, constituting 17% of total employment. Of these, 3.4 million were unionized, making for a union density of 21%. Trade is at the forefront of these numbers. It has slowed total employment growth in manufacturing, while simultaneously undermining the strength of unions in manufacturing. This has been vividly confirmed with regard to NAFTA (see below).

A FRAMEWORK FOR ANALYZING FREE TRADE

An immediate difficulty in assessing the welfare effects of free-trade reforms concerns the questions of (1) whose welfare, and (2) trade reform with whom. A theme throughout this book has been that there exists an ever-present conflict of interest between business and labor. This conflict determines how the fruits of economic activity are divided, and it is manifested in the struggle over the division of national income between wages and profit. Another feature of the real world is that countries differ in their level of economic development and prosperity.

These two features are central to any assesment of the effects of free trade. Consequently, a valid analysis of free trade must identify its effects on wage income versus profit income; and distinguish between free trade with developed (high wage/high employment) economies, and free trade with underdeveloped (low wage/surplus labor) economies.

The significance of recognizing the distinction between wages and profits is that it deconstructs the myth of a unified national interest. The vast majority of people rely exclusively on wages for their income. Contrastingly, profit income largely accrues to a small minority who represent the wealthiest segment of society. Given that wage income represents the only source of income for the vast majority of people, the contention of this chapter is that the welfare effects of free trade can largely be analyzed by reference to its impact on employment and wages.

This contrasts with orthodox trade analysis in which no weight is placed on the distinction between wage and profit income because of the assumption that all persons are identical and share equally in profits and wages. Moreover, employment is not an issue, owing to the assumption of full employment.[3] Given these assumptions, for orthodox theory, the measure of free trade becomes its effect on total national income. The argument is that if total national income is increased, then the each person must be better off; therefore, free trade is beneficial.[4] The assumptions of full employment and equally shared profits are therefore central to understanding why the views of expert economists are so different from popular readings of free trade.

Recognizing that economies are different is also critical for assessing the impact of free trade, because the effects of free trade depend importantly on the mix of economies being linked. From a structural Keynesian perspective, free trade is often best when conducted between countries that share common characteristics. Once again, this contrasts with orthodox analysis in which the greatest gains to trade arise when countries have the greatest dissimilarities.

A minimalist taxonomy therefore involves distinguishing between what may be termed developed (high wage/high employment) economies and underdeveloped (low wage/labor surplus economies). Developed economies may be identified with economies such as the U.S economy, the Japanese economy, and the economies of Western Europe; they are also sometimes referred to as the Northern economies or as the industrialized economies. Underdeveloped economies may be identified with countries such as China, Mexico, and Indonesia, and they are frequently referred to as the Southern economies.

This categorization has features in common with the distinction between capital-abundant and capital-scarce economies, which characterizes the orthodox trade theory. However, the capital-abundant/capital-scarce distinction is a narrow economic taxonomy. The developed/underdeveloped distinction is intended to be more encompassing, capturing the notion that economies are social systems and that multiple facets of these systems are relevant for understanding the impact of free trade.

The above developed/underdeveloped taxonomy recognizes that the pattern of trade depends on a range of socioeconomic characteristics. These characteristics include business' health and social welfare obligations, business' rights to pollute and obligations to prevent pollution, employee-protection laws, and worker-safety laws. In general, developed countries tend to impose heavier obligations on firms, have stronger antipollution laws, and have stonger worker-protection laws than do underdeveloped countries. These differences reflect the stronger position that workers in developed countries have secured for themselves by political action and historical good fortune.

The critical economic importance of these socioeconomic characteristics is that they alter countries' costs of production. In doing so, they change the international structure of comparative costs. In a world with free trade between developed and underdeveloped countries, these characteristics can determine the pattern of international production and trade. In this fashion, they affect employment and wages.

THE IMPACT OF FREE TRADE ON THE ECONOMY

The previous section outlined the need to (1) identify the effects of free trade on wage and profit and (2) to recognize developmental differences across countries when analyzing the welfare implications of the effects of free-trade. This section uses the above framework to analyze the potential impact of free-trade reforms on the U.S. economy.

To understand this impact, recall the characterization of the economy provided in chapter 5. This characterization rested on four principles.

1. The level of output (GNP) and employment depends on the level of demand for goods and services. Shortages of demand will tend to lower output and employment; brisk demand will tend to produce inflationary pressures on prices and wages.

2. The level of demand depends importantly on the distribution of income between wages and profits. High wages tend to stimulate demand because of their effect on the level of consumption. However, to the extent that higher wages reduce the profit rate, they can adversely affect investment spending, which reduces aggregate demand. If the former effect dominates, then higher wages are expansionary.[5]

3. The distribution of income between wages and profits depends on bargaining bewtween workers and firms. The relative bargaining positions of workers and firms depends importantly on the state of the economy, with increases in the rate of unemployment serving to weaken worker bargaining power. Worker power is also affected by the ease with which firms can replace existing workers, and by labor legislation

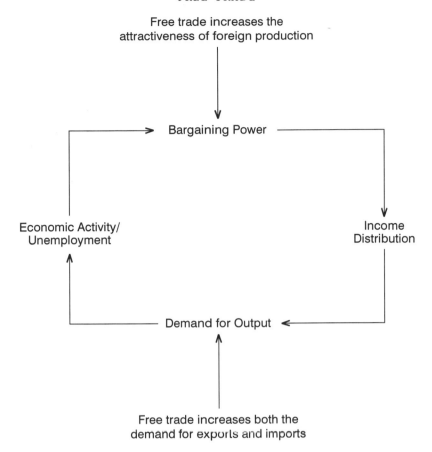

Fig. 9.2. The effect of free trade on the economic system.

providing benefits for workers and protection against employer sanctions
and layoffs.

4. Firms are driven by the search for profits, and will therefore shift
production to sites earning the highest profits.

In Chapter 5, this analytical framework was used to show how increases in
business power had affected the distribution of income and the level of
economic activity. The same framework can be used to analyze the impact
of free trade.

The potential channels of effect of free trade are shown in figure 9.2.
Free trade impacts the bargaining power of labor by affecting the relative
profitability of overseas production. The elimination of tariffs eliminates
an important cost that protects American workers from being placed in

competition with pauperized Third World workers, and from being placed in competition with economic systems in which there are no social welfare and environmental mandates.

Free trade also impacts the demand for output. To the extent that it leads to an increase in exports, this increases demand. To the extent that it leads to an increase in imports, this shifts spending away from domestically produced goods and reduces demand. Through these two channels, bargaining power and the demand for output, free trade affects income distribution and employment.

From an American perspective, there are potentially two types of reform. The first concerns trade liberalizations involving another developed country; the second concerns trade liberalizations involving an underdeveloped economy.

Developed–Developed Free Trade

This type of reform places countries which have common economic systems with broadly similar socioeconomic characteristics (i.e., employment conditions, social security laws, pollution rights, etc.) in a free-trade relationship. The similarity of systems is of critical significance, because it means that systems costs are broadly similar. As a result, the impact of these on costs is neutral, and free trade confers no competitive advantage or disadvantage on either party. In terms of figure 9.1, it means that free trade has no effect on bargaining power. The costs of production abroad are similar to those of domestic production, so that firms gain no extra leverage over labor in the form of a threat to move production abroad.

In goods markets, the abolition of tariffs and quotas lowers the price of imports: this is a source of increased well-being for all consumers, including wage earners. The opening of domestic markets to foreign producers also serves to strengthen product market competition, which promotes lower prices and improved quality on domestically produced goods. This is another source of benefit. Moreover, to the extent that firms' profit markups are driven down, prices are lowered and the purchasing power of wages increased. Finally, by creating a larger unified market, trade allows for large-scale production and spreading of fixed costs, which lowers prices and also allows a greater range of product variety.

The removal of foreign tariffs and protections increases the demand for exports. Because export demand is part of total demand, this stimulates employment and output and strengthens the position of labor in the wage bargain. However, elimination of tariffs and quotas increases imports. Because imports represent a diminuition of demand for domestically produced goods, this reduces employment and weakens the position of labor. The net effect on total demand therefore depends on the relative size of demand diversion into imports, compared to the creation of new export demand. If the net effect on demand is positive, then employment and output will increase.

The extent of export demand creation depends importantly on the availability of international finance to pay for expanded international trade. Without this finance, realizing the putative gains from free-trade reform is problematic. Developed countries like the United States have easy access to international finance because of their good standing in international credit markets. As a result, finance does not appear to be a significant obstacle to an expansion of trade.

In sum, free trade between developed countries appears to carry significant benefits. Inevitably, there is some dislocation in particular industries, because enhanced product market competition leads to an elimination of inefficient domestic producers. This dislocation adversely impacts specific groups of workers, but, for workers as a whole, the liberalization appears beneficial.[6] Prices and profit markups are reduced owing to increased competition, which increases the purchasing power of wages. Easy availability of international finance means that paying for the expansion of trade is not problematic. The net result is likely to be an expansion of demand, employment, and output in the participating countries. Had the acronym NAFTA stood for North Atlantic Free Trade Agreement, its passage would have been unopposed. Far from being protectionist, a systems-competition approach strongly advocates free trade between developed economies. When countries share common systems, free trade brings forth the full benefits of market competition, resulting in a higher standard of living for all.

Developed–Underdeveloped Free Trade

Whereas free trade among developed economies is not problematic, a systems-competition perspective suggests the opposite for free trade between developed and underdeveloped economies. Now, the economies have radically different wage levels and socioeconomic structures, which means that these factors significantly affect comparative costs. Here, the differences between the systems-competition and orthodox approaches become important.

Once again, trade opens the possibility for both increased exports and increased imports, and the demand effects of this are potentially the same as before. However, a significant difference concerns access to international finance. By and large, developed economies have unlimited access to international finance, so that financing imports from underdeveloped countries is not problematic. The same is not true of underdeveloped countries, whose low levels of wealth, high levels of debt, and generally lower standing within international financial markets limit their ability to finance purchases from developed countries. Given this finance constraint, the positive demand effects of higher exports may be quite doubtful.

So much for the demand effects, What about the bargaining power effects? Underdeveloped countries tend to have massive surpluses of labor, while being relatively short of capital (i.e., factories and machines). The reverse situation characterizes developed countries. These differences will set up incentives to relocate production. In particular, there will be an incentive to transfer production of labor-intensive goods to underdeveloped countries where labor is abundant and wages are low. The net effect of this rearrangement of global production is to reduce the demand for labor in the developed country, and this causes the share of output paid to labor (i.e., the wage share) to fall, while increasing the share paid to capital (i.e., the profit share).[7] In effect, free trade serves to unify the labor markets of developed and under-developed countries, and this puts strong downward pressure on wages in the developed country (i.e., the United States). In this fashion, free trade worsens income distribution. It is for this reason that the expansion of free trade is partly responsible for the deterioration of income distribution in the United States that was documented in chapter 4.

Apart from increasing wage competition by increasing the effective supply of labor, free trade with developing economies also hurts workers' bargaining power. Workers' power depends on their ability to find other jobs and ration their work effort. Firms' bargaining power depends on their ability to hire replacement workers at lower wages, balanced by the costs of firing existing workers and hiring and training new workers. Free trade increases firms' bargaining power by increasing the threat of employment termination, because costs of production are lower in underdeveloped countries owing to lower wages and lower costs associated with fewer environmental protection, worker safety, and social welfare mandates.[8] This is where cross-country differences in systems plays an important role.

It is also true that workers in underdeveloped countries may be less productive owing to lower levels of education and training and owing to differences in the extent of public "infrastructure" capital. However, these productivity differences are often more than offset by the scale of the wage and social overhead cost advantages, so that the net result is that firms' replacement threat is credibly enhanced by trade liberalizations. In terms of figure 9.1, free trade with underdeveloped countries increases firms' bargaining power, which promotes a shift in the distribution of income from wages to profits.

How real is this bargaining threat? Within the United States, regional cost disparities have certainly operated on worker-firm relations. Thus, a consequence of capital's increased mobility has been the establishment of competition between workers in the Sun Belt and the Rust Belt. This competition has weakened the position of workers, and it is no accident that the lion's share of productivity growth now accrues to capital. If such effects can operate within national economies, there is no reason to believe they will not operate between economies. International trade is just trade with the added feature of goods being transported across national boundaries.

NAFTA

NAFTA represents a unique example of free trade between a developed and underdeveloped economy.[9] The above analysis therefore clearly applies.[10] Thus, the import-export effects, the issue of a finance constraint on Mexico, the threat of job replacement and deterioration in workers' bargaining position, and the problem of differential social overhead costs are all present.

However, some additional issues are raised by Mexico's geographic contiguity to the United States. This is likely to strengthen the threat of job replacement because transportation costs from Mexican plants to the U.S. market are lower. Such costs represent an important source of protection to workers in developed countries, and the decline of these costs in recent years contributes to an explanation of the deterioration in labor's position.

The contiguity of Mexico raises issues related to the nature of Mexico's demand for U.S. exports. Because Mexican incomes are so low, it is unlikely that there will be significant exports of consumption goods. Instead, for the forseeable future, exports are likely to be made up of (1) semi-finished goods shipped for finishing and reexport to the United States and (2) capital goods to build new factories.

167

TABLE 9.2
United States–Mexico Merchandise Trade:
Customs Value (millions U.S. dollars)

Year	Imports	Exports	Balance
1992	35,184	40,597	5,413
1993	39,930	41,635	1,705
1994	49,493	50,840	1,348
1995	61,705	46,312	−15,393
1996	72,963	56,761	−16,202

Source: Department of Commerce.

Semifinished goods first show up as a U.S. export and then show up as a U.S. import, so that they increase the volume of both U.S. exports and imports. This is exactly what has happened since NAFTA went into effect, as shown in table 9.2. However, to the extent that value is added in Mexico, this must ultimately give rise to a worsening of the trade balance since the value of the final import exceeds that of the initial export. More importantly, such semifinished exports represent stripping out a stage of production from the U.S. economy and a transfer of that stage to Mexico. This new semifinished trade is evident in statistics showing that almost half of United States–Mexican trade is between subsidiaries of the same company or between firms with strategic alliances.[11]

With regard to U.S. exports of capital goods, the benefits are also temporary. Thus, the U.S. economy gets a short-term benefit as it exports machines to fill new Mexican factories. However, once a factory is built the capital exports cease; at that stage, the factory starts displacing U.S. production by exporting to the U.S. market.

The export of capital goods also raises the issue of *investment diversion*.[12] Such diversion arises if exports of capital goods to Mexico are the result of substitution of investment in Mexico for investment in the United States. Thus, U.S. and foreign corporations may decide to build plants in Mexico to take advantage of the lower production costs and correspondingly reduce investment in the United States. To the extent that this occurs, the gain in U.S. exports is offset by a decline in investment in the United States. Moreover, the United States loses the lasting benefits of job creation and permanently enhanced production capabilities that would have occurred in the absence of such diversion. This problem is likely very strong with NAFTA owing to Mexico's contiguity.

NAFTA has now been in effect for almost three years, and the indications are that it is having the negative effect that a structural Keynesian analysis would predict.[13] In 1992, the last year before NAFTA was approved, the U.S. trade surplus with Mexico peaked at $5.4 billion. By 1994, it had fallen to $1.3 billion, and by the end of 1996, it had become a deficit of $16.2 billion. This marks a four-year deterioration of $21.6 billion. Boosters of NAFTA claimed that every billion dollars of exports would create 19,000 jobs.[14] On that basis, NAFTA has cost 410,400 jobs. A more realistic number is 15,000 jobs per billion, which translates into a job loss of 324,000. Any which way, the number is massive. Moreover, these jobs are all in the higher-paying manufacturing sector, making the effect even more negative.

Defenders of NAFTA claim that the Mexican peso crisis of 1995 and the ensuing devaluation are responsible for these adverse developments. It is noteworthy, however, that the U.S. trade balance with Mexico had already turned into a deficit of $448 billion in the fourth quarter of 1994— before the peso crisis! Moreover, the peso was purposely pushed up as part of the selling of NAFTA to show how strong the Mexican economy was. In that fashion, the media could relay stories about the new Mexican middle class shopping at Wal-Mart in Mexico City. It is also the case that Mexico has repeatedly had such currency crises. All knew they would happen again, and the 1995 crisis is unlikely to be the last.

There is now abundant evidence of production shifting to Mexico. General Motors (GM) operates fifty-four factories in twenty-seven Mexican cities, most of them close to the border. It employs 74,500 workers, and its Mexican *maquiladora* workers gross around seventy cents an hour. Hours after NAFTA was signed, GM informed Detroit Steel of Indiana that it was shifting spring production to Mexico, thereby saving forty cents per spring.[15] GM continues to try to shift production to Mexico. The most recent instance concerns 2,700 workers at the Rochester, New York plant who make fuel injectors.[16] Goodyear is another company that has shifted production to Mexico, and between January 1995 and August 1995, its tire exports from the Mexico to the United States rose from 79,000 to 126,000.[17] More recently, Goodyear used its Mexican tire-production facilities to strengthen its bargaining position vis-à-vis its workers in the brief strike over a new employment contract in April 1997. Examples of transfers abound, and the process continues today. Osram Sylvania, Inc. plans to move its light production from Massachusetts to Mexico City to stay competitive.[18] Johnson Controls, Inc. moved production from its Milwaukee plant to Mexico.[19] As of 1997, on the Texas–Mexico border alone, there have been a total of 517 new factories set up in Mexico since NAFTA went into effect.[20]

The chilling effect of NAFTA on bargaining power has also been formally documented. In a powerful study, Kate Bronfenbrenner (1996) looked at union elections between 1993 and 1995. She found that over 50% of all employers made threats to close all or part of a plant during the organizing drive. The threat rate is significantly higher (62%) in mobile industries such as manufacturing. Twelve percent of firms actually shut down plants immediately following a union victory, and a further 3% do so before a second contract is reached. This 15% shutdown rate is triple that of the late 1980s, before NAFTA went into effect.

The findings of the Bronfenbrenner study have been confirmed by a report of the Secretariat created under NAFTA's labor side accord, which studied the problem of plant closings.[21] This report, released in June 1997, found that U.S. firms use the illegal threat of plant closings to thwart union organizing. The Secretariat reviewed more than 400 federal court and National Labor Relations Board decisions from 1989 through 1995 involving plant closings or threats thereof. It found that the employers' actions were illegal in 90% of the cases.. The Secretariat also surveyed union representatives about such activities, and the survey found a greater incidence of threats in industries more susceptible to closing, such as manufacturing, trucking, and warehousing. In effect, NAFTA has become a new union-busting weapon and has created a climate of worker intimidation that ripples throughout the labor market.

SYSTEMS COMPETITION, FREE TRADE, AND THE RACE TO THE BOTTOM

From a wider social welfare standpoint, not only do trade liberalizations with underdeveloped economies potentially disadvantage labor, they may also have adverse consequences for the socioeconomic structure. This effect can be termed the *law of the lowest standard*. Thus, to the extent that high costs of environmental protection mandates, worker-safety standards, health-care mandates, or employer social security contributions are seen as the cause of job losses or reduced wages, this will unleash political pressure to lower these politically determined costs. In this fashion, free trade can become a force for remodeling the socioeconomic system. Indeed, there is evidence that this is already happening, with business complaining about enviromental and safety mandates that make the United States internationally uncompetitive. The implication is clear: if the United States is to be competitive in the free-trade market place, these mandates will have to go. Business is already actively engaged in advancing this project.

COMMON MARKETS

The above analysis shows how the welfare effects depends on whether trade is with a developed or underdeveloped country. This contrasts with orthodox trade theory, which makes makes no such distinctions and treats free trade as unambiguously beneficial. Indeed, orthodox theory deems the greatest benefits come from free trade between developed and underdeveloped countries.

Free trade is not the solution, nor is protectionism. Instead, a systems approach to the problem of international trade suggests the adoption of *common markets*. By *common markets* is meant the establishment of binding and enforceable agreements that have trading partners adopt common environmental standards, common rights of free association for workers, common prohibitions against forced and child labor, and common prohibitions against workplace discrimination. Such requirements are often referred to as *core labor standards*. Amazingly, though the rights of intellectual property are guaranteed under NAFTA and GATT, core labor standards, which address fundamental human rights, are not.

There is also a need for *core workplace standards* that regulate conditions at work. Countries must establish basic standards regarding hours of work, minimum wages, and pension and health benefits. Core labor standards are matters of fundamental principle that can never be made contingent. Core workplace standards will inevitably reflect that state of productivity and development in a country and are therefore contingent. Establishing core workplace standards is a much trickier task, but it is one that needs to be confronted.

The United States is a common market, with states being bound by common core labor and workplace standards imposed by the Federal government. This prevents systems competition between the states and makes domestic trade a race to the top rather than a race to the bottom. It is also the case that the states right's movement—as applied to environmental standards, minimum wages, welfare, and labor laws—threatens to undo this. The European Economic Community (EEC) is also a common mar-

171

ket, and the rules governing the EEC also keep systems competition at bay, while allowing trade to take place on the basis of productive efficiency. This is what should drive trade. The goal of U.S. policy should be to foster the development of a global common market.

Given the above, some core policy conclusions begin to emerge.

1. All trade agreements should embody core labor standards.

2. Free trade between developed countries that have similar wage levels and socioeconomic structures is desirable.

3. Free trade between developed and underdeveloped countries which have fundamentally different wage levels and socioeconomic structures is problematic. Such trade requires case by case evaluation, according to the principles enumerated in 4 to 6 below.

4. Where there are differences in technical ability to produce goods, trade should be free on the grounds of technical efficiency. Thus, it makes no sense for the United States to produce coffee when climatic differences confer natural a technical advantage in the production of coffee on Latin America. This is the traditional Ricardian theory of comparative advantage, which emphasizes differences in technology as the basis for trade.

5. Where there are conditions of domestic monopoly, there should be free trade as a means of enforcing competitive behavior. In this case, free trade serves to prevent domestic monopolists from earning monopoly profits at the expense of consumers.

6. Where the only reason for trade is the low wage structure and absence of social overhead costs, then trade should be managed through imposition of a social tariff. The purpose of this tariff is to compensate for low wages and lack of commitment to social goals regarding the environment, worker health and safety, and social welfare. Where countries meet these minimum standards, there should be no tariff: where they do not, the social tariff should be imposed.

The revenues from this social tariff could be paid to the U.S. Treasury, or, alternatively, they could be paid into a fund for distribution back to the developing countries. This fund could work in many ways: revenues could be paid to the World Bank or some like organization; alternatively, revenues could be used to provide free export credits, thereby actually stimulating U.S. exports while furthering the economic development of underdeveloped countries.

The social tariff system would also provide a self-interest incentive mechanism for underdeveloped countries to improve wages and socioeconomic structures, because it would offer the prospect of unrestricted market access if they did so. Correcting the foul inequalities of development has long been one of the most intransigent policy problems; the social tariff is a policy tool that offers a plausible and efficient means of doing so.

Underlying these principles of trade is the fundamental notion that it is unacceptable for trade to be based exclusively on wage competition or competition over social welfare standards. Trade should not serve as a means of undermining the bargaining position of American workers, nor should it serve as a force for rolling back the laws and regulations governing the environment, worker safety, and social security. The goal of trade should be to export American prosperity, rather than import developing-country poverty. This is the core moral principle guiding a systems-competition approach. It contrasts with the orthodox position, in which competition that sets foreign workers against domestic workers as a means of lowering domestic wages is deemed a good.

The deception in orthodox trade theory is that it begins with the persuasive Ricardian theory of trade based on differences in technical efficiency, attributable to differences in climatic and natural resource endowments, but then ends up justifying trade on the basis of relative wages. This is classic bait and switch.

Economics is a contested social science, and there are few areas of widespread agreement. One such area of agreement is the *law of one price*, which states that where commodities are traded in an open market, there will be a tendency for similar commodities to trade at a single uniform price. Applied to free trade between the developed and underdeveloped world, it is labor that is implicitly being traded in the global market, and the pressure for price equalization will be felt on wages, conditions of employment, and attitudes toward environmental pollution in production. In a systems-competition framework, the law of one price gets expressed as the "law of the lowest standard."

THIRD WORLD ASSISTANCE AND THE DEBT TRAP

Unrestricted free trade will undermine the well-being of American workers. A common-markets approach will enhance it. One dilemma concerns the well-being of the Third World. It is quite possible that a common-markets approach would enhance the well-being of Third World workers by raising their domestic bargaining power. However, more is needed.

173

It is all too easy to talk about the economic problems of U.S. workers and their families, yet these are dwarfed by the misery that confronts most Third World workers. A strong case can be made that the rich industrialized nations have a moral responsibility to help these workers. However, foreign aid is politically unpopular given the climate of economic austerity. Consequently, if a successful case is to be made for substantive Third World assistance, it will have to be made on positive economic grounds. Appeals to moral responsibility are not sufficient, particularly if policies also result in a transfer from "have nots" in the industrialized world to the "haves" of the Third World.

That said, there is an economic case for Third World assistance that can also help workers in the First World. Helping the Third World is a win-win situation. Just as the principle of divide and rule applies in the domestic economy, so, too, it applies in the international economy. If Main Street, U.S.A. is unwilling to help Third World economies, then those economies will seek help elsewhere. All too often, this means providing multinational corporations with immunity from labor standards, workplace health and safety standards, and enviromental protection standards. In this fashion, Third World countries are able to attract industrial capital. However, in doing so they siphon jobs out of the United States and give American business the opportunity to obtain wage concessions by threatening to move. Consequently, American firms are given the incentive to take the low road, and globalization becomes a race to the bottom.

Assisting the Third World by giving them aid that is contingent on on the adoption of appropriate labor, workplace, and environmental standards, could become a means of closing off the low road. Moral and economic imperatives therefore suggest we give greater assistance. When these countries are hit by economic shocks over which they have no control, we should help them adjust to the new situation by making liquidity available. However, their difficulties should not be exploited to impose vicious labor market flexibility that eliminates the social wage, as has been International Monetary Fund practice.

The industrialized economies should also ensure that the Third World is given appropiate access to credit to finance development, and this credit must be given on reasonable terms. It is unjust that the Third World has had to pay the higher interest rates brought about by the Federal Reserve's crusade against inflation, itself designed to appease Wall Street.

Lastly, the Third World should be given debt relief. Loan forgiveness is unlikely to be popular, and policy should not focus on relief of principal: anyone who borrows should pay back what they borrow. However, for over fifteen years, the Third World has been burdened by massive debt-service payments, brought about by high real interest rates engineered by the First World's central banks. In many ways, these central banks have acted as a financial version of OPEC: just as the OPEC oil price increases sent the industrialized world into prolonged recession, so, too, have the high interest rates charged the Third World.

Giving the Third World debt-service relief would make for two types of gain. First, if given on the condition that Third World countries adopt certain standards, it would be a powerful inducement for them to sign on with enforceable core labor and environmental standards. This would facilitate the creation of a global common market, thereby helping transform globalization into a race to the top. Second, it would provide a strong economic boost to demand in industrialized countries. With reduced debt-service burdens, Third World countries would be able to use their income to purchase goods from U.S. and European factories. Exports would rise, thereby stimulating employment and raising wages. The implication is clear: appropriately designed Third World debt relief can be a win-win situation.

International Money: Who Governs?

INTERNATIONAL trade concerns the exchange of goods and services across national borders. Chapter 9 argued that trade policy needs to be considered carefully. On one hand, trade can bring benefits of lower prices and greater product diversity; on the other hand, it can give rise to a race to the bottom if it is driven purely by differences in wages or the absence of labor and environmental standards. In this event, trade unleashes the destructive forces of *systems competition*, whereby the need to retain international competitiveness forces countries to seek out the lowest common denominator regarding wages and labor, social welfare, and environmental standards.

Along with the issue of international trade is that of international money markets. These markets are where people buy and sell currencies. Such markets have always been needed in order to pay for international trade. If a person wants to buy something from a German company, then they need to acquire deutsche marks to pay for it. To do so, they use the foreign exchange (FX) market, and sell dollars in exchange for deutsche marks. As long as there is international trade, there will always be a need for international money markets to pay for trade.

However, there are now grounds for believing that the current system of international money markets has become dysfunctional. The constructive contribution to trade finance is being overshadowed by destabilizing speculation and the creation of a deflationary economic environment. International money markets have become less concerned about the mundane matter of financing trade and more concerned with speculative dealing in pursuit of financial gain. This new focus represents an extension of the dominance of finance from the domestic to the international sphere.

Two critical consequences follow from this new orientation of international money markets. First, these markets are increasingly prone to bouts of speculation that cause exchange rates to undergo dramatic swings that disrupt both international trade and employment. In this connection, there seem to be two types of speculation. One is the sudden sharp type, whereby a currency is subjected to a burst of speculative selling. The other involves a gradual persistent revaluation of a currency that occurs over a couple of years, and this revaluation is then reversed a couple of years later.

Second, international money markets now discipline government economic policy in a way that favors the interests of financial capital. Chapter 7 explored how Wall Street and the bond market have come to dominate the Federal Reserve, a dominance reflected in the Fed's fifteen-year-long crusade against inflation. The new orientation of international money markets reinforces financial capital's dominance over economic policy.

In effect, financial capital can veto policy by voting with its feet. If policy is not to the liking of wealth holders, then they can shift their holdings abroad. Selling out causes domestic interest rates to rise and the exchange rate to fall, and governments are thereby forced to reverse policy direction. In this fashion, international money has been able to discipline governments and contribute to the establishment of a contractionary economic regime that is global in scope. The problem of who governs is real.

Speculation and the New Face of International Money Markets

Behind the new focus of international money markets lie dramatic changes in computer and electronic communication technologies. These changes have linked financial markets around the world and have lowered the cost of transferring funds between financial centers. International banks operate foreign-currency trading desks in Hong Kong, London, and New York. Dealers working for these banks continuously buy and sell currencies and shift funds between countries. These shifts may be in response to fractional differences in country interest rates or in response to speculative hunches that one currency is about to appreciate and another depreciate. On their own, these technological and organizational changes would have had an enormous impact. However, their impact has been magnified by government policies eliminating controls on the international movement of money.

The changed character of international money markets is visible in both the volume and character of dealings. An indication of the scope of these changes is contained in figure 10.1, which shows the volume of dealings on the New York Stock Exchange. In 1947, the monthly volume of shares traded was 21.1 million; by 1970, it was 244.8 million; by 1980, it was 946 million; and by 1995, it had reached 7,268.1 million. Though these

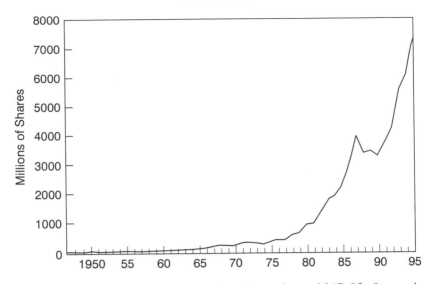

Fig. 10.1. NYSE monthly average stock market volume, 1947–95. *Source*: Author's calculations based on CITIBASE data.

numbers concern domestic stock market dealings, they are indicative of the tremendous change affecting asset market transacting.

Turning to the FX market, in 1973 daily FX trading varied between $10 billion and $20 billion per day. By 1980, the Bank of International Settlements (1993) reports that FX trading had reached a daily average of $80 billion, and the ratio of FX trading to world trade was 10:1. By 1992, daily FX trading averaged $880 billion, representing a ratio of FX trading to world trade of 50:1. In 1995, daily FX trading averaged $1260 billion, and the ratio of FX trading to world trade was nearly 70:1. The total value of the entire holdings of gold and foreign exchange held by the world's central banks was $1,500 billion, which was slightly more than one day's worth of FX trading.

The lion's share of FX dealings are no longer to finance trade: instead, they are of a short-term speculative nature. Table 10.1 shows the time to maturity of foreign exchange transactions; the bulk of these transactions are for settlement within two days. Given that these transactions are not trade-related, the implication is that they were undertaken with an eye to making a quick gain from changes in exchange rates and financial asset prices. Essentially they were speculative. The low cost of transacting means that such transactions are worthwhile even for very short holding periods and for miniscule changes in exchange rates and asset prices.

TABLE 10.1
Maturity Structure of Net Global Foreign Exchange Transactions

| | | Days to maturity | | |
| | Spot* | Forward† | | |
Year	Days ≤ 2	2 < Days ≤ 7	7 < Days ≤ 365	365 < Days
1992	47.3%	33.9%	18.2%	0.6%
1995	43.5%	38.1%	17.5%	0.8%

Source: Bank of International Settlements, 1993, 1996; cited in Eatwell 1996.

* Currency exchanges with cash settlement within two business days. Excludes the spot leg of swaps.

† Swaps, outright forwards traded on exchanges or "customized" and currency options at their notional value. Cross-country swaps of interest and/or amortization installments not included.

OVERVIEW: THE CURRENT SYSTEM

The current system of international money markets has emerged gradually over time and is characterized by a combination of flexible exchange rates and capital mobility. Why did the current system emerge? What are its problems, and what would make for a better system? These are the questions that concern the current chapter. However, before getting into the details, a little terminology.

A *flexible exchange rate system* is one in which market forces determine exchange rates, in the same way that the stock market determines stock prices: buying pressure pushes up the exchange rate, whereas selling pressure pushes it down. A *fixed exchange rate system* has governments fixing exchange rates and then intervening in international money markets to maintain them.

A system with *capital mobility* allows finance to freely move between countries: wealth holders can convert domestic money into foreign money and use the proceeds to purchase foreign financial assets. A system with *capital controls* restricts wealth holders abilities to convert domestic money into foreign financial assets.

Fixed versus flexible exchange rates and capital mobility versus capital controls are the key issues in the debate over international money markets. The evolution of the current system is shown in figure 10.2. In the 1950s and 1960s, the system was characterized by fixed exchange rates/capital

179

	Fixed Exchange Rates	Flexible Exchange Rates
Capital Controls	1950s, 1960s	1970s
No Capital Controls		1980s, 1990s

Fig. 10.2. Configuration of different policy regimes.

controls. In the 1970s, the system changed to flexible exchange rates/ capital controls. Then, in the 1980s, the system became one of flexible exchange rates/capital mobility, and that system remains today.

In an age of globally integrated economies, exchange rates affect economic performance, as illustrated in figure 10.3, in which the exchange rate affects the level of demand. If the dollar exchange rate is overvalued, U.S. goods will be internationally uncompetitive. As a result, U.S. exports will fall, while imports into the U.S. will rise as they displace purchases of American-produced goods. The net effect will be a decline in demand for American-made goods, which will cause a reduction of output in American factories, thereby causing employment to fall. Falling employment will put downward pressure on wages.

Additionally, exchange rates may affect bargaining power. When the dollar is overvalued, production abroad is more attractive, enhancing the credibility of firms' threats to relocate production. This has certainly happened in connection with Mexico, where the collapse of the peso in 1995 made it very attractive to shift production south of the border.

When there was little international trade and limited economic integration among countries, exchange rates were of reduced significance. Now that globalization is upon us, exchange rates are of much increased significance. In 1960, the combined value of U.S. imports and exports was 7% of GDP; in 1995, their combined value was 19% of GDP. Getting the exchange rate right has therefore become a matter of major importance for jobs and wages.

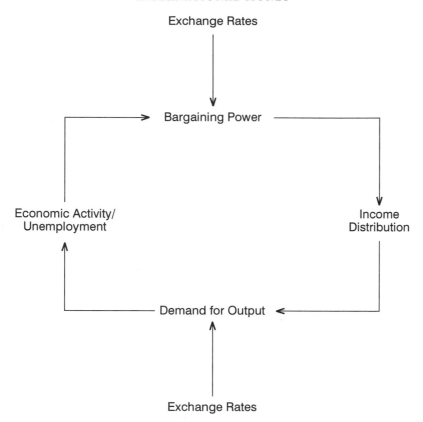

Fig. 10.3. The economic system and the influence of exchange rates.

The system of exchange rates between 1945 and the late 1970s gave preeminence to job considerations and focused on the problem of balancing exports and imports. The current system allows exchange rates to be determined by speculative financial flows. Instead of the exchange rate being determined by the real economy (i.e., the world of jobs and production), it is driven by the speculative actions of wealth holders in international money markets. Just as the stock market can be subject to booms, so, too, can individual currencies in international money markets. This means that exchange rates can be severely misaligned, giving rise to major adverse consequences for the jobs and livelihoods of ordinary people.

Worse than that, the new system allows financial capital to discipline national economic policy by threatening to move if policy is not to its liking. Thus, not only can international money markets get exchange rates wrong, but they can also prevent governments from pursuing policies to fix the effects. International money markets are the tail that should wag in response to the real forces of sensibly organized production and trade. All too often, the current system has the tail (international money markets) wagging the dog (production and trade).

WHY EXCHANGE RATES MATTER

Exchange rates are a crucial economic variable for all countries, and, for this reason, international money markets matter. The dollar exchange rate critically affects whether American industry is internationally competitive. This impact is captured in figure 10.3. If the dollar is overvalued, foreign goods become relatively cheap compared to American-produced goods. United States consumers will start to buy foreign goods and reduce purchases of American goods; foreign consumers will also reduce their purchases of American-made goods. The net result is that sales of American-made goods fall, which reduces employment in American factories. Imports rise, and exports fall, so that the trade deficit worsens.

The exchange rate affects the international competitiveness of U.S. industry. If the exchange rate is set too high, entire industries can be made uncompetitive and wiped out. Free traders continually exhort countries to specialize in the production of goods in which they have a comparative advantage over other countries. However, if international money markets misprice the exchange rate, then industries can be rendered internationally uncompetitive, no matter how efficient they are.

Just as international money markets can cause exchange rates to be mispriced, so, too, can policy. Thus, in the early 1980s the Federal Reserve's anti-inflation strategy caused a massive appreciation of the dollar (fig. 8.6). Large chunks of American industry become internationally uncompetitive, and the trade deficit exploded. Overvaluation of the dollar persisted for almost five years, and many companies went out of business or transferred production overseas. After 1985, the dollar began to depreciate, but by then the damage had been done, with the U.S. economy having suffered lasting deindustrialization.

A similar episode occurred in Britain. Over the period 1979–1981, Mrs. Thatcher's Conservative government engineered a massive appreciation of the pound, again as part of an anti-inflation strategy. The result was similar: large parts of British manufacturing industry became interna-

tionally uncompetitive and were forced to close down. British manufacturing output fell 25%, and the British economy underwent a process of
deindustrialization from which it has only just fully recovered.

The important lesson is that overvalued exchange rates matter. Even if
ultimately reversed, an extended overvaluation of the exchange rate can
cause significant deindustrialization, which causes a permanent loss of
high-paying industrial jobs. In both the U.S. and British cases, deindustrialization was not driven by a fundamental loss of competitiveness on the
factory floor. Instead, it was driven by developments in international
money markets, in part prompted by misguided anti-inflation policy.

Overvalued exchange rates negatively affect a county's international
competitiveness. Undervalued exchange rates can cause inflation. Globalization is making countries ever more interdependent. Countries rely on
imported raw materials, while the growth of trade means that they also
import more manufactured goods. No country produces everything. Instead, each produces something and then trades for what it does not have.
When the exchange rate falls, imported goods become more expensive,
which can cause inflation by triggering a price-wage spiral. The lower exchange rate raises import prices, and workers respond by seeking wage
increases in order to protect their standard of living. With imports more
expensive and less competitive, domestic firms can also raise their prices.

HISTORY: HOW FINANCE CAPITAL CAME TO DOMINATE
THE INTERNATIONAL MONETARY SYSTEM

The Bretton Woods System: Fixed Exchange Rates/Capital Controls

Figure 10.2 provides a useful means of analyzing the recent history of
international money markets. In the 1950s and 1960s, the international
financial system was characterized by the combination fixed exchange
rates/capital controls. This was the system established by the Bretton
Woods agreement of 1944.

Capital controls meant that financial capital was unable to move between countries at will, and this freed governments from the fear of capital
flight. The importance of these controls was noted by Keynes, who was
the principal architect of the Bretton Woods agreement, and who wrote,
"In my view the whole management of the domestic economy depends
upon being free to have the appropriate rate of interest without reference
to the rates prevailing elsewhere in the world. Capital control is the corol-
lary of this."[1] Keynes recognized that preventing financial capital from

moving around the globe in search of the highest interest rate keeps interest rates from being driven up in those countries that need low interest rates for full employment. In the absence of controls, financial capital will arbitrage any interest-rate gap by leaving low-interest rate countries and moving to high-interest-rate countries, thereby driving up rates in the low-interest-rate country.

The ability to arbitrage and move between financial centers is the foundation of financial capital's economic power; it fits with the logic of economic power analyzed in chapter 5. Keynes realized that freedom of international capital movement means that countries must inevitably lose control over their domestic interest rate. This can prevent full employment because countries may require different interest rate settings owing to different local economic conditions.

The Breakdown of Bretton Woods

The system of capital controls that obtained in the 1950s and 1960s allowed countries to have different interest-rate settings, and there was full employment during this period. However, fixed exchange rates became a problem.

Keynes had pushed for fixed exchange rates as part of the Bretton Woods agreement in order to counter the problems of the 1930s. During the Great Depression, countries had tried to combat unemployment by devaluing their exchange rates in the hope of gaining international competitiveness. Each country had hoped to make its goods relatively cheaper, thereby reviving demand and economic activity. However, when all tried this strategy, it merely resulted in competitive devaluations in which no country gained an advantage.

Competitive devaluation is another instance of the prisoner's dilemma: if country A devalues and country B does not, A gains a competitive advantage. Analogous reasoning applies regarding B's incentive to devalue, and, as a result, all devalue. Keynes hoped to guard against this possibility in the post-World War II era by fixing exchange rates.

However, once in place, the problems with fixed exchange rates were twofold. First, countries differ in their rates of productivity growth; thus over time, some countries gain international competitiveness, while others lose. To prevent the emergence of permanent trade deficits owing to unequal competitiveness, exchange rates need to be adjusted.

Second, fixed exchange rates cannot handle inflation. If exchange rates are to be sustainable, then all countries must have the same inflation rates.

In the absence of this, prices will be rising faster in some countries than in others, and these countries will quickly lose competitiveness. Countries must therefore run the same inflation rate. However, this effectively means surrendering national control over monetary policy, and surrendering the ability to choose the most desired feasible unemployment-inflation combination.

These two problems surfaced in the late 1960s and early 1970s. During the 1960s, the U.S. economy was at full employment and was running persistent trade deficits. Meanwhile, Europe was at full employment and running persistent trade surpluses. These surpluses were the result of improved European competitiveness that followed from the rebuilding of European industry after World War II. Owing to the U.S. trade deficits, the dollar was under continuous selling pressure, and the Federal Reserve had to intervene in international money markets to buy dollars. This meant selling gold and foreign currency held by the Fed.

Eventually, the Fed decided it could no longer do this because it risked running out of gold and foreign currency. Meanwhile, European countries were unwilling to buy dollars, because this would have meant selling their own currencies and increasing their money supplies. Since they were already at full employment, this would have increased European inflation. Thus, neither the United States nor Europe was willing to maintain the existing exchange rate, and the system collapsed in 1973.

Flexible Exchange Rates/Capital Controls

Following the end of fixed exchange rates, international money markets were characterized by flexible exchange rates with continued capital controls. Capital controls meant that countries could run independent monetary policies with different interest rates because financial capital still could not freely move between countries to force an equalization of interest rates.

The new system also allowed countries to have different inflation rates, because the exchange rate could adjust to restore any loss of international competitiveness. Countries with higher rates of inflation would find their currencies depreciating, thereby offsetting any loss of international competitiveness caused by higher inflation. Consequently, countries could choose to trade off a little less unemployment at the cost of a little bit more inflation.

The combination of flexible exchange rates and capital controls is the most desirable policy configuration and is one that we should aim to return to. It allows countries to follow independent monetary policies whereby interest rates are targeted to specific country conditions. Meanwhile, the exchange rate is set by the needs of international trade. Given capital controls, foreign exchange is bought and sold principally to finance trade. Hence, trade conditions dominate in the setting of exchange rates.

However, during the 1970s this system failed for five reasons. First, the 1970s was the period of the OPEC oil shocks, and the increase in imported oil prices caused almost all countries to experience balance-of-trade deficits. Moreover, countries were differentially affected by the oil shock, which necessitated differential exchange rate adjustments. The scale of the adjustments, their differential nature, the resulting oil and imported price inflation, and the fact that government policy responses to the oil shock differed across countries, all contributed to uncertainty and volatility in the foreign exchange markets. Rather than being seen as the product of disequilibrium generated by the oil shock, these developments were seen as reason to further change the system and get rid of capital controls.

Many countries also felt that the best way to adjust to these trade deficits was to borrow. Rather than having exchange rates adjust to equalize the balance of trade, countries would run temporary deficits that would be financed by international borrowing. This was particularly true of the Third World, and it laid the foundation for the debt crisis of the early 1980s. Such borrowing required that financial capital be internationally mobile, which in turn required relaxation of controls.

A third reason for the breakdown of the system was the gradual ability of financial capital to evade the existing system of capital controls. Capital controls represented a form of binding regulation. The fact that they were binding meant that they were successful and stopped financial capital from doing what it would have preferred to do. However, as discussed in chapter 1, this in turn set up an incentive for financial capital to innovate in order to get around the controls. The process of creative destruction operates in financial markets, just as as it does in industry.

Throughout the 1960s, there was continuous financial innovation, as evidenced by the emergence of the Eurodollar and Eurocurrency markets. To escape national jurisdictions and their associated regulations, business started placing deposits overseas. Thus, General Electric might place a dollar deposit with the London branch of Chase, and because the deposit was in London, it was free of all U.S. financial restrictions. This deposit could then be converted into deutsche marks if sentiment was that the dollar was going to fall, or it could be used to buy a German bond if interest rates in Germany were higher. In this fashion, an international money market that was free of capital controls began to emerge on its own.

As this new market emerged, it began to have larger effects on the exchange rate and domestic interest rates, because funds were increasingly channeled into it and away from national markets. The appropriate response should have been to update the system of international financial regulation to include the Eurodollar and Eurocurrency markets. This is what a structural Keynesian perspective would have advocated. Instead, policymakers decided that since the existing system was not working as well as it used to, the system of controls on capital mobility should be abolished.

The fourth reason for the ending of the system of contols on international capital mobility is the political and intellectual triumph of laissez-faire economics, with its philosophy of economic naturalism. The 1970s were a period of rising unemployment and inflation, which were both caused by the dislocation of the great OPEC oil shock. This dislocation came on top of the breakdown of the Bretton Woods agreement, which itself had been caused by a persistent U.S. trade deficit. In this environment, conservatives argued that government restrictions were the cause of the problem and should be abolished. Just as there was a need to recover natural markets in the domestic sphere, so, too, there was a need to recover them in the international sphere. This meant replacing fixed exchange rates with flexible exchange rates and eliminating capital controls.

The conservative argument marks a complete break with Keynesian economics. Keynes had argued that economies need capital controls so as to retain control over the domestic interest rate, and this control is needed because the interest rate is important for ensuring full employment. Laissez-faire economics breaks with this argument entirely by claiming that the interest rate is irrelevant for determining the level of employment. Instead, employment is determined by the free-market process operating in the labor market, and it is unaffected by interest rates. The implication is clear: there is no need for a country to control the level of interest rates, and controls on capital mobility can therefore be eliminated without adverse consequence.

More than that, eliminating controls is a good thing because owners of financial wealth can then move their wealth around the globe to get the highest rate of return. Indeed, by doing so, they earn greater foreign income to the benefit of the national economy. Thus, the new conservative economics argues that financial capital mobility actually enhances the national interest, whereas capital controls are detrimental to it.

A fifth and final reason for the elimination of capital controls concerns the need to discipline governments. As noted in chapter 7, financial capital dislikes inflation because it erodes the value of financial assets. However, flexible exchange rates allow governments to pursue independent monetary policies with differential inflation rates. Consequently, financial capital needs a means of preventing governments from pursuing inflationary policies. Capital mobility is that means, since it empowers capital to vote with its feet and escape the effects of inflation; hence another reason for financial capital to support the elimination of capital controls.

The Current System: Flexible Exchange Rates/Capital Mobility

The above arguments explain how we have arrived at our current system. This system, with its absence of capital controls, has had significant negative effects and is an important factor explaining the emergence of global economic stagnation.

From a structural Keynesian perspective, interest rates affect employment by affecting level of demand. The abolition of capital controls means that countries have lost control of their interest rates, which are now set by international money markets. In its global search for highest rates, financial capital now sets domestic interest rates. In countries around the world, interest rates have been pushed too high for full employment; this is evident from Canada to Western Europe to Australia.

The combination of exchange rate flexibility and capital mobility has also turned international money markets into asset markets, so that they are now dominated by speculative forces. When capital controls are in place, the needs of trade finance are the dominant force determining the exchange rate. When financial capital is free to move, the dominant force becomes the portfolio decisions of wealth holders. Investors now constantly switch between currencies, looking to make a quick buck. The international money market becomes like the stock market, and thus it, too, can be roiled by speculative fevers and bubbles.

As argued earlier, the exchange rate affects industrial competitiveness. If seriously misaligned, it can cause permanent deindustrialization that is unwarranted by the underlying reality of shop-floor productivity. Yet the current system allows exactly this possibility, and it is the direct result of the abolition of controls on capital mobility.

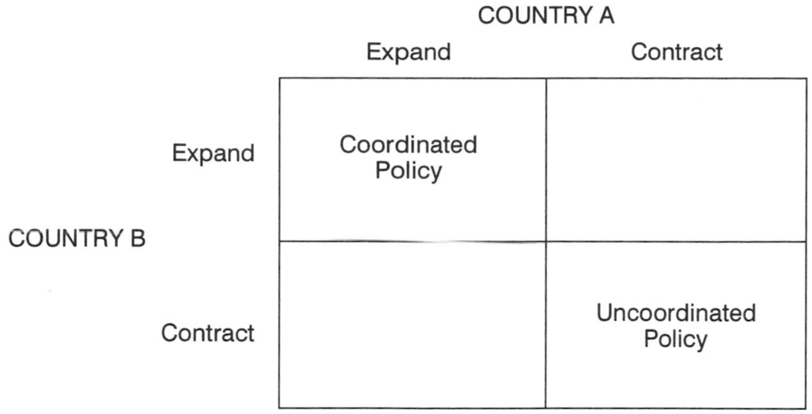

COUNTRY A

	Expand	Contract
Expand	Coordinated Policy	
Contract		Uncoordinated Policy

COUNTRY B

Fig. 10.4. The prisoner's dilemma and macroeconomic policy.

Lastly, the abolition of controls has contributed to locking countries into deflationary economic policies. This compounds the problems associated with exchange rates being driven by asset market speculation. Once again, the problem is one of the prisoner's dilemma (fig. 10.4). Two countries (A and B) can follow expansionary or contractionary policies. Countries are best off if both expand, in which case they both have full employment. However, international capital mobility gives them a perverse incentive to contract.

Countries that pursue expansionary policies are likely to experience capital flight because financial capital dislikes inflation. Capital therefore moves to countries where there is less risk of inflation. Such flight pushes interest rates higher and depreciates the exchange rate. Instead, to curry favor with the bond market, countries may pursue policies of fiscal austerity. Meanwhile, central banks may raise their domestic interest rates fractionally to reduce the likelihood of capital flight. However, when all central banks do this, the net result is higher global interest rates, which are contractionary.

In effect, the threat of capital flight gives financial capital a veto over policy, and the result is a tendency toward contractionary policy. No country can escape this trap acting alone. If one decides to expand alone, it suffers from capital flight. A structural Keynesian perspective recognizes that institutional reform is needed to induce countries to opt for expansion. Restricting international capital mobility and coordinating economic policy can solve the problem. If both countries pursue coordinated

189

moderate expansions, then each has full employment with balanced trade and a balanced budget. Countries import from each other, thereby producing balanced trade; full employment raises tax revenues and lowers welfare payments, thereby balancing the government budget.

WHERE NEXT? WHAT IS THE RIGHT WAY TO ORGANIZE INTERNATIONAL MONEY MARKETS?

We have now completed an examination of the the different systems of international money that have prevailed over the last forty years. Where is the system headed, and what is the right way to go? These are the questions addressed in the balance of this chapter.

The Wrong Way: Fixed Exchange Rates/Capital Mobility

The combination of flexible exchange-rates and capital mobility has transformed the process of exchange-rate determination into one resembling a speculative asset market. As a result, exchange rates are highly volatile, and the exchange rate can diverge from real world fundamentals for long periods of time. These divergences carry major economic costs in the form of lost jobs and even permanent deindustrialization.

This high level of volatility is being used to make a case for returning to fixed exchange rates. However, such a change would aggravate the situation and further entrench the dominance of financial capital. It would force countries to follow strict zero-inflation policies in order to maintain their fixed exchange parity, and this would create higher unemployment according to the logic of the Phillips curve.

Fixed exchange rates with capital mobility represents the worst possible combination. It would lock countries into following tight money policies that keep the lid on inflation in order to preserve the exchange rate. Anytime financial interests disliked policy, they could sell out, thereby causing an exchange-rate crisis and forcing governments to reverse policy. Such a combination also risks globalizing the problems that have afflicted Southeast Asia. Finance capital can be expected to speculate against weaker central banks, thereby generating rolling financial crises. To defend themselves, these banks will be forced to raise interest rates, thereby potentially causing a global deflationary economic spiral.

In effect, the fixed exchange rate/capital mobility arrangement is the

INTERNATIONAL MONEY

modern descendant of the gold standard. The only difference is that governments are not obliged to convert their monies into gold. However, each government is obliged to convert its money into foreign currency. Given limited government holdings of foreign currency, this is analogous to a gold supply constraint. The gold standard was one of the principal factors contributing to the Great Depression. It did so by locking countries into deflationary regimes in which monetary policy was tied up protecting the exchange rate and could not be used to lower interest rates to achieve full employment. A fixed exchange rate/capital mobility system would do the same.

The Right Way: Flexible Exchange Rates/Capital Controls

The right way is to maintain the existing system of flexible exchange rates, but limit financial capital mobility. This was the system that applied in the 1970s. It was mistakenly done away with because of the problems of that decade. However, these problems were the result of the OPEC oil crisis rather than the system.

Foreign exchange market speculation and volatility is not the result of flexible exchange rates. Rather, it is the result of capital mobility, which has allowed financial capital to flow around the world in search of quick speculative gains. This has transformed FX markets into financial asset markets, so that exchange rates are no longer driven by the needs of trade finance.

Similarly, the incentive for governments to pursue contractionary policies is not driven by flexible exchange rates. Once again, capital mobility is the problem: it exposes governments that pursue expansionary policies to the risk of being chastized by capital flight and facing a sell off in bond and foreign exchange markets.

Restoring controls on financial capital mobility would put an end to many of these problems. At the same time, retaining flexible exchange rates would mean that there is an automatic system for correcting trade imbalances. This adjustment mechanism would not be contractionary, because it would merely involve a change in the price at which one money exchanged for another. Moreover, governments could pursue expansionary policies without risking punishment by capital flight.

The dominance of economic naturalism has mistakenly led us to believe that capital controls are wrong and unnatural. The abolition of these controls has not created natural international financial markets; they have

191

merely created markets in which financial capital is dominant. Capital controls are feasible. Financial capital moves through the banking system, and wherever it moves, it leaves a footprint in the form of a transactions record. Consequently, it can be controlled. What is needed is a rediscovery of political will.

Some policy suggestions are as follows.

1. Domestic residents could be subjected to restrictions on the quantity of financial capital they can export. Each taxpayer could be allocated a capital export license, and they could then be allowed to buy and sell these licenses. A market for such licenses would develop, and those without capital to invest abroad would be able to sell their licenses. This means that the private gain of capital exports would not accrue to only the rich.

2. The destabilizing influence of foreign inflows of hot money could be neutralized by imposing a minimum required stay, perhaps six months. This is a regulation that Chile has successfully imposed. Forcing capital inflows to commit to a stay discourages purely speculative inflows. At the same time, it has no effect on long-term inflows and therefore does no harm to long-term inward foreign investment.

3. Short sales of currency by individuals and corporate nationals could be subject to a requirement that they be accompanied by a non-interest-bearing deposit with the central bank equal to 50% of the short sale.[2] Having sellers make a noninterest-bearing deposit would raise the cost of speculating against a currency and therefore discourage speculation.

This regulation would apply to foreign subsidiaries located in a country, as well as to subsidiaries and affiliates of corporate nationals located abroad. There are good reasons to believe that the preponderance of short sales of domestic currency come from domestic nationals, because their income flows are denoted in the currency, and their exchange risk is therefore significantly curtailed.

4. Finally, governments could impose a Tobin (1978) transaction tax. This tax, perhaps equal to 0.125% of the value transacted, would be placed on every FX transaction. Raising the cost of buying and selling currency would serve to discourage speculation. Those investing in a country for the long haul would not find this small tax onerous. Those planning an in-and-out trip in the hope of a quick speculative gain would find it a burden. Thus, speculative transacting would be discouraged, while long-term investing would be unaffected. At the same time, a lot of

tax revenue would be raised owing to the magnitude of international financial capital flows. This revenue could either go to funding productive public investment, or it could be used for purposes of debt relief in the Third World.

The major problem with the Tobin tax is that it needs to be imposed globally. In the absence of global enforcement, the geographical location of dealings will simply shift to those countries without the tax. Consequently, countries imposing the tax would lose financial sector business, without diminishing speculation. A successful Tobin tax therefore requires cross-country policy coordination.[3]

✳ CHAPTER 11 ✳

Structural Keynesianism
and Globalization

Throughout the last ten chapters, three key concepts have repeatedly appeared. The first is the Keynesian concept of aggregate demand. The level of aggregate demand for goods and services determines the level of output, and the level of demand is itself affected by the distribution of income.

The second is the concept of bargaining power. The distribution of bargaining power between business and labor determines the distribution of income between wages and profits.

The third concept is that of the prisoner's dilemma, a situation that repeatedly afflicts both individuals and governments. It generates a perverse set of incentives that induces individuals and policymakers to make choices that result in everybody being less well-off than they could be.

Chapter 1 introduced a distinction between the philosophies of economic naturalism and structural Keynesianism. Economic naturalism represents the economy as if it were "natural"; hence, the notion of a natural rate of unemployment, a natural rate of interest, and a natural rate of growth. The significance of the appeal to nature is that it creates a mentality of economic fatalism. If the economy is fixed by nature, then there is nothing we can do about it, and the role of economic policy is correspondingly diminished.

Structural Keynesianism fundamentally contests the mentality of economic fatalism. Aggregate demand is subject to management through monetary and fiscal policy. Bargaining power is affected by labor laws, by the extent of unionization, by laws governing workplace safety standards, by welfare and unemployment insurance arrangements, and by trade policy: all of these are the product of design. Lastly, outcomes in situations marked by the prisoner's dilemma depend on institutional arrangements. If the right institutions are in place, the good outcome can be achieved. Hence, tax treaties can prevent corporate tax auction frenzies; common markets can prevent international trade from becoming a race to the bottom; and economic policy coordination can encourage countries to pursue the path of expansion rather than that of contraction.

GLOBALIZATION AND THE PROBLEM OF
ECONOMIC LEAKINESS

Globalization has recently become a popular term used to describe our new economic condition. Globalization refers to the process promoting increased international trade, increased integration of financial markets, and the development of mobile multinational methods of production.

With globalization has come increased integration of national economies, which poses real problems for achieving an expansionary economic climate. Each country now has an incentive to rely on other countries to stimulate economic activity and then piggyback on their expansion. When all pursue this strategy, however, no country expands, and all get caught in a deflationary trap. Once again, the prisoner's dilemma is visible.

Globalization has fundamentally changed the economic landscape, and the policies that were successful in the Golden Age (1945–1970) will no longer suffice. Structural Keynesianism recognizes this, for globalization is merely a catchword for profound structural change brought about by the process of creative destruction. Economic policy must now operate in an economic environment in which national economies are becoming increasingly integrated through international trade, while production has become highly mobile and multinational in character.

Increased trade gives rise to *macroeconomic leakiness*, whereby demand leaks out of national economies through an increased propensity to import. Increased integration of international money markets gives rise to *financial leakiness*, whereby financial capital flees at the prospect of lower unemployment and marginally higher inflation. Increased mobility of production gives rise to *microeconomic leakiness*, whereby jobs leak out of an economy if labor markets are not sufficiently flexible or profit taxes are relatively unfavorable. The ongoing process of globalization means that the scale of these leaks is increasing, and new sources of leakiness are being introduced.

The increased integration of the United States in the global economy is captured in table 11.1. This shows the degree of openness, as measured by the ratio of imports plus exports to total gross domestic product. A measure of zero corresponds to a totally closed economy that has no imports or exports. Economic openness has increased almost everywhere: in the United States, the measure of openness has increased 152%, but even now the United States remains relatively closed compared to European economies.

195

TABLE 11.1
Openness of OECD Countries, 1966–95 (percent)

Country or Region	1966	1995	Change 1966–95
United States	9.9	23.6	138
Canada	39.1	72.3	95
Japan	19.4	16.8*	−13
Germany	51.1†	63.4*	24
United Kingdom	37.8	57.3	52
France	25.0	44.5	78
Italy	28.1	43.2*	54
Austria	51.4	76.2	48
Belgium	73.5	137.2*	87
Denmark	58.5	63.3	8
Finland	41.3	67.5	63
Netherlands	89.8	100.0	11
Norway	83.2	70.6	−15
Portugal	54.1	61.0*	13
Spain	20.2	47.3	134
Sweden	43.8	75.3	72
Switzerland	58.7	66.9	14
G-7	30.1	45.9	53
Europe	51.2	69.6	36

Source: Author's calculations using IMF statistics. G-7 and Europe computed as simple averages.

Note: Openness = (Exports + Imports)/Gross Domestic Product.
* 1994 data. † 1979 data.

The significance of openness is that it makes economies sensitive to imported price inflation resulting from exchange-rate depreciation, and it makes economies subject to large leakages of demand through import spending. Both of these features encourage contractionary policies. Fear of imported inflation keeps countries from pushing for lower interest rates; fear of trade deficits keeps them from pursuing full-employment policies.

THE STRUCTURAL KEYNESIAN RESPONSE TO GLOBALIZATION

Guided by the philosophy of economic naturalism, policymakers have concluded wrongly that it is impossible to sustain activist growth promoting economic policy in this new environment. Instead, they have adopted a model of economic austerity, the hallmarks of which are zero tolerance of inflation, high interest rates, lower fiscal deficits, elimination of public investment, and an attack on the social wage.

In response to macroeconomic leakiness, policymakers have cut back on government spending and operated the economy with more unemployment. In response to financial leakiness, they have raised interest rates and placed a floor under the unemployment rate (the natural rate) to prevent inflation. Lastly, in response to microeconomic leakiness they have pushed labor market flexibility by undercutting unions, reducing the value and accessibility of welfare and unemployment insurance, and debasing the minimum wage. The specific mix of policy varies by country.

This austerity model poses real risks. In the absence of an expansionary environment, the Schumpeterian process of creative destruction described in chapter 2 will promote a steady increase in productive capacity that is unmatched by growth of demand. This will produce unemployment, and it will also give firms an incentive to retain market share by cutting costs through squeezing wages. In this fashion, the focus of private economic activity will be subtly shifted to distributional conflict rather than growth. Moreover, unemployment will likely foster protectionism.

Structural Keynesianism suggests an alternative set of policies for dealing with the new situations posed by globalization. These policies are predicated on an understanding of the economic significance of aggregate demand, bargaining power, and the problem of the prisoner's dilemma.

Figure 11.1 is a two-by-two matrix in which policies are described as "maintenance of the wage floor" and "expansionary macroeconomic policy." Box B corresponds to the U.S economy, where the wage floor has been undermined through the adoption of labor-market flexibility, but macroeconomic policy has been comparatively expansionary. The result has been increased income inequality, accompanied by job creation. Box C corresponds to Europe, where the wage floor has been maintained, and labor-market flexibility has been resisted (at least up until now). However, macroeconomic policy has been contractionary owing to extensive macroeconomic and financial leakiness. The result has been unchanged income inequality but massively increased unemployment.[1]

Structural Keynesianism identifies box A (maintained wage floor/expansionary macroeconomic policy) as the right policy combination. Unfortunately, guided by economic naturalism, the current direction of policy is the exact opposite. Thus, policymakers around the world are pushing toward box D, with its combination of undermined wage floor/contractionary macroeconomic policy.

In Europe, the push is to lower the wage floor and reduce worker protections under the guise of creating greater labor-market flexibility.[2] In

WAGE FLOOR MAINTAINED

	Yes	No
A. Structural Keynesianism		**B.** U.S.
C. Europe		**D.** Economic Naturalism

EXPANSIONARY MACRO POLICY

Yes

No

Fig. 11.1. Taxonomy of policy configurations.

addition, the provisions of the Maastricht Treaty, which govern the creation of a single European currency, demand that governments reduce their budget deficits to below 3% of GDP. This is contractionary at a time when Europe is in deep recession.

The United States is pushing for tighter fiscal policy through a reduced budget deficit, while the Federal Reserve remains under the influence of the theory of the natural rate of unemployment and is inclined to tighten monetary policy.

This push toward box D also reflects the prisoner's dilemma character of today's globalized economic environment. Increased competition in international trade exerts a persistent pressure to improve competitiveness, and this has encouraged countries to implement policies that lower the social wage. Greater economic integration means that economies are becoming more open and characterized by greater import demand leakages. This means that domestic macroeconomic policy has become less capable of stimulating domestic employment, because a greater proportion of any domestic demand stimulus now leaks abroad as imports. Consequently, countries that try to expand domestic demand are left burdened with both trade and fiscal deficits. This is the principal lesson of the failed Mitterrand government economic experiment in the early 1980s, and it explains why European governments have been unwilling to adopt sufficiently expansionary policies.[3]

Given this adverse environment, there is no single policy that can restore high-wage full employment. Instead, a successful program will have to be multidimensional. The outline of such a program is as follows.

1. *Labor Market Reform.* Rather than aiming for increased labor-market flexibility and lower wages predicated upon reduced worker protections, labor market reform should focus on raising wages by restoring the balance of power between business and labor. This balance has tilted in favor of business owing to technological and organizational innovations. It has also been affected by the decline of unions and by free trade, which has increased firms' threat to shift production abroad. In the face of these structural changes, policy should aim to rectify this imbalance by strengthening the wage floor through higher minimum wages and improved unemployment benefits and coverage. In addition, labor laws should be amended to level the labor-market playing field regarding workers' ability to form and join unions.

2. *Monetary Policy.* The doctrine of the natural rate of unemployment, which maintains that monetary policy is handcuffed by a binding employment constraint, should be abandoned. In its place, monetary policy should be guided by a pragmatic stance, that seeks to lower unemployment, while experimenting to locate where inflation actually starts to accelerate. Given the high level of corporate profitability and continued productivity growth in manufacturing, there is room for noninflationary wage increases. The bond market's implicit domination of monetary policy, which is evidenced by the policy goal of zero inflation, should be replaced by an outlook that balances concerns with employment, wages, and inflation.

3. *Fiscal Policy.* The notion of a saving shortage, which has fueled the push for fiscal austerity, should be rejected. Industrialized economies are awash with savings, as evidenced by the increase in stock prices and other financial asset prices. Saving does not cause investment; rather, investment causes saving. Increasing investment in turn calls for easier monetary policy and lower interest rates. Public investment is important for both growth and the quality of life; it should be funded for both reasons. A more progressive system of taxation, combined with the elimination of corporate welfare, can help restore income equality as well as fund increased public investment.

4. *International Trade Policy.* International trade is in principle good, conferring the benefits of product diversity, economies of scale, and increased product market competition. However, where trade is exclusively driven by low wages or by the absence of environmental regulations and labor standards, it should be carefully managed. This is the only means of preventing international trade from undercutting domestic wages. Free trade is the wrong approach to international trade; so,

too, is protectionism. What is needed is a common-markets approach that has countries adopting common environmental standards, common rights of free association for workers, common prohibitions against forced and child labor, and common prohibitions against workplace discrimination.

5. *International Money Markets.* International money markets also need to be regulated through the imposition of appropriately designed capital controls, trading taxes, and trading requirements. This would reduce speculative distortions of the exchange rate and prevent financial capital from exercising a veto over domestic economic policy. This problem has been particularly severe in Europe, where policy has been held hostage by the threat of speculative attacks against the exchange rate.

6. *International Economic Policy Coordination.* Increased openness has increased the size of import demand leakages, while increased integration of international money markets has made financial capital more mobile and skittish in response to policies it dislikes. Economic policy coordination has therefore become a necessary condition for acheiving sustained economic prosperity in the new globalized economic environment. By ensuring concurrent economic expansion across countries, coordination can mitigate the problems of trade deficits and capital flight. Countries will import from one another, thereby reducing the problem of trade deficits. Concurrent expansion means that interest rates and inflation will follow similar trends in all countries, thereby reducing the incentive for capital flight. Coordination enables countries to stay the expansionary course. In its absence, the forces promoting the economics of austerity and lowering of the wage floor must inevitably assert themselves.

CONCLUSION

Economic policy is now being driven by the notion of a natural economy and being designed to recapture that economy by shrinking government, eliminating labor-market protections, and eliminating all controls on trade and international movements of financial capital. The notion of a natural economy is a dangerous illusion. It promises to create markets in which business dominates labor and governments. This will exacerbate the problem of income inequality and force governments to adopt policies of economic austerity that lead to higher unemployment. Such policies may even ultimately prove bad for business and profits.

Contributing to these developments is the new world of globalization. Globalization is not a natural process. It is an economic process prompted by technical and organizational innovations driven by the search for profit. Globalization can be a positive force if managed and directed properly. Left to its own devices, however, the economic leakiness that it creates can become a highly destructive force.

Countries are afflicted in different degrees by each type of leakiness. For the United States, microeconomic job leakiness has been a problem. At the moment, the U.S. economy is in the midst of a sustained economic expansion. A combination of relief that downsizing has slowed, an optimistic psychological disposition, and a tendency to short-term memory have together contributed to a belief that all is well and that there is no need to change course.

Despite the expansion, the U.S. economic bottle remains half full. Wage growth is extremely fragile, and wages remain significantly below levels of twenty years ago. Recalling the corridor analogy of chapter 6, the task confronting economic policymakers is to construct spacious and strong corridors, while fostering a robust economic environment that allows market forces to fill those corridors with productive economic activity. At the moment, technological and organizational innovation, deregulation, and the corporate capture of economic policy are contributing to pulling down the existing corridors for the benefit of some and the disadvantage of many. This act of demolition has even prompted an economic boom, albeit one marked by wage stagnation.

What if we do not rebuild our economic corridors? One possibility is that the existing situation of full employment with substantial income inequality will prove durable. If it does not, a combination of unemployment and income inequality could prove socially and politically combustible.

Recipe for a Depression

Economists are hardly renowned for their ability to predict the course of economic activity.[1] In 1929, Irving Fisher, the greatest of all American economists, confidently predicted that the stock market would go on to new record highs and that there was no end in sight to the expansion of economic prosperity. Two months later, Wall Street experienced the Great Crash, and the economy had already entered what was to become the Great Depression.

As of the moment of writing, the U.S. economy is in the midst of an economic boom that has generated a new sense of well-being. Thus, in May 1997, *Time* magazine ran the story "Too Good To Be True? By Almost Any Measure, Life Is Swell in the U.S. What Went Right?" Part of this new well-being is plain old-fashioned business-cycle euphoria, which always sweeps up people in the last stages of the cycle. Part is the result of diminished expectations, combined with relief that employment downsizing has finally slowed. Thus, wage and income growth that would have been deemed totally unsatisfactory a decade ago are now embraced as outstanding economic performance. Finally, the U.S. economy has pushed the unemployment rate down to 4.9%. Even if pay is much more unequal than it used to be, jobs are at least plentiful, and that is a source of psychological relief.

Challenging the current euphoria has the appearance of raining on the parade. However, without seeking to predict when the next recession will occur, there are grounds for believing that it will prove deep, to the point of potentially becoming a depression. The changes associated with the move from Main Street to Mean Street capitalism have been of sufficient magnitude, and the stabilizing structures associated with the Golden Age of 1950–70 have been so eroded, that the economy is now vulnerable to the types of seismic shock that generated the Great Depression. Rather than retreating from the edge, policy continues to disembowel the economy's automatic stabilizers that were put in place by New Deal legislation and the Keynesian revolution in economic policy that followed World War II.

HOUSEHOLD DEBT AND THE DANGER
OF WAGE DEFLATION

One indication of the return to an era of dangerous economic fragility is the recession of 1990. In many regards this recession remains very poorly accounted for. The commonly told story is that the Iraqi invasion of Kuwait and the ensuing spike in oil prices gave a nasty sudden shock to the confidence of American consumers, and this caused a decline in consumer spending that pushed the economy into recession. This recessionary shock was then amplified by the large debt that American households and corporations had built up during the 1980s.

The household debt part of this story concerns structural developments associated with the emergence of the Mean Street economy (the growth of debt as a means of sustaining living standards), and it is indeed important for understanding our new fragility. However, the consumer shock story has all the hallmarks of the snowball theory of avalanches. Moreover, it illustrates the complete confusion that characterizes modern economics. On the one hand, consumers are told to spend, spend, spend! On the other, they are told to save, save, save!

Chapters 3 and 4 documented how the Golden Age of the period 1945–70 has been replaced by a new Leaden Age. Whereas the economy used to be characterized by rapid productivity growth and rising standards of living for all, it is now characterized by slow productivity growth and increased income inequality. This waning of prosperity reflects a shift from Main Street capitalism to Mean Street capitalism. The hallmark of the former was that it generally worked for the benefit of the average citizen by sharing the fruits of productivity growth. The hallmark of the latter is an economic environment that pits citizen against citizen for the benefit of those who own and manage America. This change is a direct result of the refashioning of the nation's economic architecture, and a reversal of the policies associated with the Golden Age. It has opened the possibility of another depression.

Since the Second World War, the U.S. economy has had nine recessions, defined as two consecutive quarters of declining output. The normal pattern has involved an increase in the unemployment rate accompanied by "disinflation," a decrease in the rate of inflation. The most severe of these recessions was that of 1981–2, when unemployment exceeded 10% for the first time since the 1930s.

203

The last recession, which began in 1990, appears to be qualitatively different from preceding recessions in that the process of disinflation has continued throughout the recovery period. Thus, rather than picking up, inflation has continued to fall during the recovery, and we now have close to zero inflation. Even as the unemployment rate was hitting a twenty-three year low of 4.9% in April 1997, the annual rate of inflation was only 2.5% and dropping. Thus, if the economy were to enter a new recession, it would likely experience deflation: prices and wages would actually fall.

Falling prices and wages are now a real possibility. The globalization of the economy means intense import competition which exerts downward pressure on prices. The decline in union strength means that unions no longer protect most workers against pay cuts. Many households increasingly rely on overtime earnings (average manufacturing overtime hours hit an all-time high in 1997), and such earnings will quickly shrink in a recession. Finally, many companies have now shifted to bonus and other incentive pay schemes that are contingent on profitability, and recessionary effects that adversely impact profits will now be magnified through their impact on wages.

If prices and wages start to fall, the burden of interest payments on the debts of consumers and business would increase enormously, thereby causing a collapse of consumer spending and capital spending by business. For this reason, deflation has historically been associated with periods of economic *depression*. A reasonable definition of *depression* is a period of prolonged unemployment in excess of 10% accompanied by deflation. The recession of 1981–82 showed that rates of unemployment in excess of 10% are again possible, while the most recent recession has raised the specter of deflation. The twin characteristics of depression are therefore now potentially in place.

The high-level of indebtedness in the U.S. economy implies that if prices and wages start falling, spending and fresh borrowing will most likely collapse, and bankruptcies will rocket. The economy could then find itself in a contractionary spiral, with wage deflation feeding a collapse in spending, and collapsing spending feeding further wage deflation.

PROLONGED RECESSIONS, FRAGILE RECOVERIES

Just as the causes of the recession have been poorly explained, the subsequent prolonged recession and weak recovery also give cause for concern. Though some economists have dated the end of the recession in the third

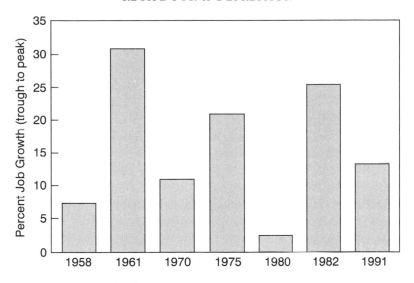

Fig. 12.1. The strength of economic recoveries.

quarter of 1990, substantive recovery did not really begin until the second half of 1993, and for a full three years the economy was effectively dead in the water. This type of prolonged recession has been absent from U.S. economic experience since World War II and marks a return to an earlier history of the business cycle.

Much has been made of the strength of the current recovery. However, job creation during the current expansion has actually been very weak (figs. 12.1, 12.2). Figure 12.1 shows the percentage growth in private-sector jobs since the beginning of economic recovery for the last seven expansions. Expansions are of different length, and longer expansions can be expected to create more jobs. Figure 12.2 therefore shows a measure of standardized job creation: this is obtained by taking the percentage growth in jobs and dividing it by the number of months in the expansion. According to this standardized measure, the current expansion has the lowest rate of job creation of all.

Throughout this period of putative recovery, consumer confidence has exhibited considerable fragility. As of the moment, consumer confidence is again riding high. This can be attributed to diminished expectations and relief that employment downsizing has slowed. However, even though the employment front looks good, wages are below the level of the last business cycle peak: measured in 1996 dollars, the average hourly wage for a nonsupervisory worker was $12.14 in 1989 versus $11.82 in 1996.

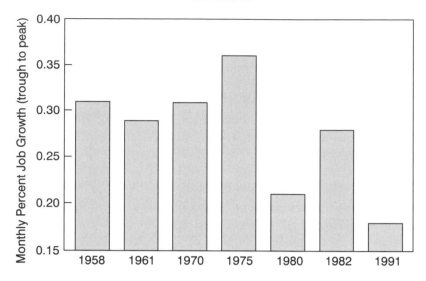

Fig. 12.2. Economic recovery strength standardized for recovery duration.

Median family income (measured in 1995 dollars) was $42,049 in 1989 versus $40,611 in 1995. As in the 1980s, there are indications that the sense of prosperity is being created by borrowing. In 1994, household financial debt grew 8.7%; in 1995, it grew 8.2%; and in 1996, it grew 7.8%. This creates a temporary sense of affluence, but ultimately the debt has to be paid back with interest.

THE FRAGILE HOUSEHOLD

The above description of the prolonged 1990 recession and its subsequent weak recovery are the symptomology of the new fragile economy. Behind this propensity to fragility lie the decisive structural changes that have been identified and examined in earlier chapters of the book. First, and foremost is the underlying deterioration in the robustness of product market conditions. Ultimately, a system of mass production requires steady stable demand conditions predicated upon mass consumption. However, this fundamental requirement has been persistently undermined by the developments of the last twenty-five years.

The silent depression that has embraced ordinary American households during this period has eroded the purchasing power of wages, and shifted the distribution of income away from wages toward profits and the salaries of executives. More than anything else this has created structural weakness in demand. This development has been obscured, and its impact delayed, by the tremendous growth of household debt that began in the 1980s. As a result, debt served to fill the gap in demand that would otherwise have emerged.

Expansion of household debt has always been an important source of demand growth in the U.S. economy, paving the way for expansion of the mass market. However, in past decades, household borrowing was predicated on the confident presumption of rising incomes to pay it back and was therefore "demand leading." Today, with declining wages, debt is being incurred to maintain existing living standards and fill the gap in demand that would otherwise emerge. Debt has therefore changed from being "demand leading" to being "demand maintaining."

However, this demand-maintaining capacity of new borrowing has been increasingly undermined by the cumulative expansion of household indebtedness, because debt involves debtor households making interest payments to creditor households. In general, low- and middle-income households are net debtors, while high-income households (of which there are few) are net creditors. Consequently, over time, the process of demand-maintaining borrowing has the paradoxical effect of aggravating the underlying problem of deteriorating income distribution.

Unfortunately, even this process of demand-maintaining borrowing must ultimately come to an end as households run into their debt ceilings. The end of this process can be temporarily delayed by either raising debt ceilings and allowing greater household leverage, or by lowering credit requirements and lending to less credit-worthy households. Indeed, both features have been at work, as is evidenced by the flood of invitations to obtain credit cards and by the lowering of mortgage lending ceilings from the old "four times gross income" to the new "three times gross income." However, even this process of delay is fragile, because households may put a voluntary end to it when they realize the financial vulnerability to which they are exposing themselves. It is this feature, rather than the invasion of Iraq, that likely explains the onset of the recession of 1990.

Once households run out of income to service existing debt and borrowing stops, the problem of maintaining demand becomes immediately apparent. Unfortunately, this then produces destabilizing feedbacks, which amplify the problem. Thus, reduction in borrowing lowers demand, which then causes firms to reduce output and employment. This lowers wage income and further undermines households willingness and ability to borrow, thereby amplifying the underlying problem of demand.

These problems would be bad enough in an economy with strong labor markets. They are likely to be compounded in an economy in which labor is weak, because there is the danger that firms will be able to force wage concessions, which would worsen the financial conditions of households and raise debt burdens. If such a wage deflation gets started, it could generate a total collapse in demand and employment. Exactly these type of conditions (which are discussed in detail below) now characterize the U.S. economy, and, for this reason, we all have cause to worry about the next recession.

THE END OF AUTOMATIC STABILIZATION POLICY

Just as household borrowing can sustain the economy, so can borrowing by the Federal government. During the 1980s, the Federal government ran massive deficits that were financed by borrowing, and this borrowing served to fund government spending and employment of which contributed significantly to demand. A large component of this spending was the defense buildup which was a classic example of military Keynesianism (by no means the best sort of Keynesianism!) at work. The impact of this spending was also augmented by the large tax cuts that were given to the wealthiest households in the country, though a better policy would have been to give the tax cuts to ordinary households who spend a greater share of their income. Aside from issues of equity, this would have achieved the same economic outcome with with less expenditure and smaller deficits.

This period of maintaining demand through Federal deficit spending is also coming to an end, and there are now political pressures to contract government spending, which will have a negative effect on demand. Thus, there is a risk that both the household sector and the government sector may be forced into a deflationary posture at the same time. The pressure for this move is largely political and related to misunderstanding of govenment deficits. Though deficits can be extreme and dangerous, there are little grounds for believing this to be the current case in the U.S. economy in which the deficit has fallen to less than 2% of gross national product.

Just as individual households borrow to finance home and car purchases, and total household borrowing has grown as the economy has grown, we should expect government to borrow to finance expenditures on public infrastructure such as highways, sewers, schools, airports, and public buildings. Moreover, the government plays a critical role in providing banks and the financial sector with liquid financial instruments to hold as part of their portfolios. In a growing economy with a growing financial system, we should therefore expect government to borrow both to fund its expenditures and to lubricate the financial system.

Though it is impossible to say exactly what the optimal level of the deficit should be, it was certainly too high during the Reagan era. However, we have now moved to the opposite extreme of deficit phobia, and this phobia is being opportunistically and dangerously exploited to refashion government in the spirit of Mean Street capitalism. The clearest example of this is the call for a balanced budget amendment requiring zero deficits. As chapter 8 showed, such an amendment would lock the Federal government into dangerously destabilizing financial practices. Thus, in recessions when tax revenues fall owing to lower economic activity, the government would either have to cut spending or increase taxes to balance its budget, and both of these measures would reduce demand and aggravate the recession.

Even if a balanced budget amendment is not passed, we are now embarked on a political trajectory (shared by Republicans and Democrats alike) intended to diminish enormously the economic role of government. This diminuition threatens to cannibalize the system of automatic stabilizers that was built into the economy in the period after World War II, as well as reversing the process of putting a human face on capitalism, which was accomplished through regulation of workplace conditions and terms of employment. Over the last fifty years, government has been a progressive force in labor markets, and as government employment has grown, it has exerted a beneficial impact on wages and employment conditions throughout the economy; shrinking the size of government will diminish the impact of this effect.

Attempts to reform welfare by subcontracting the functions of the Federal government out to state governments are another source of threat to the system of automatic stabilizers. The Federal government has run programs on the basis of defined standards, and it has been willing to fund these programs independent of the number of claimants. However, the proposed new arrangements are based on the principle of block grants to the states, and it is therefore likely that they will be unresponsive to cyclical fluctuations in need. In this case, the Federal government will no longer automatically pump more welfare spending into the economy during recessions, when need rises.

Lastly, these shifts to deflationary fiscal practice are occurring at a time when the composition of the Federal outlays has become less effective at maintaining demand. The principal reason for this is the massive increase in the national debt attributable to the excessive Reagan-era deficits, which in turn have caused an enormous increase in interest payments. This increase in interest service has been compounded by the Federal Reserve's policy of high interest rates, which has been used to discipline labor and shift income away from wages to profits. As a result, interest payments now constitute 16% of Federal outlays, and since the debt is primarily held by the most wealthy 1% of households, it has become the largest single transfer program. The catch is that it is a transfer program based on the "reverse Robin Hood" principle of transferring income from the poor to the rich. The net effect is therefore deflationary, because ordinary Americans spend most of their income, whereas the wealthy hoard most of theirs.

The Deflationary Fed

The other great instrument of economic stabilization policy has been monetary policy conducted by the Federal Reserve Bank. Monetary policy involves using the Fed's control over the money supply and the availability of credit to control the level of interest rates. In the past, the Fed used this power to ensure high levels of employment. Chapter 7 showed how there has been a retreat from this policy goal over the last twenty years, and today the Fed is exclusively committed to achieving zero inflation. Inflation rather than full employment has therefore become the goal of Fed policy.

The Fed's changed policy stance has contributed to interest rates being higher in the 1980s and 1990s than there were in the period 1950 to 1970. This has weakened the position of labor and contributed to the shift in income distribution from profits to wages. The danger is that the Fed is now inclined to interpret any signs of wage increases as a sign of inflation, and responds by raising interest rates. Since wage increases are the way labor gets to share in productivity growth, this policy is tantamount to siding with corporate and financial capital. Moreover, when the Fed raises interest rates, the higher debt burden of households means that this causes additional economic pain for households.

The Fed now defends its tight money policies by saying that monetary policy has to be forward looking and preemptive with regard to inflation. Defenders of the Fed claim it is always criticized because the Fed's job is to "take away the punch bowl just when the economic party is warming up": the problem is that "most working Americans haven't been invited to the party."

The preemption approach risks the Federal Reserve spooking itself into a false belief that inflation is accelerating and thereby mistakenly raising rates. This is a dangerous game that may trigger the next downturn. Given the current fragility of the economy, there is the risk of prematurely truncating the recovery and sending the economy into a tailspin. Once the amplifying effects of a downturn are in place, it is not clear that reversing interest rates will be able to pull the economy back up. This is surely the lesson of the last recession, which took three years of interest rate cuts to produce a meaningful recovery.

A key factor in shaking off the last recession was the wave of mortgage refinancings and household loan consolidations that took place in the early 1990s. These refinancings reduced the amount of debt service that households had to pay, and gave households a desperately needed shot in the arm that helped stave off a deeper recession. However, this process of refinancing is ultimately limited by the number of old mortgages and debts taken on when interest rates were at their peak, and gradually this stock has been exhausted. When this factor is combined with the shift to variable-rate mortgages, on which rates have been lower so that refinancing is not worthwhile (except for reasons of rate lock-in), it is unlikely that refinancing can continue to provide the same stimulative force. Consequently, demand will be more fragile in the next recession, and recovery harder to achieve.

There are also other barriers to refinancing and low rates. During the last recession, house prices fell, and many homeowners saw their equity wiped out. This elimination of equity is itself a barrier to refinancing because banks refinance without equity, and if housing prices fall in the next recession, this will provide another obstacle. At the same time, the lowering of credit standards by banks has raised the risk of default. This risk must in turn be reflected in market rates, which means there are barriers to how low the Fed will be able to push market rates in the event of another recession.

DEMOGRAPHICS AND ECONOMIC DEPRESSION

Another factor making for increased likelihood of an economic depression is the widely acknowledged aging of the baby-boom generation, and the generalized graying of America. It is widely recognized that there is a life cycle to household expenditure patterns, with people tending to borrow and spend more than their income when they are young and while raising children. In middle age, after child rearing is over, households begin to save more to pay off their debts and to make provision for old age. Older people are also significant savers, perhaps to cover against the risk of living longer than their means will provide for and perhaps to leave bequests.

The massive size of the baby-boomer cohort, combined with the fact that baby-boomers delayed the starting of families, mean that these life-cycle forces have worked in the economy's favor for the last twenty years. This helps explain the enormous increase in household borrowing in the 1980s, and it served to mitigate the adverse consequences of the worsening of income distribution. However, this demographic effect is now drawing to a close, and the inexorable force of demographics is now turning against the U.S. economy. Having been expansionary in nature, demographics are now taking on a deflationary character. Moreover, this demographic juggernaut is unlikely to be turned around by the influx of young immigrants, because these immigrants enter on the lowest economic rung. They therefore have low incomes, poor job prospects, and little access to credit, so that their net contribution to demand will not compensate for the aging of white middle-class America.

Finally, this demographic development is compounded by the system of financing social security. Under current arrangements, contributions to social security are paid into a trust fund, to be notionally held until retirement. Given the current age distribution, payments into the fund vastly exceed payments out owing to the large number of baby boomers who are still working. This situation will to continue through the first decade of the twenty-first century, and it means that payments into the fund will be a net deflationary drain out of the economy. In recent years, this effect has been countered by the huge government deficits that have more than offset them. However, recent moves to balance the Federal budget mean that this deflationary effect will be increasingly felt, and it will impart a deflationary bias to the underlying economic structure.

Labor Markets and Business Domination

Perhaps the single most important factor in the growing fragility of the American economy concerns developments in labor markets, which have produced declining wages and a tremendous increase in job insecurity. These developments represent the product of both structural change within the economy and adverse economic policy. They have formed a core part of the book. The adverse wage consequences of increased capital mobility were examined in chapter 5, while the adverse wage effects of unrestricted free trade were examined in chapter 9. Chapter 8 examined the "Raw Deal," with its goal of removing government from the labor market and undercutting the wage floor. Most important of all has been the decline of the extent of unionization in the American economy, which was examined in chapter 3.

The net effect of these developments has been a significant weakening of the position of American workers vis-à-vis firms. This weakening has manifested itself in declining job security and declining wages, and the trend shows no sign of abating. These structural changes mean that the general level of wages is more likely to crumble in an economic downturn.

Businesses are increasingly willing to subcontract work and use low-paid temporary (but in fact semipermanent) workers provided by firms such as Manpower, Inc. In a downturn, the availability of large numbers of unemployed workers, coupled with easy replacement, would make wage concessions relatively easy to obtain. In this regard, the recession of 1982–3 is a significant harbinger, because it marked the first time in the post-World War II era that concessions and givebacks were widespread. Were this to happen on a larger scale, household debt burdens would become intolerable, consumer spending would collapse, and financial markets would be confronted by a wave of defaults. In such a scenario, economic activity would plummet, and it is hard to see how policy could turn the situation around.

CONCLUSION

The last twenty-five years have witnessed a persistent deterioration in the constitution of demand in the U.S. economy. This weakening has been predicated on structural changes in labor markets that have undermined the position of American workers and given rise to a worsening of income distribution and increased job insecurity. This outcome has also been fostered by restrictive monetary policy, ill-considered free-trade arrangements, and labor-market policies that have subverted unions. The effects of these changes have been obscured by a debt binge by households and government and by favorable demographic factors. However, households now face increasing financial constraints, government faces political constraints that limit its economic freedom, and the favorable demographic situation is reversing itself. Under such conditions, there are reasonable grounds for believing that the next economic recession could spiral into a depression.

✳ *Epilogue: Ending Economic Fatalism* ✳

CHAPTER 1 introduced an economic philosophy that I called structural Keynesianism. Chapter 11 summarized some of the economic policy implications of such an approach. Let me close by briefly addressing some of the political implications.

Structural Keynesianism maintains that economic outcomes depend on a combination of economic structure (i.e., rules, regulations, and institutions), economic policy, and the enterprise and initiative of business and individuals. Structure and policy are the province of collective action: only enterprise and intitiative are the province of individual action.

The laissez-faire model of conservative economics emphasizes enterprise and intiative. Structure is notionally absent, as evidenced by the appeal to the fiction of natural markets. Policy is a matter of reestablishing these natural markets, which are really just markets in which business dominates labor. This involves repealing existing policy and creating a minimalist libertarian government that enforces particular laws of property and contract. Government is restricted to acting as policeman, judge, and jailer.

Structural Keynesianism's emphasis on designed structure and policy highlights the necessity of collective action, which brings us back to the political dimension behind our current stagnation. Developing the theoretical underpinnings and technical details of a policy agenda is one necessary ingredient for fixing our disordered economy. The other is a massive transformation of the way in which people understand and read the economy, and the creation of a willingness to collectively engage in a redesign.

There is a need for a new popular understanding that breaks with economic naturalism and its prescription of fatalism. People should see institutions such as unions and minimum wages, not as unnatural distortions, but as fundamental props to prosperity. Monetary policy and the Federal Reserve should not be the private domain of bankers and economists. Rather, our ordinary economic conversation should be informed by and inform these matters.

With this new understanding must then come a popular engagement with the political process that ensures that legislators and policymakers craft the right structure and policy agenda. Rather than fatalistically accepting the economy we have, we can instead, within the constraints defined by our knowledge and endowments, design a Main Street economy that delivers for all. This is the political implication of structural Keynesianism's identification of the need for designed structure and policy.

214

✳ *Notes* ✳

CHAPTER 1
DEBUNKING ECONOMIC NATURALISM

1. For instance, The *Washington Post* business section led with the headline "The Thriving Economy That Keeps Surprising: In Past Decade, U.S. Transformed Itself," Saturday, May 3, 1997, p. I11.

2. See Mishel, Bernstein, and Schmitt, *The State of Working America*, p. 140.

3. Keynes, *The General Theory of Employment, Money and Interest*, p. viii.

4. Quoted from Minsky, "Financial Integration and National Economic Policy."

5. Firms may also lobby to get regulations repealed, lobbying being another way of circumventing regulation. This explains why business has pushed so hard for the emasculation of government's regulatory capacity.

6. See Fukuyama, *The End of History and the Last Man*.

CHAPTER 2
MAKING SENSE OF THE ECONOMY AND ECONOMICS

1. The process of creative destruction is outlined in chapter VII of Schumpeter's *Capitalism, Socialism, and Democracy*.

2. See Gordon, *Fat and Mean*.

3. The term "Golden Age" is attributable to Marglin and Schor (eds.), *The Golden Age of Capitalism*.

4. Keynes, *The General Theory of Employment, Interest, and Money*, p. 383.

5. This reasoning is embodied in the famous Stolper-Samuelson theorem: Stolper and Samuelson, "Protection and Real Wages."

6. Smith, *An Inquiry into the Nature and Causes of The Wealth of Nations*, Vol. I, chap. 8.

7. The term "silent depression" is drawn from Peterson, *Silent Depression: The Fate of the American Dream*.

CHAPTER 3
PLENTY OF NOTHING: AN OVERVIEW

1. Statistic provided by Whalen, "The Anxious Society.

2. See Mishel, Bernstein, and Schmitt, pp. 200–202.

3. The number of instances in which there is actual replacement are relatively few. The reason why the frequency of "actual" replacement is low, and why it is

not a good indicator of the changed state of the game, is that replacement is seldom needed by firms to achieve their goals. All that is needed is that firms have a "credible threat" of replacement, which is enough to get workers to give in.

CHAPTER 4
THE STATE OF THE AMERICAN DREAM

1. All numbers are in constant 1987 dollars.

2. Average compensation was arrived at by taking average hourly wages and multiplying by (Total compensation per the national income and product accounts/total wages and salaries per the national income and product accounts).

3. "After 5,000 Years on the Job, You Too Could Earn This Much," *Christian Science Monitor,* April 22, 1997.

4. *New York Times,* March 3, 1996. Recession Jan.–July, 1980. Recession July–Dec., 1981. Recession Jan.–Nov. 1982. Recession July–Dec., 1990. Recession Jan.–March, 1991. 1994 and 1995 = estimated.

5. Data in the following paragraphs are drawn from Bluestone and Ghilarducci 1996b, "Still Working, Still Poor."

6. Reported in Danziger and Weinberg, "Market Income, Income Transfers, and the Trend in Poverty."

7. Rose, "Declining Job Security and the Professionalization of Opportunity."

8. These data are reported in Bluestone and Ghilarducci 1996b.

9. Schor, *The Overworked American.*

10. See for instance, Baily, Burtless, and Litan, *Growth with Equity.*

11. Madrick, *The End of Affluence.*

CHAPTER 5
THE LOGIC OF ECONOMIC POWER, PART I:
DIAGNOSING THE PROBLEM

1. Much of this chapter derives from my article "Capital Mobility and the Threat to American Prosperity" (Palley 1994c).

2. "Workers of the World, Get Smart," *New York Times,* July 20, 1993, p. A19.

3. Keith Bradsher, "Productivity Is All, but It Doesn't Pay Well," *New York Times,* June 25, 1995, News of the Week in Review, p. 4.

4. Howell and Weiler, "Explaining the Collapse of Low-Skill Earnings."

5. See Juhn and Murphy, "Inequality in Labor Market Outcomes."

6. Gordon, *Fat and Mean.*

7. Davis and Topel, "Comment."

8. Howell and Wolff, "Trends in the Growth and Distribution of Skills in the U.S. Workplace."

9. Wieler, "Can Technological Change Explain Increasing Inequality within Age, Schooling, and Gender Groups?"

10. The conference proceedings were published in *Economic Policy Review*, Federal Reserve Bank of New York, 1 (January 1995).

11. "Is VW's New Plant Lean, or Just Mean?" *New York Times*, November 11, 1996, p. D1.

12. See "Choppy Waters Ahead," *Financial Times*, April 25, 1997, p. 16.

13. "Edging Up," *Wall Street Journal*, June 3, 1997.

14. See "Full Time, Part Time, Temp—All See the Job in a Different Light," *Wall Street Journal*, March 18, 1997, p. A10.

15. See "Many Firms Press States For Concessions," *Wall Street Journal*, March 8, 1995, p. A2.

CHAPTER 6
THE LOGIC OF ECONOMIC POWER, PART II:
POLICIES FOR PROSPERITY

1. Material for this section is drawn from Friedman and Prosten, "How Come One Team *Still* Has to Play with Its Shoelaces Tied Together?"

2. Weiler, "Promises to Keep."

3. Bronfenbrenner, *Successful Union Strategies For Winning Certification Elections and First Contracts.*

4. Nobile, "Yes, We Allow No Solicitation Today."

5. McDonough, "Maintain a Union-Free Status."

6. The source for the statistics cited here and in paragraphs below is Friedman and Prosten, "How Come One Team *Still* Has to Play with Its Shoelaces Tied Together?"

7. This metaphor is attributable to the late Hyman Minsky.

CHAPTER 7
THE TRIUMPH OF WALL STREET: FINANCE AND
THE FEDERAL RESERVE

1. Corrigan, "The Trilogy of Central Banking in a Contemporary Setting."

2. See Tobin, "Inflation and Unemployment." The argument is that moderate inflation raises prices in sectors with full employment, thereby choking off demand in those sectors. At the same time, this lowers relative prices in sectors with unemployment, thereby increasing demand and employment in those sectors.

3. In later versions of natural-rate theory that include rational expectations, there is no trade-off at all. Systematic monetary policy cannot lower the rate of unemployment, and any attempts to do so produce higher inflation. See Lucas, "Some International Evidence on Output-Inflation Trade-offs."

217

4. See Friedman, M., "The Role of Monetary Policy" and Phelps, "Money Wage Dynamics and Labor Market Equilibrium."

5. This section detailing the spread of natural-rate theory within the *Economic Report of the President* is drawn from Gordon, "Six-Percent Unemployment Ain't Natural."

6. See Mishkin, "Does Anticipated Policy Matter? An Econometric Investigation."

7. See Palley, "Escalators and Elevators." A similar argument for the Phillips curve has also been made by Akerloff et al., "The Macroeconomics of Low Inflation."

8. See Gordon, "The Un-Natural Rate of Unemployment." Rissman, "Wage Growth and Sectoral Shifts"; Palley, "Does Inflation Grease the Wheels of Adjustment?"; Blanchflower and Oswald, The Wage Curve.

9. See Tullock, *The Politics of Bureaucracy*; Niskanen, *Bureaucracy and Representative Government*.

10. Within this framework, government and bureaucratic corruption can certainly exist. However, it is more analogous to ordinary criminal economic activity that affects the efficiency and efficacy of government, rather than class-based action that affects the stance of government vis-à-vis society at large. The exception to this would be the system of bureaucratic socialism associated with the former Soviet Union, which brought into existence a new bureaucratic capitalist class. In that society, government was identical with, and controlled by, that bureaucratic capitalist class which jad effectively replaced the standard capitalist class.

11. An early statement of this point of view was provided by Boddy and Crotty, "Class Conflict and Macro Policy."

12. This refinement is attributable to Epstein, "A Political Economy Model of Comparative Central Banking."

CHAPTER 8
FROM NEW DEAL TO RAW DEAL: THE ATTACK ON GOVERNMENT

1. See Bluestone and Ghilarducci, "Making Pay Work: Wage Insurance for the Working Poor."

2. Cited in The *New York Times,* November 18, 1996.

3. Mishel and Schmitt, "Cutting Wages by Cutting Welfare."

4. See "Welfare Recipients Taking Jobs Often Held by the Working Poor," Louis Uchitelle, *New York Times,* April 1, 1997.

5. At the end of the day, it is not clear that deregulation has produced significant additional price reductions, because prices would have fallen anyway owing to ongoing productivity growth and technological advance. Immediately following deregulation there have been price reductions, but prices and industry concentration have tended to increase once the dust has settled. Moreover, wages have fallen in deregulated industries, as has union coverage of workers. With regard to

banking deregulation, consumers as tax payers were forced to pick up the half trillion dollar cost of the Savings and Loan collapse.

6. "Nothing Succeeds Like Excess," *New York Times,* August 28, 1988.

7. The base period is 1955.1 because the period 1947.1–1954.4 is economically unrepresentative. In the late 1940s, the U.S. economy was still adjusting to the end of World War II, and this pushed the consumption share to artificially high levels. The early 1950s were marked by the Korean War, which artificially depressed the consumption share and massively increased the defense expenditure share. By 1955, the defense expenditure share had begun falling and had attained a level more representative of ordinary times.

8. "Nothing Succeeds Like Excess," *New York Times,* August 28, 1988.

9. Monetarists refer to "inside" and "outside" lags. Inside lags refer to the time needed for government to adjust its policies; outside lags refer to the time needed for policies to have an economic effect once they are implemented.

10. The specific details of the crowding-out mechanism depend on the type of macroeconomic model adopted. In the neo-Keynesian ISLM model, crowding out works by assuming a positively sloped LM schedule, and assuming that investment spending depends negatively on interest rates and is independent of the level of output. In the classical macro model, it is assumed that total output is fixed, so that increases in government spending have to be accommodated by reduced private consumption and investment spending.

11. If a private household repays its debts, these repayments are treated as saving. The exact same logic applies to government repayment of debt.

12. Zeile, "U.S. Intrafirm Trade in Goods."

13. This section is drawn from Palley, "State of the Union."

CHAPTER 9
FREE TRADE AND THE RACE TO THE BOTTOM

1. This chapter is largely drawn from Palley, "The Free Trade Debate: A Left Keynesian Gaze."

2. This argument is made by Richards, "Income Inequality and Trade: How to think, What to Conclude."

3. This assumption is referred to as the "representative" consumer assumption.

4. If confronted by the distinctions between wage and profit income, the response of orthodox economics is that, "in theory, lump-sum redistributions can make everyone at least as well-off as they were before the reform. The fact that such redistributions are not possible in the "real world" is deemed of no consequence.

5. These conflicting tendencies of higher real wages are examined in Bhaduri and Marglin, "Unemployment and the Real Wage."

6. The normative criterion used to assess the welfare effects of trade reforms is well-being of workers. In some countries, it is harder to talk about a representative

219

worker. This is particularly true of countries with large agricultural sectors, in which case there may be a divide between the well-being of rural and urban workers. In the United States, agricultural employment is a small fraction of total employment, so that this problem is not salient.

7. See Stolper and Samuelson, "Protection and Real Wages."

8. Per orthodox trade theory, these differences can also matter. Thus, production of goods that are pollution- or safety-intensive will be shifted to underdeveloped countries where the cost of pollution or safety is lower. Because there is also full employment, developed countries derive an additional benefit to the extent that the "bads" associated with pollution and personal injury are shifted to the underdeveloped country.

9. The economic impacts of NAFTA are extensively explored in the December 1993 issue of the *Review of Radical Political Economics*, which was exclusively devoted to this subject.

10. The welfare effects of trade liberalizations for underdeveloped countries are not the symmetric opposite of those for developed countries. In the case of NAFTA and Mexico, there is a division between urban and rural workers, so that the device of a representaive worker will not suffice for analyzing NAFTA's welfare effects on Mexico. Urban workers potentially gain from NAFTA, whereas rural workers lose owing to the liberalization of trade in agricultural products. Moreover, an increase in urban-sector jobs does not mean that urban-sector wages will increase. Mexico has a labor surplus and a rapidly growing workforce, and the loss of jobs in the agricultural sector will compound the problem of urban unemployment. The one clear winner is the oligarchy that owns Mexican industry. This illustrates the need to analyze trade liberalizations on a country-by-country basis.

11. See "Trade Knits U.S. and Mexico Ever More Tightly," *Los Angeles Times*, May 5, 1997.

12. This issue is emphasized by Koechlin in "NAFTA and the Location of North American Investment."

13. An excellent survey of the misleading way in which NAFTA was sold to the American public is provided by Lee, "False Prophets: The Selling of NAFTA."

14. See Hufbauer and Schott, "NAFTA: An Assessment."

15. *Time*, June 13, 1993, p. 18

16. See "GM Braces for Widening Disputes with Union," *Wall Street Journal*, April 30, 1997.

17. See *New York Times*, September 26, 1995.

18. See *Boston Globe*, March 9, 1997.

19. See *Milwaukee Journal Sentinel*, March 9, 1997.

20. "Borderline Working Class: In Texas, Labor Is Feeling Trade Accord's Pinch," *New York Times*, May 8, 1997.

21. The report is summarized in "Daily Labor Report," No. 111, June 1997, pp. A.1–2.

CHAPTER 10
INTERNATIONAL MONEY: WHO GOVERNS?

1. Keynes, Letter to R. F. Harrod, 19 April 1942.
2. This policy proposal is contained in Eichengreen and Wyplosz 1993.
3. In addition, the Tobin tax does not distinguish between speculative trades and bona fide trades to finance international trade.

CHAPTER 11
STRUCTURAL KEYNESIANISM AND GLOBALIZATION

1. See Bernstein and Mishel, "A Comparison of Income, Wages and Employment Trends of the Advanced Industrial Economies."
2. This is the policy that the OECD has endorsed in its jobs strategy recommendations. See *OECD Economic Surveys, United States, 1996.*
3. The Mitterrand economic experiment is examined in Lombard, "A Reexamination of the Reasons for the Failure of Keynesian Expansionary Policies in France, 1981–1983."

CHAPTER 12
RECIPE FOR A DEPRESSION

1. This chapter is drawn from my article, "The Forces Making for an Economic Collapse."

* *References* *

Akerlof, G. A., Dickens, W. T., and Perry, G. L. 1996. "The Macroeconomics of Low Inflation." *Brookings Papers on Economic Activity* 27(1):1–26.

Anderson, A. 1989. *A Progressive Answer to the Fiscal Deficit.* Washington D.C.: Economic Policy Institute.

Aschauer, D. A. 1991. *Public Investment and Private Sector Growth: The Economic Benefits of Reducing America's Third Deficit.* Washington D.C.: Economic Policy Institute.

Baily, M. N., Burtless, G., and Litan, R. E. 1994. *Growth with Equity: Economic Policymaking for the Next Century.* Washington D.C.: The Brookings Institution.

Baker, D., and Mishel, L. 1995. "Profits Up, Wages Down." Briefing paper. Washington, D.C.: Economic Policy Institute.

Bernstein, J., and Mishel, L. 1995. "A Comparison of Income, Wages and Employment Trends of the Advanced Industrial Economies." Pp. 197–229 in L. Mishel and J. Schmitt, eds. *Beware the U.S. Model: Jobs and Wages in a Deregulated Economy.* Washington, D.C.: Economic Policy Institute.

Bhaduri, A., and Marglin, S. 1990. "Unemployment and the Real Wage: The Economic Basis for Contesting Political Ideologies." *Cambridge Journal of Economics* 4(June):103–15.

Blanchflower, D., and Oswald, J. 1994 *The Wage Curve,* Cambridge: MIT Press.

Blecker, R. A. 1990. "Are Americans on a Consumption Binge? The Evidence Reconsidered." Economic Policy Institute, Washington D.C.

Bluestone, R., and Ghilarducci, T. 1996a. "Making Pay Work: Wage Insurance for the Working Poor." Levy Institute Public Policy Brief, No. 28, p. 15.

———1996b. "Still Working, Still Poor: Beyond Full Employment." Paper presented at the Levy Institute Conference held to commemmorate the 50th anniversary of the Full Employment Act, April 1996.

Boddy, R., and Crotty, J. 1975. "Class Conflict and Macro Policy: The Political Business Cycle." *Review of Radical Political Economics* 7:1–19.

Bowles, S., and Gintis, H. 1982. "The Crisis of Liberal Democratic Capitalism: The Case of the United States." *Politics and Society* 11:51–93.

Bronfenbrenner, K. 1990. *Successful Union Strategies For Winning Certification Elections and First Contracts: Report to Union Participants.* "Part I: Organizing Survey Results, Summary of Results from 1986–88 Survey of 261 Lead Organizers." New Kensington, Pa.: Penn State.

———1996. *Final report: The Effects of Plant Closing or Threat of Plant Closing on the Right of Workers to Organize.* New York State School of Industrial and Labor Relations, Cornell University, Ithaca, N.Y.

REFERENCES

Corrigan, E. G. 1992. "The Trilogy of Central Banking in a Contemporary Setting." *Seventy-Eighth Annual Report of the Federal Reserve Bank of New York*, pp. 5–13.

Danziger, S. H., and Weinberg, D. H. 1992. "Market Income, Income Transfers, and the Trend in Poverty." Paper presented in Madison:Institute for Research on Poverty, University of Wisconsin.

Davidson, P. 1994. *Post Keynesian Macroeconomic Theory: A Foundation for Successful Economic Policies for the Twenty-First Century*. Aldershott, U.K.: Edward Elgar.

Davis, S. J., and Topel, R. H. 1993. "Comment." *Brookings Papers on Economic Activity* 1.

Dembo, D., and Morehouse, W. 1995. *The Underbelly of the U.S. Economy*. Council on International and Public Affairs. New York: Apex Press.

Eatwell, J. 1996. "International Capital Liberalisation: An Evaluation." Report to UNDP (SSA no. 96–049), August.

Economic Report of the President. 1997. Washington: U.S. Government Printing Office.

Eichengreen, B., and Wyploz, C. 1993. "The Unstable EMS." Unpublished paper, presented to the Brookings Panel on Economic Activity, April 1993.

Eisner, R. 1986. *How Real is the Federal Deficit?* New York: Free Press.

———.1996. "A New View of the NAIRU," manuscript, Northwestern University, June.

Epstein, G. 1992. "A Political Economy Model of Comparative Central Banking." *Review of Radical Political Economics* 24:1–30.

Federal Reserve Bank of New York. 1995. *Economic Policy Review* 1(Jan.:1–72.

Freeman, R. B. 1995. "Are Your Wages Being Set in Beijing?" *Journal of Economic Perspectives* 9(Summer):15–32.

Friedman, B. 1988. *Day of Reckoning*. New York: Random House.

Friedman, M. 1962. *Capitalism and Freedom*. Chicago: University of Chicago Press.

———.1968. "The Role of Monetary Policy." *American Economic Review* 58(May):1–17.

Friedman, S., and Prosten, R. 1993. "How Come One Team *Still* Has to Play with Its Shoelaces Tied Together?" *Industrial Relations Research Association*, Proceedings of the 1993 Spring Meeting.

Fukuyama, F. 1992. *The End of History and the Last Man*. New York: Free Press.

Gordon, D. M. 1987. "Six-Percent Unemployment Ain't Natural: Demystifying the Idea of a Rising 'Natural Rate of Unemployment.' " *Social Research* 54(2) (Summer):223–46.

———.1988. "The Un-Natural Rate of Unemployment: An Econometric Critique of the NAIRU Hypothesis." *American Economic Review* 78(2) (May):117–23.

224

———.1996. *Fat and Mean*. New York: Free Press.

Harris, E. S., and Steindl, C. 1991. "The Decline in U.S. Saving and its Implications for Economic Growth," *Federal Reserve Bank of New York Quarterly Review*, 1991:1–19.

Howell, D. R. 1997. "Institutional Failure and the American Worker: The Collapse of Low-Skill Wages." Levy Institute Public Policy Brief, No. 29.

Howell, D. R., and Wieler, S. 1996. "Explaining the Collapse of Low-Skill Earnings: Implications for Education and Training Policy," unpublished, New School for Social Research, New York.

Howell, D. R., and Wolff, E. N. 1991. "Trends in the Growth and Distribution of Skills in the U.S. Workplace." *Industrial and Labor Relations Review* 44(April):486–502.

Hufbauer, G. C., and Schott, J. J. 1993."NAFTA: An Assessment." Washington, D.C.: Institute for International Economics.

Juhn, C., and Murphy, K. 1995. "Inequality in Labor Market Outcomes." *Economic Policy Review*, Federal Reserve Bank of New York 1 (Jan.):26–32.

Keynes, J. M. 1936. *The General Theory of Employment, Interest, and Money*. London: Macmillan.

———. 1980. "Letter to R. F. Harrod, 19 April 1942." In *The Collected Writings of J. M. Keynes*, edited by D. Moggridge, Vol. XXV, Chap. 3. London: Macmillan.

Koechlin, T. 1993. "NAFTA and the location of North American Investment: A Critique of Mainstream Analysis." *Review of Radical Political Economics* 25 (December):59–71.

Lee, T. M. 1995. "False Prophets: The Selling of NAFTA." Economic Policy Institute Briefing paper, Washington, D.C.

Lombard, M. 1995. "A Re-examination of the Reasons for the Failure of Keynesian Expansionary Policies in France, 1981–1983." *Cambridge Economic Journal* 19:359–72.

Lucas, R. E., Jr. 1973. "Some International Evidence on Output-Inflation Tradeoffs." *American Economic Review* 63:326–34.

Madrick, J. 1995. *The End of Affluence*. New York: A. Knopf.

Marglin, S., and Schor, J. B., eds. 1990. *The Golden Age of Capitalism: Reinterpreting the Postwar Experience*. Oxford: Clarendon Press.

McDonough, P. S. 1990. "Maintain a Union-Free Status." *Personnel Journal* 69 (April):108–14.

Minsky, H. 1993. "Financial Integration and National Economic Policy." Paper presented at the Post-Keynesian Workshop, University of Tennessee, Knoxville.

Mishel, L., Bernstein, J., and Schmitt, J. 1997. *The State of Working America, 1996–97*. Washington, D.C.: Economic Policy Institute.

Mishel, L., and Schmitt, J. 1996. *Cutting Wages by Cutting Welfare*. Briefing Paper. Washington, D.C.: Economic Policy Institute.

Mishkin, F. S. 1982. "Does Anticipated Policy Matter? An Econometric Investigation," *Journal of Political Economy* 90 (Feb.):22–51.

Munnel, A. 1990. "Why has Productivity Growth Declined? Productivity and Public Investment." *New England Economic Review* 1990 (Jan.–Feb.):3–22.

Niskannen, W. A. 1971. *Bureaucracy and Representative Government.* Chicago: Aldine-Atherton.

Nobile, R. J. 1991. "Yes, We Allow No Solicitation Today." *Personnel* 68 (March):11.

Organization for Economic Cooperation and Development. 1997. *OECD Economic Surveys, 1995–1996: United States.* Paris: OECD.

Palley, T. I. 1994a. "Escalators and Elevators: A Phillips Curve for Keynesians." *Scandinavian Journal of Economics* 96:111–16.

———. 1994b. "The Free Trade Debate: A Left Keynesian Gaze." *Social Research* 61(Summer):379–94.

———. 1994c. "Capital Mobility and the Threat to American Prosperity." *Challenge* (Nov.–Dec.):31–40.

———. 1996a. "The Institutionalization of Deflationary Monetary Policy." *Economies et Societes, Monnaie et Production.* X:247–68.

———. 1996b. "The Forces Making for an Economic Collapse." *The Atlantic Monthly* (July) 278:44–58.

———. 1996c. "The Savings-Investment Nexus: How it Works and Why it Matters." Center for Economic Policy Analysis, Working Paper No. 1.

———. 1997a. "State of the Union: The Sorry Politics of the Balanced Budget." *Challenge* 40 (May–June):5–13.

———. 1997b. "Does Inflation Grease the Wheels of Adjustment? Evidence from the U.S. Economy." *International Review of Applied Economics.*

Papadimitriou, D. B., and Wray, L. R. 1994. "Flying Blind: The Federal Reserve's Experiment with Unobservables." The Jerome Levy Economics Institute, Public Policy Brief, 15.

Peterson, W. C. 1994. *Silent Depression: The Fate of the American Dream.* New York: W. W. Norton.

Phelps, E. 1967. "Money Wage Dynamics and Labor Market Equilibrium." *Journal of Political Economy* 75 (July–August):678–711.

Richards, J. D. 1995. "Income Inequality and Trade: How to Think, What to Conclude." *Journal of Economic Perspectives* 9 (Summer):33–56.

Rissman, E. 1993. "Wage Growth and Sectoral Shifts: Phillips Curve Redux." *Journal of Monetary Economics* 31:395–416.

Rose, S. 1995. "Declining Job Security and the Professionalization of Opportunity." Research Report No. 95–04, Washington, D.C.: National Commission for Employment Policy.

Schor, J. B. 1991. *The Overworked American: The Unexpected Decline of Leisure.* New York: Basic Books.

Schumpeter, J. A. 1976. *Capitalism, Socialism, and Democracy.* New York: Harper Colophon Books.

Smith, A. 1936. *An Inquiry into the Nature and Causes of The Wealth of Nations.* London: Macmillan edn.

Stolper, W. F., and P. A. Samuelson. 1941. "Protection and Real Wages." *Review of Economic Studies* 9(November):58–73.

Summers, L. H., and A. Alesina. 1993. "Central Bank Independence and Macroeconomic Performance: Some Comparative Evidence." *Journal of Money, Credit, and Banking* 25:151–62.

Tobin, J. 1972. "Inflation and Unemployment." *American Economic Review* 62:1–18.

———. 1978. "A Proposal for International Monetary Reform." *Eastern Economic Journal* 4:153–59.

Tullock, G. 1965. *The Politics of Bureaucracy.* Washington, D.C.: Public Affairs Press.

Weiler, P. 1983. "Promises to Keep: Securing Workers' Rights to Self-Organization under the NLRA." *Harvard Law Review* 96(June):1769–1827.

Wieler, S. S. 1994. "Can Technological Change Explain Increasing Inequality within Age, Schooling, and Gender Groups?" Paper presented at the Eastern Economic Association, March.

Whalen, C. J. 1995. "The Anxious Society: Middle Class Insecurity and the Crisis of the American Dream." *Levy Institute Report* 5(October 1995):9–11.

Wolff, E. N. 1996. "Trends in Household Wealth during 1989–1992." Unpublished manuscript, New York University.

Wood, A. 1995. "How Trade Hurt Unskilled Workers." *Journal of Economic Perspectives* 9(Summer):57–82.

Zeile, W. J. 1997. "U.S. Intrafirm Trade in Goods." *Survey of Current Business* 77(February): 23–38.

227

* Index *

accountability: of central banks with independence, 105; lack of Federal Reserve, 122

aggregate demand: as Keynesian concept, 5, 194; of structural Keynesianism, 5, 194

Aid to Families with Dependent Children (AFDC), 129–30

Anderson, A., 136

arbitrage law: applied to firm's transaction costs, 78–79; related to interest rates, 86

Aschauer, D. A., 143

balanced-budget amendment (BBA): effect if passed, 44, 150–54, 209; function of, 149–50

balance-of-power hypothesis, 73–74, 95

banking system: influence on Federal Reserve, 122–23

bankruptcy, 204

bargaining power: as determinant of income distribution, 29, 75, 194; determinants of, 75–76; economic policy effect on, 87; firms' transaction costs effect on, 79; free trade effect on, 166; government regulation's effect on workers', 127–28; NAFTA effect on, 170; in natural market, 91; workers' reduced, 80, 82–83, 90

BBA. See balanced-budget amendment (BBA)

Bensinger, Richard, 96

Blanchflower, D., 116

Blecker, Robert, 136

bonds, government: under proposed BBA, 153

borrowing: government, 208–9; household, 206–8, 212

Bretton Woods system: breakdown of, 187; fixed exchange rates/capital controls, 183

Bronfenbrenner, Kate, 95, 170

budget deficit. See deficit, budget

bureaucratic-failure theory, 117–18

Bush administration: fiscal policy, 42–44; laissez-faire policies of, 80

business: in bargaining process, 29; as dominant social force, 20–21; effect on conflict in capitalism, 16; in process of creative destruction, 17. See also corporations; firms; multinational corporations

business domination: economics of, 24; over government and labor, 7; reflected in NAFTA and GATT, 156; role of economic policy in establishing, 19

capacity utilization: levels (1948–95), 53–54; underuse of, 57, 65

capital: bargaining power of, 92; shift in balance of power to, 73–74, 82, 95. See also financial capital

capital controls: with breakdown of Bretton Woods, 187; of Bretton Woods system, 183–84; effect of abolition of, 46–47, 86, 91; with flexible exchange rates, 185–88, 191–93; of Keynes's economic theory, 187; in money markets, 179; 1930s era, 88. See also capital mobility

capitalism: Cold War victory of utopian, 12; corporate, 22; current version of, 12; economic booms of, 3–4; forms of, xv, 11–12, 102; free-market, 8; of 1950–70 period, 12; of structural Keynesianism, 5–6; transition to Mean Street, 13, 48–49

capitalist economies: conflict in, 15–16; creative destruction process in, 29; exploitation and unequal distribution of income, 6

capital mobility: with abolition of controls on, 46–47, 188; in current money markets, 179–80; as determinant of bargaining power, 75; with fixed exchange rate, 191; restoring controls on, 191; role in disordered economy, 29; Tobin tax related to, 94. See also capital controls

About the author

Thomas I. Palley is Assistant Director of Public Policy (Economics) at the AFL-CIO and the author of *Post-Keynesian Economics: Debt, Distribution, and the Macro Economy.*